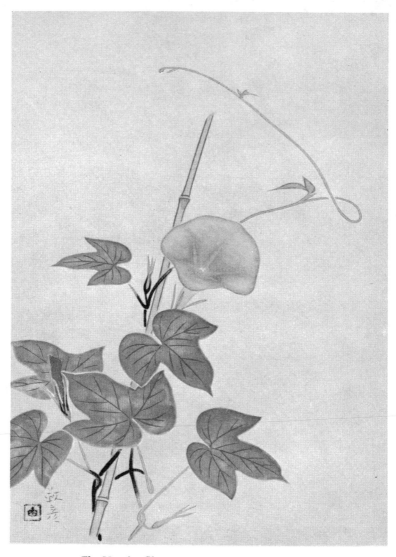

**The Morning-Glory**

By Yukihiko (安田靫彦), a contemporary painter

# Masterpieces of Japanese Poetry
# Ancient and Modern

## （古 今 名 歌 集）

Translated and Annotated

By

## MIYAMORI ASATARŌ
(Surname)        (Personal name)
（宮 森 麻 太 郎）

### IN TWO VOLUMES

### VOL. II.

With Numerous Autographs and Full-page Pictures
Coloured and Uncoloured

## GREENWOOD PRESS, PUBLISHERS
### WESTPORT, CONNECTICUT

Originally published in 1936
by the Maruzen Company Ltd., Tokyo

First Greenwood Reprinting 1970

SBN 8371-2944-3 (SET)
SBN 8371-2946-X (VOL. 2)

# CONTENTS

## Vol. II

# LIST OF PICTURES AND AUTOGRAPHS

## VOL. II

iv

## Poets of the Yedo Period (1603–1867)

### 佐 川 田 昌 俊
#### Sakawada Masatoshi (1580–1643)

Masatoshi was a retainer of Nagai Naokatsu, a famous warrior under Tokugawa Ieyasu. He took part in the battle of Ōsaka in 1604. In his day he was well known as a poet, and the following is one of his masterpieces.

### 待　花 昌　俊

吉野山　花待つ頃の　朝な朝な
心にかゝる　峯の白雲

#### Hana wo Matsu

*Yoshino-yama　Hana matsu koro no　Asa na asa na*
*Kokoro ni kakaru　Mine no shira-kumo.*

### Waiting for Flowers Masatoshi

Waiting, morning by morning,
For the cherries to flower on Yoshino-Yama,
The white clouds clinging to the mountain tops
Cling heavily round my heart.

### 楫 取 魚 彦
#### Katori Nahiko (1623–1782)

A native of Sawara in the Province of Shimōsa, Nahiko studied Japanese classics under Kamo no Mabuchi. He was proficient in versification and painting.

## 雪中の鶯 魚彦

春や來ぬ　冬やのこれる　あまぎらひ
ふりしく雪に　うぐひすのなく

### Setchū no Uguisu

*Haru ya kinu　Fuyu ya nokoreru　Amagirai*
*Furi-shiku yuki ni　Uguisu no naku.*

## The *Uguisu* in Snow Nahiko

**Has spring come round?**
**Is winter lingering?**
**Amid the thickly falling snow**
***Uguisu* sing.**

The reader doubtless remembers that the *uguisu*, the sweetest of Japanese songsters, is the messenger of spring.

## 德 川 光 圀
### Tokugawa Mitsukuni (1628–1700)

A grandson of the Shōgun Ieyasu, Mitsukuni was the lord of Mito Castle, Hitachi Province. He ruled his clan with leniency and was one of the ablest daimiōs. He was well versed in almost all branches of knowledge then available. The most important of his several noteworthy undertakings was the compilation of the *Dai-Nihon-Shi* or "History of Great Japan", in which popular errors concerning the history of the Imperial family are corrected, and loyalty to the Emperor is powerfully inspired. For this work he gathered together many learned scholars and historians, to whom he himself gave valuable assistance. It is remarkable that in those days, when the Tokugawa Shōgun ruled Japan *de facto*, Mitsukuni, himself a member of the Tokugawa family, earnestly advo-

" Waiting for Flowers "—Masatoshi

Handwritten by the poet

" The *Uguisu* in Snow "—Nahiko

Handwritten by the poet

cated loyalty to the Emperor.  On this account, soon after the Restoration of 1868, the Emperor conferred on him posthumous honours—the Junior First Court Rank.  And in 1882 a Shintō shrine called Tokiwa Jinja was dedicated to his spirit.

## 蓮　葉　　　　　　　　　光　圀

夕立の　涼しく過ぐる　蓮葉に
入日かがやく　露のしら玉

### Hachisu-Ba

*Yūdachi no　Suzushiku suguru　Hachisu-ba ni*
*Irihi kagayaku　Tsuyu no shiratama.*

### Lotus Leaves　　　　　　Mitsukuni

Over the lotus leaves
A refleshing shower has run;
Now, on the white jewels of dew
The splendour of the setting sun!

## 月　　　　　　　　　　光　圀

荒磯の　岩に砕けて　散る月を
一つになして　歸る浪かな

### Tsuki

*Ara-iso no　Iwa ni kudakete　Chiru tsuki wo*
*Hitotsu ni nashite　Kaeru nami kana.*

## The Moon                              **Mitsukuni**

Against the rough rocks of the beach
   The moon breaks into myriad beams;
But lo! the billows collect them again,
   And roll them back, made into one, meseems.

### 僧　契　沖
#### Priest Keichū (1640-1701)

Keichū was the chief priest of the Myōhōji Temple in the neighbourhood
of Amagasaki, in Settsu Province. An authority on Japanese literature and a
prolific poet, he wrote many literary books, including the *Manyō-Shū Daishōki,*
annotations on the *Manyō* anthology.

### 春 の 河 舟                          契　沖

吹く風に　岸の柳は　靡けども
ゆくとも知らぬ　春の河舟

### *Haru no Kawa-Fune*

*Fuku kaze ni　Kishi no yanagi wa　Nabike-domo*
*Yuku tomo shiranu　Haru no kawa-fune.*

## A River-Boat in Spring              **Keichū**

The willows on the shore,
   As the spring wind blows, gently sway;
But does the river-boat move on?
   I cannot say.

It is a balmy spring day. The flowing branches of willow-trees on the
shore of a river sway gently and gracefully; but a boat sailing on it moves so
sluggishly that the poet cannot perceive its progress.

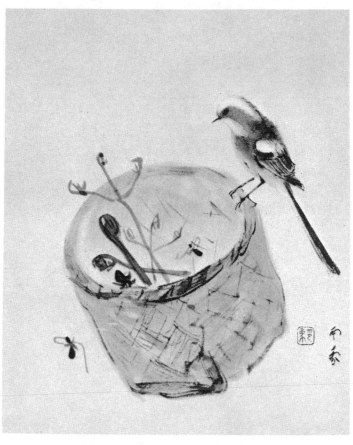

**Spring in Mountains**
(violets, brackens and *enaga*, a kind of titmouse)

By Inshō (堂本印象), a contemporary painter

花　　　　　　　　　　契　沖

花を思ふ　心は山に　春霞
かかりし日より　かかりそめてき

## Hana

*Hana wo omō　Kokoro wa yama ni　Haru-gasumi*
*Kakarishi hi yori　Kakari-some teki.*

## Flowers　　　　　　Keichū

A passionate longing
For the cherry bloom
Began to haunt my mind,
When spring mists did begin to haunt the hills.

春 の 夜 の 月　　　　契　沖

夕雲雀　芝生に落ちて　聲やめば
山よりのぼる　春の夜の月

## Haru no Yo no Tsuki

*Yū-hibari　Shibafu ni ochite　Koe yameba*
*Yama yori noboru　Haru no yo no tsuki.*

## The Spring Moon　　　　Keichū

The evening larks dropt on the lawn,
　　And their songs having come to a pause,
From yonder mountain,
　　The beautiful spring moon arose.

## 大 石 良 雄
### Ōishi Yoshio (1659–1703)

Ōishi Yoshio was the leader of the world-renowned Forty-seven Rōnins, who nobly revenged their dead lord, Asano, upon the latter's mortal enemy, the mean wretch Kira. At the tomb of their lord in the graveyard of the Sengakuji Temple, where they had brought Kira's head, Yoshio composed the following *jisei* or "death-verse", in anticipation of an official sentence to commit suicide.

## 辭　世　　　　　良　雄

あら樂や　思ひは晴るる　身は捨つる
うき世の月に　かかる雲なし

### *Jisei*

*Ara raku ya　Omoi wa haruru　Mi wa sutsuru*
*Ukiyo no tsuki ni　Kakaru kumo nashi.*

### The Death Verse　　　Yoshio

**Oh, blest relief! My wish fulfilled!**
**My life I now lay down!**
**No longer in this passing world**
**One cloud to dim my moon!**

*Omoi wa haruru* or "My desire has cleared up" are *engo* or "related words" to *kumo* or "clouds".

## 荷　田　春　滿
### Kada no Azumamaro (1668–1736)

Azumamaro was a Shintō priest in Kyōto and an authority on Shintō. He wrote several literary books.

月  春 滿

嵐吹く　音もおよばぬ　雲の上は
いかに靜けく　月のすむらむ

### Tsuki

*Arashi fuku   Oto mo oyobanu   Kumo no ue wa*
*Ikani shizukeku   Tsuki no sumuran.*

### The Moon  Azumamaro

Above the clouds,
　Beyond the tempest's sound,
How bright and how serene
The moon is found!

\*　　\*　　\*　　\*　　\*

Be still, sad heart!  and cease repining;
Behind the clouds is the sun still shining.

From "The Rainy Day", by Henry W. Longfellow

## 賀 茂 眞 淵
### Kamo no Mabuchi (1697–1769)

Mabuchi was born the son of a Shintō priest in the western suburbs of Hamamatsu, in the province of Tōtōmi.  In 1733 he went to Kyōto to study Japanese classics under Kada no Azumamaro, continuing his studies later at Yedo. When he was fifty years old he became a lecturer on Japanese classics to Tayasu Munetake, the second son of the Shōgun Yoshimune; in which position he remained for fourteen years.  During these years he steadily wrote literary books and taught Japanese classics and versification to many people, among whom may be numbered the celebrated scholars and poets, Moto-ori Norinaga,

Arakida Hisa-oi, Katō Nao-e, Tachibana Chikage, Murata Harumi and Katori Na-hiko. Throughout his life he devoted his best energies to the study of the *Manyō-Shū;* and his studies in this anthology are the most noted among the books—over fifty—which he wrote. His style of versification, according to his pupil Chikage, underwent three changes: in the first period, his verses are akin to those of the *Kokin Shū* and *Shin Kokin Shū;* in the second period, they are of a purely *Manyō* style; and in the third period, they have for their ideal the verses of the *Kojiki* and the *Nihongi.* His poems, however, may be considered to be, on the whole, of a *Manyō* style mixed with something of a *Shin Kokin* style.

Mabuchi, Murata Harumi, Tachibana Chikage and Hirata Atsutane are the greatest Japanese classical scholars in the latter part of the Tokugawa period.

## 山　櫻　　　　　眞　淵

うらうらと　のどけき春の　心より
にほひいでたる　山ざくら花

### *Yama-Zakura*

*Ura-ura to　Nodokeki haru no　Kokoro yori*
*Nioi-idetaru　Yama-zakura bana.*

### Cherry-Blossoms　　　　**Mabuchi**

The mountain cherry-blossoms
Have come forth, brightly shining,
Out of the very heart of
Serene and balmy spring.

## あ　ら　し　　　　眞　淵

しなのなる　すがのあら野を　とぶ鷲の
つばさもたわに　ふく嵐かな

**A portrait of Kamo no Mabuchi**

Painted by Uchiyama Shinryū (内山眞龍),
the poet's pupil
In the possession of Dr. Sasaki Nobutsuna

### *Arashi*

*Shinano naru   Sugano arano wo   Tobu washi no*
*Tsubasa mo tawani   Fuku arashi kana.*

### The Tempest                    Mabuchi

Over the wilds of Sugano
   The storm wind has a blast so violent,
Even a flying eagle's wings thereby
   Are blown and bent.

*Sugano arano* or "the wilds of Sugano" was an extensive wilderness in Suga-no-gō, Higashi-Chikuma County, Shinano Province. The wilderness in question was famous from the *Manyō Shū* period, so Mabuchi lays the scene in it.

### 海 眺 望                    眞 淵

雲や波　波や雲かと　大ぞらに
さながら及ぶ　海のおもかな

### *Umi no Chōbō*

*Kumo ya nami   Nami ya kumo ka to   Ōzora ni*
*Sanagara oyobu   Umi no omo kana.*

### A View of the Sea                Mabuchi

Clouds or waves?  Waves or clouds?
   I hardly know—so high
The face of the sea seems mounted up
   Into the great sky.

明　月　　　　眞淵

こほろぎの　待ちよろこべる　長月の
清き月夜は　更けずもあらなん

*Meigetsu*

*Kōrogi no    Machi-yorokoberu    Nagatsuki no
Kiyoki tsukiyo wa    Fukezu mo aranan.*

**The Brilliant Moon**　　　**Mabuchi**

This brilliant moonlight night, for which
　　The crickets longed, and now are gay—
Oh, I wish that this September night
　　Would never wear away!

はるのはて　　　　眞淵

櫻だに　まだ散りのこる　此春を
幾日もなしと　誰かいふらむ

*Haru no Hate*

*Sakura dani    Mada chiri-nokoru    Kono haru wo
Ikuka mo nashi to    Tare ka yūran.*

**The Close of Spring**　　　**Mabuchi**

Who dares assert
　　There are only a few more days of spring,
When even cherry-flowers
　　Are still upon their branches lingering?

"Flowers"—Keichū

Handwritten by the poet

"The Close of Spring"—Mabuch

Handwritten by the poet

To realize the significance of this verse, the reader should remember that the cherry-blossom, the most beautiful of Japanese flowers, is the representative flower of spring.  This poem may be considered a eulogy of the cherry-blossom.

## 荷 田 在 滿

### Kada no Arimaro (1706–1751)

The nephew of Kada no Azumamaro, Arimaro was adopted as heir by his uncle.  He was an authority on ancient rites and Japanese classics.  He served Lord Tayasu Munetake as a literary adviser for some years, and later opened a private school to which numerous pupils flocked.

### わ が 命 在 滿

戀死なば　あはれとだにも　人や見む
つれなきものは　命なりけり

## *Waga Inochi*

*Koi-shinaba　Aware to da nimo　Hito ya min
Tsurenaki mono wa　Inochi nari keri.*

## My Life  Arimaro

**If I should die of love, perchance
She might pity me;
O life, a heartless thing
I feel thee now to be!**

Paraphrase in prose:  If I should now die of love, my beloved might be sorry for me; but I do not die.  It seems to me that my life is unkind in not leaving me.

## 田 安 宗 武
### Tayasu Munetake (1714–1771)

Munetake was the second son of the Shōgun Tokugawa Yoshimune and the father of Matsudaira Sadanobu, Lord of Kawagoe, a famous statesman.  He was a poet, fond of music and well versed in literature, a subject on which he wrote several books.

雁　　　　　　　　　宗 武

さざなみの　比良の山べの　花さけば
堅田にむれし　雁かへるなり

### Kari

*Sazanami no   Hira no yamabe no   Hana sakeba*
*Katata ni mureshi   Kari kaeru nari.*

### Wild Geese　　　　　Munetake

**When on Mount Hira**
　　**The cherry blossoms burst forth,**
**The wild geese flocking at Katata**
　　**Fly back north.**

"The Evening Snow on Mount Hira" and "The Wild Geese Alighting at Katata" are among the famous "Eight Beauties of Ōmi".

Mount Hira is also famous for cherry-blossoms.

*Sazanami* or "ripples" is the pillow-word belonging to all places in the district of Shiga, in the province of Ōmi.

文月佃島にて　　　　宗 武

眞帆ひきて　よせ來る船に　月照れり
樂しくぞあらむ　その船人は

### Fuzuki Tsukudajima nite

*Maho hikite   Yose-kuru fune ni   Tsuki tereri*
*Tanoshiku zo aran   Sono funa-bito wa.*

## On Tsukuda-Isle in July               Munetake

Upon the incoming ship, with sails full set,
    The glory of the moon is poured.
How happy must they be—
    Those sailor-men on board!

## 雪                                        宗 武

酒のみて　見ればこそあれ　この夕べ
雪ふみ分けて　往きかふ人は

### Yuki

*Sake nomite   Mireba koso are   Kono yūbe*
*Yuki fumi wakete   Yuki-kō hito wa.*

## Snow                                    Munetake

A cup in hand, I can enjoy
    This evening snow;
And yet—how does it fare outside
    With those who through the storm must go?

## 郭 公                                      宗 武

心よげに　草木繁れる　夏山に
煩はしくも　ほととぎす鳴く

### Hototogisu

*Kokoroyoge ni   Kusaki shigereru   Natsuyama ni*
*Wazurawashiku mo   Hototogisu naku.*

#### The *Hototogisu*                          Munetake

Upon the summer mountain where
   Grasses and trees grow pleasantly,
The *hototogisu* are crying
   Annoyingly.

This is the only verse I have come across that speaks depreciatingly of the *hototogisu*'s notes.  This idea, so contrary to traditional thought, and apparently based upon the poet's actual feelings, is appreciated by some annotators.

### 萩 の 花                          宗 武

昨日まで　盛りをみむと　思ひつる
萩の花散れり　今日の嵐に

### Hagi no Hana

*Kinō made   Sakari wo minto   Omoitsuru*
*Hagi no hana chireri   Kyō no arashi ni.*

#### The Lespedeza Flowers                          Munetake

The lespedeza flowers
   For whose full bloom I longed till yesterday—
Alas! they have been scattered by
   The tempest of to-day.

**Lespedeza Flowers in Morning Breeze**

By the late Hyakusui (平福百穂)

佃　島　　　　　　宗　武

かく來ては　珍らしみ聞けど　此波の
夜な夜な響く　あまの伏屋は

### Tsukudajima

*Kaku kite wa Mezurashimi kikedo Kono nami no*
*Yona yona hibiku Amano fuseya wa.*

## On Tsukuda Island　　　　Munetake

**To-day for the first time coming here,**
**I list to the waves with delight;**
**But how may they strike the fisherman's ear,**
**By whose hut they are sounding night after night?**

This verse was composed when the poet visited Tsukudajima, a small island lying in the mouth of the Sumida River, which flows through the east of Tōkyō.

## 小　野　古　道
### Ono Furumichi (18th century)

Ono Furumichi, whose real name was Hasegawa Ken-eki (長谷川謙益), was a physician by profession, but he was a good poet and a pupil of Kamo no Mabuchi. He left a collection of his verses.

鶯　　　　　　　古　道

百鳥の　いづれはあれど　鶯の
なく一聲に　春は來にけり

### *Uguisu*

*Momodori no   Izure wa aredo   Uguisu no*
*Naku hito-koe ni   Haru wa kini keri.*

### The *Uguisu*                    Furumichi

'Tis true,
   A thousand birds may sweetly sing;
But one voice of an *uguisu*
   Has brought the spring.

河 津 美 樹

**Kawazu Umaki** (1721–1777)

An officer of the Tokugawa Government, who left a collection of his verses.

古 戰 場 に て                    美 樹

もののふの　艸むすかばね　年ふりて
秋風寒し　きちかうが原

### *Kosenjō nite*

*Mononofu no   Kusa musu kabane   Toshifurite*
*Akikaze samushi   Kichikō-ga-Hara.*

### At an Old Battlefield                    Umaki

The autumn wind blows mournfully
   Here in the Kikyō Plain,
Where warriors' bones are mossy, mouldering
   With years of snow and rain.

Kichikō-ga-Hara or more popularly Kikyō-ga-Hara, in Shinano Province, was in the poet's day an extensive plain, where in May, 1553, a battle was fought between the troops of Ogasawara Nagatoshi and the famous general, Takeda Shingen, resulting in a crushing defeat of the former.

## 小 澤 蘆 庵
### Ozawa Ro-an (1725–1803)

Ro-an was a samurai of the Owari Clan; but resigning his post, he resided in Kyōto, later in Ōsaka. He studied Japanese and Chinese literature under celebrated scholars. Afterwards he became known as a poet and earned his living by lecturing on Japanese classics and verse-making. A man of intrepid spirit, Ro-an was proficient in fencing and *koto*-playing. He produced many literary works.

## 富 蘆 庵

人の世の　富は草葉に　おく露の
風をまつ間の　光なりけり

### *Tomi*

*Hito no yo no　Tomi wa kusaba ni　Oku tsuyu no
Kaze wo matsu ma no　Hikari nari keri.*

### Riches　Ro-an

The riches of this world—
Alas! but beads of dew
Sparkling on the grass a while,
Waiting—till by the wind down hurled.

## 谷　川 蘆 庵

響き來る　松の嵐に　うづもれて
絶間がちなる　谷のみづおと

### Tani-gawa

*Hibiki kuru   Matsu no arashi ni   Uzumorete*
*Taema gachi naru   Tani no mizu-oto.*

### The Mountain Brook                    Ro-an

Drowned in the roar of the wind
Whistling through the pines,
The murmur of the mountain brook
Ceases now and again.

### 草　木                    蘆　庵

思ふこと　云はで止まめや　心なき
草木も風に　聲たてつなり

### Kusa-Ki

*Omou-koto   Iwade yama-meya   Kokoro-naki*
*Kusaki mo kaze ni   Koe tatetsu nari.*

### Grasses and Trees                    Ro-an

How can I give up
　　Speaking what is in my mind?
Even inanimate grasses and trees
　　Utter sounds against the wind.

### 犬　の　聲                    蘆　庵

里の犬　聲のみ月の　空に澄みて
人はしづまる　宇治の山陰

### Inu no Koe

*Sato no inu   Koe nomi tsuki no   Sora ni sumite*
*Hito wa shizumaru   Uji no yama-kage.*

## The Barking of Dogs                    Ro-an

Only the barking of the village dogs
    Sounds in the moonlit sky;
The people of Uji, the mountain hamlet,
    Asleep all quiet lie.

## こ と の 葉                    蘆 庵

ことの葉は　人の心の　聲なれば
おもひをのぶる　ほかなかりけり

### Koto-no-Ha

*Koto-no-ha wa   Hito no kokoro no   Koe nareba*
*Omoi wo noburu   Hoka nakari keri.*

## A Poem                    Ro-an

A poem is the voice
    Of a man's heart;
So, simply to express his thoughts
    Is all the poet's part.

## 鶯 の 聲                    蘆 庵

何事の　はらだたしかる　折にしも
聞けばゐまるる　鶯のこゑ

## *Uguisu no Koe*

*Nanigoto no   Haradata-shikaru   Ori ni shimo*
*Kikeba emaruru   Uguisu no koe.*

## An *Uguisu*'s Song

**Ro-an**

Even when inclined to anger
Over anything,
I break into a smile on hearing
An *uguisu* sing.

## 本 居 宣 長
### Moto-ori Norinaga (1730–1801)

Norinaga was the son of a rich merchant at Matsuzaka, in the Province of Ise. But, having no propensity for business, he went up to Kyōto in his youth to study literature and medicine. But throughout the Empire he became known as a great authority on Japanese classics. Afterwards he served Lord Tokugawa of Kishū as both a physician and a Japanese scholar. He wrote a number of books on Japanese classics.

## 櫻　花

宣　長

散るまでは　世の營みも　すてて見む
花の日數は　いくばくもあらず

## *Ōkwa*

*Chiru made wa   Yo no itonami mo   Sutete min*
*Hana no hikazu wa   Ikubaku mo arazu.*

**"A Eulogy on My Portrait"—Norinaga**

Both poem and picture done
by the poet in his sixtieth year

### Cherry Blossoms
Norinaga

Setting aside my worldly affairs,
    On the cherry-bloom I will gaze,
Every day till it withers; for
    The flowers will last so few days.

肖 像 自 讃　　　　　宣 長

敷島の　やまと心を　人間はば
朝日ににほふ　やまざくら花

### Shōzō Jisan

*Shikishima no    Yamato-gokoro wo    Hito towaba*
*Asahi ni niou    Yamazakura-bana.*

### A Eulogy on My Portrait
Norinaga

If one should ask of me
    "What is the spirit of Japan?"
I would point out the mountain cherry-bloom
    Bright glowing in the morning sun.

*Shikishima* is a "pillow-word" of *Yamato* or "Japan", and *Yamato-gokoro* means the soul of the Japanese. *Shikishima* is derived from the name of a district in the Province of Yamato, where, stood, tradition says, the palace of the Emperor Kimmei (reigned 540–571); and *Yamato*, the name of a province, is often used as an equivalent to "Japan".

*Niou* has two meanings: to smell fragrant; to shine brightly. Here it is used in the latter sense.

This verse was written in the poet's sixtieth year, as a eulogy of his portrait painted by himself. The poet likens his purity of heart and nobility of mind to the mountain cherry-blossom, the fairest and purest of all Japanese flowers; and since he considers himself to be a typical Japanese, this verse is intended to be applied to the Japanese character in general. Norinaga, when forty-three, wrote another poem on his portrait from his own brush, accompanied by a picture of a branch of cherry-blossoms in a vase:

めづらしき　こまもろこしの　花よりも
あかぬ色香は　櫻なりけり

*Mezurashiki   Koma morokoshi no   Hana yorimo*
*Akanu iroka wa   Sakura nari keri.*

**Beautiful indeed are some**
**Korean and Chinese flowers;**
**But peerless in colour and in scent**
**Are these cherry-blossoms of ours.**

The poet compares himself to the cherry blossom, and considers himself superior in character to great Koreans and Chinese.

It is evident, therefore, that the former poem—the one written in his sixty-first year—is another eulogy of his own character and, at the same time, of the Japanese character in general; and it is wrong to construe this poem, as many scholars do, as a eulogy of the Japanese warrior who is ready to die for Emperor and country, in the full vigour of life and beauty, as the petals of the cherry-blossom flutter, while still lovely, to the earth.

✳　　　✳　　　✳　　　✳　　　✳

Heart of our Land,
Heart of Yamato,
If one should ask you
　　　What it may be;
Fragrance is wafted
Through morning sunlight
Over the mountain where
　　　Cherry-trees bloom.　Trans. by an anonymous writer

**"A Eulogy on My Portrait"—Norinaga**

Both poem and picture done by the poet in
his forty-third year
The poem is accompanied by the remark,
" It expresses my mind which cannot be seen
through a mirror."

If one should ask you
What is the heart
Of Island Yamato—
It is the mountain cherry-blossom
Which exhales its perfume in the morning sun.

Trans. by W. G. Aston

Isles of blest Japan!
    Should your Yamato spirit
Strangers seek to scan,
    Say—scenting morn's sunlit air,
Blows the cherry wild and fair.        Trans. by Nitobe Inazō

Should one ask me
    What is the soul of Japan, (This is my reply:)
    Behold, the mountain cherry flower,
    Glowing in the morning sun!

Trans. by Wadagaki Kenzō

    O Sacred Isles!  Would strangers know
The spirit of Yamato's hero race?
    Point where the cherry-blossoms blow,
Veiling the rugged mountain's frowning face,
    Sun-flushed and heavenly fair,
    Scenting the mountain air!        By Clara A. Walsh

The spirit of Yamato's isles
    If, chance, a stranger should inquire
Go show the morning sun that smiles
    Upon the mountain-cherry fair!

Trans. by Saitō Hidesaburō

Wem wohl der Geist Yamatos
Mag zu vergleichen sein?
Dem Duft der Kirschen blüte
Im Sonnenaufgangschein.        Übertragen von Georg Brandes

Vomit vergleichbar
Ist wohl Yamatos Seele,
Des Flussbeteilands?
In Morgenglut dem Dufte
Der Bergeskirschenblüte!　　　Übertragen von Julius Kurth

## 櫻　　　　　　　　宣長

鶯の　聲ききそむる　あしたより
待たるるものは　櫻なりけり

### Sakura

*Uguisu no　Koe kiki-somuru　Ashita yori*
*Mataruru mono wa　Sakura nari keri.*

### The Cherry-Blossoms　　　Norinaga

From the morning when I first
Hear the *uguisu* sing,
How passionately do I long
For the cherries' blossoming!

## 吉野山の櫻　　　　宣長

見渡せば　ただしら雲ぞ　にほふなる
櫻やいづら　みよし野の山

### Yoshino-Yama no Sakura

*Miwataseba　Tada shirakumo zo　Niō naru*
*Sakura ya izura　Mi-Yoshino no yama.*

### The Cherry Blossoms on Mount Yoshino   Norinaga

Upon Mount Yoshino
White clouds gleam all around;
I wonder in what part of it
The cherry-flowers may be found!

An intense and imaginative admiration of Mount Yoshino, covered with cherry-flowers, leads the poet to express himself with a little poetic license.

The cherry-flowers look to him like white clouds, so he wonders in what part of the mountain the flowers may be found.

菫　　　　　　　　　宣 長

朝戸出の　庭の芝生に　昨日まで
しらぬ菫の　花さきにけり

### *Sumire*

*Asa-tode no   Niwa no shibafu ni   Kinō made*
*Shiranu sumire no   Hana saki ni keri.*

### Violets   Norinaga

In early morning, going out
To my garden, I found blooming there
In the turf some violets, of which,
Till yesterday I was quite unaware.

い　の　ち　　　　　宣 長

世にあれば　今年の春の　花も見つ
うれしきものは　命なりけり

### Inochi

*Yo ni areba   Kotoshi no haru no   Hana mo mitsu*
*Ureshiki mono wa   Inochi nari keri.*

## Life                                                    **Norinaga**

**Since I live within this world,**
**This spring again I've seen the flowers;**
**Ah! how enjoyable it is—**
**This life of ours!**

### 伴　蒿　蹊
#### Ban Kōkei (1732–1806)

The poet's real name was Sukeyoshi (資芳), Kōkei being his *nom de plume.*
His other pen name was Kanden (閑田). The son of a rich merchant of Ya-
wata in the Province of Ōmi, he was also engaged in business, and in spare
hours studied literature. Later he devoted himself to the study of Japanese
and Chinese classics and Buddhism. He became widely known as a poet and
a prose writer. He enjoyed the favour of the friendship of the Emperor Ōgi-
machi and Prince Chikataka. He wrote many books on literature.

### 山　水                                              蒿　蹊

末遂に　海となるべき　山水も
しばし木の葉の　下くゞるなり

### Yamamizu

*Sue tsuini   Umi to narubeki   Yama-mizu mo*
*Shibashi ko no ha no   Shita kuguru nari.*

### The Mountain Brook    Kōkei

The mountain brook, which finally
Is destined to become the sea,
Goes hidden underneath a pile
Of fallen leaves, a little while.

Needless to say, this is a didactic verse teaching that a man who is bound to achieve great things is humble.

### 橘　千　蔭

#### Tachibana Chikage (1734–1804)

The son of Enao (枝直), a *yoriki* or lower official of the Tokugawa Government, Chikage succeeded to his father's office, which he later resigned on account of illness. He studied Japanese versification under his father and Kamo no Mabuchi, the great poet. He became a good poet, was skilled in calligraphy and painting. He was proficient in writing *kyōka* or "humorous verses", and wrote several books, including "Brief Annotations on the *Manyō Shū* Anthology." It is well to note that he was generally known by another name, Katō Matazaemon.

### 菫　の　床    千　蔭

あけたてば　霞に消ゆる　雲雀だに
菫の床は　忘れざるらむ

### Sumire no Toko

*Ake tateba   Kasumi ni kiyuru   Hibari dani
Sumire no toko wa   Wasure zaruran.*

### The Bed of Violets

Chikage

Even the larks which vanish into mists,
When breaks the dawn,
Will surely not forget
The fragrant bed of violets.

### ほととぎす

千 蔭

隅田川　堤に立ちて　舟待てば
みなかみ遠く　鳴くほととぎす

#### *Hototogisu*

Sumida-gawa　Tsutsumi ni tachite　Fune mateba
Minakami tōku　Naku hototogisu.

### The Cuckoo

Chikage

On the banks of the Sumida River,
While awaiting the ferryboat,
Sudden, I heard, far away up the stream,
A cuckoo's note.

### 夕 顔

千 蔭

かはほりの　飛びかふ軒は　くれそめて
猶くれやらぬ　夕顔の花

#### *Yūgao*

Kawahori no　Tobikō noki wa　Kure-somete
Nao kure-yaranu　Yūgao no hana.

**"The Bed of Violets"**
—**Chikage**
In the poet's own handwriting

**"The Notes of Skylarks"**
—**Hijimaro**
In the poet's own handwriting

**The picture** by Busei (喜多武清 1776-1856)

### Evening-Glories Chikage

**About the eaves, where bats go flitting by,**
**Darkness is deepening fast;**
**But the white gleaming of the evening-glories**
**Is not yet quenched in dusk.**

Evening twilight has begun to enwrap all things save where the *yūgao* or "evening-glories" (a kind of convolvolus which blooms in the evening) gleam white and beautiful. かはほり or *kawahori* is the old spelling of こうもり or *kōmori*.

### 栗 田 土 麿
#### Kurita Hijimaro (1737–1811)

Kurita Hajimaro was a priest of the Hachiman Shrine at Hirao Village, in the Province of Tōtōmi. He studied Japanese poetry under Kamo no Mabuchi and Moto-ori Norinaga.

### 羇 中 戀 土 麿

はろばろに　海山こえて　來ぬれども
戀の奴は　おくれざりけり

#### Kichu no Koi

*Haro-baro ni　Umi-yama koete　Kinure domo*
*Koi no tsubune wa　Okurezari keri.*

### Love in My Journey Hijimaro

**Over mountains, over seas,**
**I travelled far away;**
**Yet Love, my servant, never failed**
**To follow day by day.**

*Okure zari keri*, literally, means "Never lagged behind"—a striking phrase. *Tsubune* (奴) or "servant" is an ancient word. *Shimobe* or *yakko* is modern.

## 雲雀の聲　　　　　土　麿

聲をのみ　聞きてぞ思ふ　鳴く雲雀
あやなの野邊の　春の霞や

### *Hibari no Koe*

*Koe wo nomi   Kikite zo omō   Naku hibari*
*Ayana no nobe no   Haru no kasumi ya.*

## The Notes of Skylarks　　　Hijimaro

Only hearing the notes
    Of skylarks which sweetly sing,
I think how heartless are the mists
    Wrapping the fields of spring!

*Ayana no* means "unreasonable" or "heartless".

### 村　田　春　海
**Murata Harumi (1740–1805)**

Harumi was a great authority on Chinese and Japanese classics, and a prominent poet. He also had great skill in calligraphy. He was appointed a literary adviser to the Lord of Shirakawa in Oshū.

## 富　士　山　　　　　春　海

心あてに　見し白雲は　麓にて
おもはぬ空に　はるる富士のね

### Fuji San

*Kokoro ate ni   Mishi shirakumo wa   Fumoto nite*
*Omowanu sora ni   Haruru Fuji no ne.*

## Mount Fuji                    Harumi

The bank of snowy clouds, wherein
I thought Mount Fuji to espy,
Is now found at its foot.  The peak
Towers majestic in the unsuspected sky.

## 曉天千鳥                    春　海

沖つ風　雲居に吹きて　有明の
月にみだるる　村千鳥かな

### Gyōten no Chidori

*Okitsu-kaze   Kumoi ni fukite   Ariake no*
*Tsuki ni midaruru   Mura-chidori kana.*

## Plovers in Dawn Sky          Harumi

The open sea wind blowing hard,
High in the sky,
Amid the moonlight of the dawn,
Flocks of plovers, straggling, fly.

## 時　雨                    春　海

雲過ぐる　みねは夕日の　かげ見えて
麓のさとに　時雨ふるなり

## *Shigure*

*Kumo suguru   Mine wa yūhi no   Kage miete
Fumoto no sato ni   Shigure furu nari.*

## A Winter Shower

**Harumi**

The evening sun is shining bright
  Upon the peak from which the clouds have passed,
While in the village at its foot
  A winter shower is falling fast.

## ゆ く 春

春 海

花ははや　須磨も明石も　散りにけり
浦傳ひして　春やくれゆく

## *Yuku Haru*

*Hana wa haya   Suma mo Akashi mo   Chiri ni keri
Ura zutai shite   Haru ya kure-yuku.*

## Departing Spring

**Harumi**

Lo, at Suma and Akashi
  The flowers have drifted quite away;
Spring is leaving, step by step,
  Along the bay.

Suma and Akashi are beautiful shores of the Inland Sea.
*Hana* or "flowers" means "cherry flowers".

矢 部 正 子
**Yabe Masa-ko** (1745–1773)

Divorced from her ill-behaved husband, Masa-ko became an attendant to a young daughter of a daimiō; but when she was twenty-seven, bereft of her only child, she became a Buddhist nun. She studied poetry under the famous poet, Ozawa Ro-an.

夏草の風 正 子

咲き交る 早百合撫子 うちなびき
風の姿を 見るすすしさ

*Natsu-gusa no Kaze*

*Saki-majiru Sayuri nadeshiko Uchi-nabiki*
*Kaze no sugata wo Misuru suzushisa.*

### The Breeze on Summer Flowers **Masa-ko**

**When I see the breeze's own fair form,**
**Where the wild flowers mingled grow—**
**Fringed pink and early lily swaying**
**In its breath—the coolness, oh!**

僧 豪 潮
**Priest Gōchō** (1749–1835)

Gōchō was a priest of the Ryōgon-in Temple on Mount Hiei, in Ōmi Province. He was well known for his strict observance of Buddhist commandments and his rigorous asceticism.

朝 顔 豪 潮

朝がほの はかなきことを ゆふべには
わすれて明日の 花を待ちけり

## *Asagao*

*Asagao no Hakanaki koto wo    Yūbe niwa*
*Wasurete asu no    Hana wo machikeri.*

### The Morning-Glories    Gōchō

The evanescence of my morning-glories
I have forgotten in the evening,
And am only looking forward
To the morrow's blooming.

### 賀 茂 季 鷹
#### Kamo no Suetaka (1752–1842)

Suetaka was a priest of the Shintō Temple at Kamo, Kyōto.  In his younger
days he studied poetry under Tachibana Chikage at Yedo.

### 月 前 梅    季 鷹

梅が香の　かをらざりせば　窓の内に
まだ影寒き　月を入れめや

### *Getsuzen no Ume*

*Ume ga ka no    Kaora zari seba    Mado no uchini*
*Mada kage samuki    Tsuki wo ire me ya.*

### The Plum-Blossoms under the Moon    Suetaka

But for the fragrance of the plum-bloom,
Why should I let
The still cold moon
Inside the window yet?

It was still early spring and the moon shone cold; but the sweet odour of the plum-flowers in his garden delighted the poet so much that he opened the shuttered window in spite of the chilly air, so that the moonbeams streamed in.

## 武藏野の月　　　季 鷹

するがなる　富士のねかけて　すむ月を
武藏野の原に　出でて見る哉

### Musashi-no no Tsuki

*Suruga naru　Fuji-no-ne kakete　Sumu tsuki wo
Musashino no hara ni　Idete miru kana.*

## The Moon Above Musashi Plain　　Suetaka

Out to Musashi Plain I come
　To see the clear moonbeams, and how they light—
So far they shine—in Suruga
　Mount Fuji's height.

## 服 部 中 庸
### Hattori Nakatsune (1756–1824)

A man of Matsuzaka, Ise Province, Nakatsune was a pupil of Moto-ori Norinaga and wrote some books on Moto-orism. By profession he was a physician.

## 嵐　山　　　中 庸

櫻さく　春は幾日も　あらし山
花のさかりは　心してふけ

### *Arashi-Yama no Hana*

*Sakura saku   Haru wa ikuka mo   Arashi-Yama*
*Hana no sakari wa   Kokoro shite fuke.*

## Mount Arashi                      Nakatsune

**The cherry-flowers on Mount Arashi**
**Last but very few days;**
**Oh, wind, blow not with violence,**
**While they delight our gaze.**

The word *arashi* is used in a threefold sense: firstly, it is the name of the famous hill, Arashi-Yama, in the neighbourhood of Kyōto, noted for cherry-flowers; secondly, it is used in the sense of *araji* or "there are not", so that *ikuka mo araji* means "there are not many days"; and thirdly, it is used in the sense of *arashi* or "tempest", or, more precisely, "wind".

### 賴 杏 坪
#### Rai Kyōhei (1756–1834)

A native of Takewara, a village in Aki Province, Kyōhei studied Chinese classics at Ōsaka and Yedo.  He became an important retainer of Lord Asano of the Aki Clan, and contributed greatly to the finances of the clan.  He was proficient in Chinese poetry and calligraphy.

### 花　見                     杏 坪

今日ひとひ　身を鶯に　なしはてて
花あるかたに　うかれてぞゆく

### *Hana-Mi*

*Kyō hitohi   Mi wo uguisu ni   Nashi-hatete*
*Hana aru kata ni   Ukarete zo yuku.*

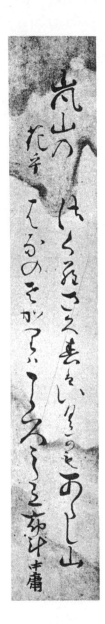

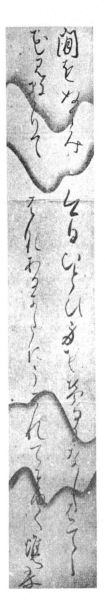

**"Mount Arashi"—Nakatsune**

In the poet's own handwriting

**"Flower-Viewing"—Kyōhei**

In the poet's own handwriting

### Flower-Viewing                    Kyōhei

Changing myself to an *uguisu*,
For this one day, all day,
Where there are flowers, there will I wander,
Lightsome and gay.

### 松 平 定 信
#### Matsudaira Sadanobu (1757–1829)

The seventh son of Tayasu Munetake, *Rōchū* or Minister of the Shōgun's Government, Sadanobu was adopted by Matsudaira Sadakuni, the Lord of the Shirakawa Castle in Ōshū. He became Minister of the Shōgun's Government and contributed a great deal to political improvement. He was well versed in Japanese history and versification; also skilled in painting. Left a collection of his own verses.

### あ け ぼ の                    定 信

さく花の　梢しらみて　あをやぎに
まだ夜をのこす　あけぼのの空

### *Akebono*

*Saku hana no   Kozue shiramite   Aoyagi ni*
*Mada yo wo nokosu   Akebono no sora.*

### Dawn                    Sadanobu

Upon the boughs of cherry-bloom
Dawn glimmers white,
Though among green willow leaves
Lingers the night.

In the twilight of early dawn, day seems already breaking where cherry-blossoms gleam white, while it is still dusky where green willow leaves sway in the breeze.

## 僧　良　寛
### The Priest Ryōkwan (1757–1831)

Born of a good family of Izumozaki in the Province of Echigo, Ryōkwan gave his hereditary rights to his younger brother and spent most of his life as an itinerant priest. He was a prominent poet and a skilful calligrapher, and left a collection of his own verses. He is famous for his eccentric behaviour.

## 月　夜　　　　良　寛

いざ歌へ　われ立ち舞はむ　ぬば玉の
こよひの月に　いねらるべしや

### *Tsukiyo*

*Iza utae　Ware tachi-mawan　Nubatama no
Koyoi no tsuki ni　Ineraru beshi ya.*

### A Moonlight Night　　　Ryōkwan

Come, friend, be gay and sing;
　　I'll rise and dance!　To-night
How can we sleep at ease
　　When the moon shines so bright?

## 鶯　　　　　　良　寛

うぐひすの　聲をききつる　あしたより
春のこころに　なりにけるかも

**Ryōkwan with his Bowl**

By the late Hyakusui (故平福百穂)
From the frontispiece to " The Life
of Ryōkan " By Sōma Gyofū

## *Uguisu*

*Uguisu no   Koe wo kiki tsuru   Ashita yori*
*Haru no kokoro ni   Nari ni keru kamo.*

### The *Uguisu*                    Ryōkwan

**The morning when I heard
The first *uguisu* sing,
My mind became
The mind of spring.**

At first sight this verse seems to be commonplace but as one repeatedly recites it, one is irresistibly charmed by its magic. It is not a mere fantasy but the spontaneous outburst of an actual experience.

It may well be imagined that the snow was still lingering about the poet's hermitage in the mountain. He longed passionately for spring, but everything seemed to suggest that it was far away. However, early one morning, quite unexpectedly, to his boundless delight, an *uguisu*, the messenger of spring, was heard to sing sweetly at some distance. The poet, for the first time, became aware of the arrival of spring, and suddenly experienced the ecstasy of the sweet and gay season. Therefore, it seems, he burst into the above lines.

## 形　見                    良　寛

形見とて　何か殘さむ　春は花
山ほととぎす　秋はもみぢ葉

### *Katami*

*Katami tote   Nani ka nokosan   Haru wa hana*
*Yama-hototogisu   Aki wa momiji-ba.*

### My Legacy
Ryōkwan

What shall I leave as my legacy?
   Cherry-blossoms in spring,
Hill cuckoos in summer,
   Maples in autumn, I will bring.

Before *Yama-hototogisu, natsu wa* "in summer" is understood.

The poet is thoroughly identified with Nature.  His heart and soul are lodged in the cherry-blossom, the cuckoo and the maple leaf.  He, therefore, would leave them as his memorials to his friends.

### 籠 の 鳥
良 寛

ひさかたの　くもゐの上に　鳴く雲雀
今を春べと　かごぬちに鳴く

### Kago no Tori

*Hisakata no　Kumoi no ue ni　Naku hibari*
*Ima wo harube to　Kago-nuchi ni naku.*

### A Bird in a Cage
Ryōkwan

The skylark which might soar
   High in the blue and gaily sing—
Oh, hark!—is singing in its cage,
   Proclaiming that it now is spring.

### 松 の 音
良 寛

里べには　笛や太鼓の　音すなり
み山はさはに　松の音しつ

### *Matsu no Oto*

*Satobe niwa   Fue ya taiko no   Oto su nari
Miyama wa sawani   Matsu no oto shitsu.*

## The Murmuring of Pine Trees          Ryōkwan

**Down in the villages
Flutes and drums are sounding;
Here in the mountain—
Pines' multitudinous murmuring.**

It is the opinion of Sōma Gyofū that this verse was composed on an August night when the *Bon* dances—open-air dances performed for the consolation of the dead on three or four August nights in succession (*Bon* being an abbreviation for *Urabon* derived from the Sanskrit Ullambana)—were in progress to the accompaniment of flutes and drums. In connection with the phrase, "Here in the mountain", we may remind the reader that the priest-poet lived in a hut on a mountain.

Down in the village merry dances were going on, while in the mountain, where the poet lived, the wind whispered through the pine-trees, a sound which was congenial to the hermit.

"The last phrase, *sawani matsu no oto shitsu*, or 'the pine-trees murmur in abundance' is an extremely beautiful one", says Saitō Mokichi. "This phrase is very brief but has much significance".

鉢 の 子          良 寛

みちのべに　菫つみつつ　鉢の子を
忘れてぞ來し　その鉢の子を

### *Hachi-no-Ko*

*Michinobe ni   Sumire tsumitsutsu   Hachi-no-ko wo
Wasurete zo koshi   Sono hachi-no-ko wo.*

### The Bowl                                    Ryōkwan

Gathering violets,
Growing by the wayside,
I left my bowl,
My dear bowl, behind me.

The *hachi-no-ko* or "bowl" is a wooden, iron or earthen bowl which a mendicant priest carries for receiving alms, *ko* or "child" being a dimunitive with an implication of affection.

The bowl is the most important possession for a mendicant priest, yet this poet-priest, it seems, often forgot his bowl while gathering violets.

秋の時雨の降らぬ間に          良 寛

水やくまむ　薪やこらむ　菜やつまむ
秋の時雨の　ふらぬその間に

### Aki no Shigure no Furanu Mani

*Mizu ya kuman    Takigi ya koran    Na ya tsuman*
*Aki no shigure no    Furanu sono ma ni.*

### Before the Autumn Shower Falls        Ryōkwan

Before the autumn shower falls,
I will draw water,
I will cut firewood,
Greens I will gather.

The simple life of a hermit simply described.

## 鉢 の 子　　　　良 寛

みちのべに　すみれつみつつ　鉢の子を
わが忘るれども　とる人はなし

### Hachi-no-Ko

*Michinobe ni Sumire tsumitsutsu　Hachi-no-ko wo*
*Waga wasururedomo　Toru hito wa nashi.*

### The Bowl　　　　Ryōkwan

True, at the wayside, gathering blue violets,
　　Forgetful, I may leave behind me my bowl,
But no one will care to take and keep it,
　　Dear though it is to my soul.

## 鶯のこゑ　　　　良 寛

薪こり　この山かげに　斧とりて
いくたびかきく　鶯のこゑ

### Uguisu no Koe

*Takigi kori　Kono yamakage ni　Ono torite*
*Ikutabi ka kiku　Uguisu no koe.*

### The *Uguisu*'s Voice　　　　Ryōkwan

While with an axe I am chopping wood
　　Under this mountain,
I hear the voice of *uguisu*
　　Often and often.

## 菫　　　　　　　　良　寛

飯乞ふと　わが來しかども　春の野に
菫つみつつ　時をへにけり

### Sumire

*Ii kō to　Waga koshi kadomo　Haru no no ni*
*Sumire tsumi-tsutsu　Toki wo heni keri.*

### Violets　　　　　　Ryōkwan

I started out to beg for rice,
　　But in the meadows grew intent
On gathering spring violets,
　　And so my time has all been spent!

### 植　松　有　信
**Uematsu Arinobu (1760–1819)**

A man of Owari Province, Arinobu was the chief disciple of Moto-ori No-
rinaga.　Being a woodcarver by profession, he carved the wood blocks for many
of his master's books and thus contributed a great deal to the spread of Moto-
orism.　He wrote some books on Japanese literature.

## 花　　　　　　　　有　信

旅寐して　家路のみかは　日數さへ
花にわするる　春の山里

### Hana

*Tabine-shite　Ie-ji nomi kawa　Hi-kazu sae*
*Hana ni wasururu　Haru no yama-zato.*

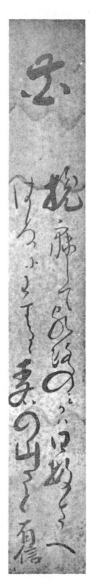

**"Flowers"—Arinobu**

In the poet's own handwriting

**"When Seriously Ill"—Hirotsuna**

In the poet's own handwriting
(See Page 603)

## Flowers

**Arinobu**

Travelling in spring among mountain villages,
Charmed by the beauty of the flowers,
I have forgotten about the way to my home,
And even how many days have been passing.

## 香 川 景 樹

### Kagawa Kageki (1768–1843)

Suminori (純德)—for this was the poet's first name—was the second son of Hayashi Zembei, a samurai of lower rank, of the Tottori Clan in Inaba Province. He was such a prodigy, it is said, that he composed a poem when he was six years old. In his town, he studied poetry under Shimizu Sadakata and Chinese classics under Hori Nanko. At the age of seventeen, he went up to Kyōto to continue his studies, and while studying he supported himself by shampooing at night. He took lessons from Kagawa Kagemoto (香川景柄), an instructor in poetry by hereditary profession. On account of his poetical genius, he became a favourite with his master, who soon adopted him as his heir. Then the young poet-to-be assumed the name of Kagawa Kageki, after his father-in-law. Since the Kagawas were retainers of the noble Tokudaiji family, Kageki also became their retainer, and in his old age he was granted the Junior Fifth Rank and the honorary title of Lord of Higo.

In his thirties, Kageki was recognised as a poet in the Kyōto poets' circles, and his style and theory gradually gained ground, until at last they enjoyed an undisputed sway in the poetical world of all Japan. He earned his living as an instructor in poetry, and in the course of his whole life, it is said, he had about one thousand pupils. He wrote some books on poetry and left a collection of his verses called *Kei-en Isshi* (桂園一枝) or "A Branch from the Garden of the Katsura-tree", "Kei-en" being his *nom de plume*. For further information about his poetical career see Page 33 (Introduction).

It is well here to note that the proper pronunciation of the Chinese characters 景樹 which represent the poet's name is Kageshige, but they are generally pronounced Kageki and even the poet himself came to adopt this pronunciation later in his life.

蝶　　　　　　　　　　　景　樹

大空に　戯るる蝶の　一つがひ
目にもとまらず　なりにけるかな

## Chō

Ōzora ni　Tawaruru chō no　Hito-tsugai
Me ni mo tomarazu　Nari ni keru kana.

### Butterflies　　　　　　　Kageki

Dancing through the air—
A pair of butterflies—
Flitting up till lost to sight
In the infinite skies!

春　の　野　　　　　　　景　樹

春の野の　うかれごころは　果もなし
とまれといひし　蝶はとまりぬ

## Haru no No

Haru no no no　Ukare-gokoro wa　Hate mo nashi
Tomare to üshi　Chō wa tomarinu.

### The Spring Fields　　　　　Kageki

In the fields in spring, there is no end
To my jollity!
I told a butterfly to alight,
And it lighted on me!

**A Portrait of Kagawa Kageki**

Painted by Inoue Tadaoki (井上忠興), the poet's son-in-law
In the possession of Dr. Sasaki Nobutsuna

The last two lines are suggested by the children's song:—

蝶々　蝶々　菜の葉にとまれ
菜の葉がいやなら　手にとまれ

*Chōchō　chōchō　Na-no-ha ni tomare*
*Na-no-ha ga iya nara　Te ni tomare.*

Butterfly, little butterfly,
Light upon the rape leaf;
But if thou dost not like the rape leaf,
Prithee, light upon my hand.

## 雲　雀　　　　　景　樹

おもしろく　さへづる春の　夕ひばり
身をばこころに　まかせはてつつ

### *Hibari*

*Omoshiroku　Saezuru haru no　Yū-hibari*
*Mi wo ba kokoro ni　Makase hatetsutsu.*

## Skylarks　　　　Kageki

The skylarks of an eve in spring
Soar and sing with ecstasy,
Yielding up their bodies all
To their spirits perfectly.

In this verse the poet imagines himself to be a farmer, busily engaged in tilling land, who, laying his hoe aside, gazes up with envy at skylarks soaring freely and singing merrily in the evening sky.

燕 　　　　　　　　　　　　　景 樹

かたらはん　友にもあらぬ　燕すら
遠く來るは　うれしかりけり.

### Tsubame

*Katarawan　Tomo nimo aranu　Tsubame sura
Tōku kitaru wa　Ureshikari keri.*

### Swallows　　　　　　　　　**Kageki**

**Although the swallows are not like
The friends with whom I freely may
Hold converse, what a joy it is
To meet these birds from far away!**

松 と 月 　　　　　　　　景 樹

殘りなく　松の姿は　あらはれて
いまだ離れぬ　山の端の月

### Matsu to Tsuki

*Nokori-naku　Matsu no sugata wa　Arawarete
Imada hanarenu　Yama no ha no tsuki.*

### Pine-Trees and the Moon　　**Kageki**

**The forms of all the pine-trees
Have stood forth into sight;
But yet the moon has not left
The rim of the mountain height.**

The full moon has half appeared on the top of the eastern mountain, and all the pine-trees growing on it have already thrown their fantastic shadowy forms against the sky—a beautiful effect!

### 寒　　月　　　　景　樹

照る月の　影の散り來る　ここちして
夜行く袖に　たまる雪かな

#### *Kangetsu*

*Teru tsuki no　Kage no chiri-kuru　Kokochi shite*
*Yoru yuku sode ni　Tamaru yuki kana.*

### The Cold Moon　　Kageki

Behold! upon my sleeves,
As I was strolling in the moonlit night,
White snowflakes drifted thickly down,
Like moonbeams raining bright.

*Kangetsu* or "the cold moon" means "the winter moon".

"It is no uncommon phenomenon in Kyōto, where the poet lived, because of its geographical position, that snowflakes fall while the moon shines".—Kubota Utsubo.

### 夜は明けたり　　　　景　樹

燈の　影にて見ると　思ふ間に
文の上白く　夜は明けにけり

#### *Yo wa Aketari*

*Tomoshibi no　Kage nite miru to　Omō mani*
*Fumi no e shiroku　Yo wa akeni keri.*

### Day has Dawned                    Kageki

**While I thought still**
**That I was reading by a light,**
**Behold! upon the book**
**Day has dawned white.**

While the poet was absorbed in reading an interesting book, ere he was aware, day has dawned.

*Fumi no e shiroku* or, "White upon the book", is considered by Kubota Utsubo to be a clever impressionistic description.

### 山　櫻                    景　樹

照る月の　影にて見れば　山櫻
枝うごくなり　今か散るらむ

### *Yama-Zakura*

*Teru tsuki no   Kage nite mireba   Yama-zakura*
*Eda ugoku nari   Ima ka chiru ran.*

### Mountain Cherry-Trees          Kageki

**Clear in the bright moonlight,**
**The branches of the mountain cherry-trees**
**Are swaying; and I wonder if**
**The flowers are scattering in the breeze.**

The moonlight is so brilliant that the poet cannot see the scattering petals; but judging from the swaying branches, he imagines that they may be fluttering down.

**Wild Geese**

By Bunchō (谷文晁 1764-1841)

雁 　 景 樹

はるばると　かすめる空を　うちむれて
きのふもけふも　歸る雁がね

### Kari

*Harubaruto　Kasumeru sora wo　Uchitsurete*
*Kinō mo kyō mo　Kaeru karigane.*

### Wild Geese　Kageki

Far in the distance, across the hazy sky,
　I saw the wild geese flock and fly away;
Yesterday I saw them take their flight,
　Also to-day.

少　女 　 景 樹

わか草を　駒にふませて　かいまみし
少女も今は　老いやしぬらむ

### Otome

*Wakakusa wo　Koma ni fumasete　Kaimamishi*
*Otome mo ima wa　Oi ya shinuran.*

### A Maiden　Kageki

The girl of whom in olden days
I once caught glimpses through a hedge,
Making my horse tread on young grass—
Alas! she, too, by now must have grown old!

菊　映　水　　　　　　　　　景　樹

いづくより　駒うち入れむ　さほ川の
さざれにうつる　しら菊の花

### Kiku Mizu ni Eizu

*Izuku yori   Koma uchi-iren   Saho-gawa no*
*Sazare ni utsuru   Shira-giku no hana.*

## Chrysanthemums Reflected in the Stream   Kageki

At what spot shall I plunge my horse
Into the Saho River's bosom?
Lo! white chrysanthemums are reflected
Over the pebbles at the bottom.

The Saho-gawa is the upper stream of the Yamato River, which flows through the outskirts of Nara; and on its beauty several poets of the Nara Period wrote excellent poems.

It seems that the poet imagines himself to be a young man of the Nara Period. He comes on horseback to a shallow ford of the Sahogawa, intending to cross it; but he finds that white chrysanthemums growing on the banks are reflected everywhere in the clear water running over pebbles in the river-bed, and hesitates, lest his horse should disturb the beautiful picture.

あ　ひ　る　　　　　　　　　景　樹

鴨河に　浮ぶあひるの　朝な朝な
たらすなりゆく　數ぞ悲しき

### Ahiru

*Kamo-gawa ni   Ukabu ahiru no   Asa-na asa-na*
*Tarazu nari-yuku   Kazu zo kanashiki.*

**Chrysanthemums**

By Kwashū (菊池華秋),
a contemporary painter

### Ducks                                    **Kageki**

**How sad to see the ducks**
**Which swimming go**
**Upon the Kamo River, morn by morn**
**A smaller number show!**

(*Kei-en Isshi*, Section "Winter")

The poet was sorry to find that numerous ducks kept free on the Kamo
River by a poultryman, lessened in number morning by morning, as one after
another they were killed.

### 木 枯 の 風                              景　樹

おぼつかな　木の間に見ゆる　三日月も
散るばかりなる　木枯の風

### Kogarashi no Kaze

*Obotsuka na　Ko no ma ni miyuru　Mikazuki mo*
*Chiru bakari naru　Kogarashi no kaze.*

### The Winter Gale                         **Kageki**

**It seems as if the fury**
**Of the winter gale**
**Would blow down, too, the slender crescent moon**
**Between the tree trunks gleaming pale.**

*Mikazuki mo* means "the crescent, too," i. e. together with the leaves of
trees scattered by the tempest.

The winter gale is blowing so hard that the leaves of trees are falling, and
it seems as if the crescent hanging low behind the trees may be blown down
too.

きりぎりす　　　　　景 樹

敷妙の　夜床のしたの　きりぎりす
わがささめ言　人に語るな

### Kirigirisu

*Shikitae no    Yodoko no shita no    Kirigirisu*
*Waga sasame-goto    Hito ni kataru na.*

## The Cricket　　　　　**Kageki**

**O, cricket, chirruping**
**Under my bed,**
**Do not tell other men**
**My whispers with my beloved.**

*Shikitae* is a pillow-word pertaining to *toko* or "bed".
*Kirigirisu* nowadays means "grasshoppers", but in the poet's day it often meant "cricket".

### 平 田 篤 胤
#### Hirata Atsutane (1776–1843)

Atsutane, the son of a samurai of the Kubota Clan, was deeply read in Japanese and Chinese classics and a great authority on Shintō. He wrote numerous books, principally on Shintō, and, it is said, had over a thousand pupils.

神のみちびき　　　　　篤 胤

なすわざを　己が力と　人や思ふ
神のみちびく　身を知らずして

## *Kami no Michibiki*

*Nasu-waza wo   Ono ga chikara to   Hito ya omou*
*Kami no michibiku   Mi wo shirazushite.*

### The Guidance of the Gods         Atsutane

**Men think that by their own good strength**
 **They do each deed,**
**Not knowing that in all it is**
 **The gods who lead.**

### 清 水 濱 臣
#### Shimizu Hama-omi (1778–1824)

A native of Yedo, Hama-omi was a physician by profession. But he was widely known as a poet and a prose writer. He wrote many books on poetry and left a collection of his own verses.

### 櫻　花         濱 臣

君も舞へ　我も歌はん　咲く花の
醉をすすむる　今日にやはあらぬ

### *Okwa*

*Kimi mo mae   Ware mo utawan   Saku˙hana no*
*Ei wo susumuru   Kyō ni ya wa aranu.*

### Cherry-Blossoms         Hama-omi

**Well, dance, my friend;**
 **I will sing gay.**
**The cherry-blossoms incite us**
 **To drink and make merry to-day.**

## 木 下 幸 文
### Kinoshita Takabumi (1779–1821)

A native of a village in Bitchū Province, Takabumi studied poetry under Kagawa Kageki at Kyōto, and became one of his ten chief pupils. Later he resided at Ōsaka; and his fame spreading far and near, he flourished as an instructor in poetry. He wrote several books, including "Notes on the *Manyō Shū* Anthology" and "A Diary of Travels".

## 貧　窮 幸 文

かにかくに　疎くぞ人の　なりにける
貧しきばかり　悲しきはなし

### Hinkyū

*Kani kakuni   Utoku zo hito no   Narini keru*
*Mazushiki bakari   Kanashiki wa nashi.*

### Poverty Takabumi

In this way, in that way,
Most of my friends are estranged;
Nothing so much saddens
As poverty.

## 島 の 秋 幸 文

しら浪の　たちめぐらせる　わたつみの
沖つ島山　紅葉しにけり

## Shima no Aki

*Shiranami no    Tachi-meguraseru    Watatsumi no*
*Okitsu-shima yama    Momiji shi ni keri.*

### Autumn in an Island                    Takabumi

The island in the great sea
Surrounded by white waves—
Its hills are all aflame
With crimson-tinted leaves.

### 熊 谷 直 好
#### Kumagai Naoyoshi (1782-1862)

Naoyoshi was a native of Suō Province. In his youth, he studied poetry under the famous poet, Kagawa Kageki. He became known for his poetic gift, and was one of the "Ten Disciples" of Kageki. He wrote several books on poetry, and left a collection of his own verses.

### 世 の 中                    直 好

花も見つ　月をも愛でつ　世の中に
あるかひなしと　いふは誰が言

### Yo no Naka

*Hana mo mitsu    Tsuki omo medetsu    Yono naka ni*
*Aru kai nashi to    Yū wa ta ga koto.*

### Human Life                                       Naoyoshi

We've seen the cherry-blossom,
We've viewed the harvest moon.
Who dares to say this life
Is not worth living after all?

### 雪                                                直 好

朝風は　たたずもあらなん　しら雪の
ふりしづめたる　峯のまつ原

### Yuki

*Asakaze wa　Tatazu mo aranan　Shirayuki no*
*Furi-shizumetaru　Mine no matsubara.*

### Snow                                             Naoyoshi

Oh, that the morning wind may not blow through
　　The pine grove on the mountain's brow,
Which has been hushed to stillness
　　By a fall of snow.

### うるはしき夜                                      直 好

月影の　いたらぬ隈に　螢飛び
思ひすてても　寝られざる夜や

### Uruwashiki Yoru

*Tsuki-kage no　Itaranu kuma ni　Hotaru tobi*
*Omoi-sutetemo　Nerarezaru yo ya.*

**Mount Fuji**

By Mitsuzane
(土佐光孚 1800-1852)

"Snow"—Naoyoshi

Handwritten by the poet

### A Beautiful Night                    Naoyoshi

Fireflies flitted in those dark spots
Where the moonlight did not fall.
Although I strove to put the memory by,
That night I could not sleep at all.

Needless to say, the poet was so much haunted by the beautiful scene,
combining the glorious moon and the bright fireflies, that he could not sleep
all night.

### 螢                    直 好

露ふかき　若葉がくれに　飛びくれば
螢のかげも　緑なりけり

### *Hotaru*

*Tsuyu fukaki　Wakaba gakure ni　Tobi-kureba
Hotaru no kage mo　Midori nari keri.*

### Fireflies                    Naoyoshi

When they come to flit, half-hidden,
The tender leaves between,
Deeply drenched in evening dew—
The fireflies' glow is also green!

### 長柄川畔にて                 直 好

渡守　呼べどこたへす　長柄川
岸には蟲の　こゑばかりして

### *Nagara-gawa no Hotori nite*

*Watashi-mori   Yobedo kotaezu   Nagara-gawa*
*Kishi niwa mushi no   Koe bakari shite.*

## On the Shore of the Nagara River     Naoyoshi

The ferryman I call,
But he does not reply;
On the shore of the Nagara
Only insects cry.

The Nagara-gawa is a river in the Province of Mino, noted for its fine views and an extremely curious method of fishing with the help of cormorants, called *u-kai*.

The ferryman does not answer, but the insects cry sweetly, as if in response.

燕         直 好

人だにも　忘れはてたる　わが宿に<br>歸る燕の　あはれなるかな

### *Tsubame*

*Hito da nimo   Wasure-hate taru · Waga yado ni*
*Kaeru tsubame no   Aware naru kana.*

## Swallows     Naoyoshi

To my cottage
Quite forgotten even by men,
The swallows have returned again.
How pitiful!

## 柳 原 安 子

**Yanagiwara Yasu-ko** (1783–1866)

The daughter of Ōgimachi Sanjō Sane-atsu, Yasu-ko married Yanagiwara Tadamitsu. She was the greatest woman pupil of the famous poet, Kagawa Kageki.

君 ゆ け ば　　　　　　安 子

君ゆけば　かへらむ日まで　世の中に
花も紅葉も　あらじとぞおもふ

### *Kimi Yukeba*

*Kimi yukeba　Kaeran hi made　Yo no naka ni*
*Hana mo momiji mo　Araji tozo omou.*

### When You Depart　　　**Yasu-ko**

When you have gone away,
　　No flowers more, methinks, will be—
No maple leaves in all the world—
　　Till you come back to me.

This verse is evidently addressed to the poetess' husband who is departing on a long journey.

行 く 春　　　　　　安 子

うたたねの　いめのまもなく　春くれて
青葉がくれを　とぶ胡蝶かな

### *Yuku Haru*

*Utatane no   Ime no ma mo naku   Haru kurete*
*Aoba gakure wo   Tobu kochō kana.*

## Departed Spring          Yasu-ko

In less than the space of a dozing dream,
  Spring is away,
And already, half-hidden among green leaves,
  Butterflies play.

## 歸　雁          安　子

急ぎても　かへる雁かな　越路には
櫻にまさる　花やさくらむ

### *Kigan*

*Isogite mo   Kaeru kari kana   Koshiji ni wa*
*Sakura ni masaru   Hana ya sakuran.*

## Wild Geese Flying Home          Yasu-ko

Behold the wild geese flying back
  In hurry and in flurry!
May be in Koshiji are found
  Some flowers fairer than the cherry.

*Koshiji* is the ancient name of Echigo and six other northern provinces.
  The poetess humorously refers to the wild geese, which fly back to the north
in early spring, before the cherry flower opens.

## 橘 守 部

**Tachibana Moribe** (1785–1849)

A native of Ise Province, Moribe resided in Yedo. He was a famous expounder of Shintō, and a good poet. He wrote many literary books and left a collection of his verses.

元 日　　　　　　　　　守 部

むつきたつ　けふとて遠つ　祖の世の
太刀とりはきて　君ををろがむ

### Gwanjitsu

*Mutsuki tatsu　Kyō tote tōtsu　Oya no yo no*
*Tachi tori-hakite　Kimi wo orogamu.*

### On New Years's Day　　　　**Moribe**

New Year to-day having come,
　　I wear the sword of my ancestor,
And reverentially worship
　　His Majesty the Emperor.

*Mutsuki* is the archaic refined name of January in the lunar calendar.

卯 の 花　　　　　　　守 部

咲きつづく　卯の花垣を　行過ぎて
にはかに暮れし　ここちこそすれ

### Unohana

*Saki-tsuzuku   Unohana-gaki wo   Yuki-sugite*
*Niwakani kureshi   Kokochi koso sure.*

### Unohana                                          Moribe

**Passing beyond a long, long hedge**
**Of *unohana* in bloom, snow-white,**
**It seemed as if on a sudden the day**
**Had darkened into night.**

*Unohana* means the flowers of an *utsugi*.  The *utsugi* is a shrub, five or six
feet in height, with graceful snow-white flowers and fruit used for medical pur-
poses.  It blooms in early summer.  It is often cultivated for a hedge.

It was already dark; but while the poet walked along a long hedge consist-
ing of *utsugi*, with beautiful snow-white flowers, it was light as day, so that when
he passed beyond the hedge it seemed as if suddenly pitchdark night had fallen.

### 石 川 依 平
#### Ishikawa Yorihira (1791–1859)

Born the son of a farmer in Datemura, Sano County, Tōtomi Province,
Yorihira took lessons in versification from Moto-ori Haruniwa, and became a
famous poet.  He wrote a few books on literature and had numerous pupils.

### 菫                                          依 平

野べみれば　雲雀の牀も　匂ふまで
芝生の菫　花さきにけり

### Sumire

*Nobe mireba   Hibari no toko mo   Niō made*
*Shibafu no sumire   Hana saki ni keri.*

### Violets

Yorihira

Lo! in the field the violets bloom
In such abundance,
That even the nests of the larks
Are full of fragrance.

千 種 有 功

**Chigusa Arikoto** (1797–1854)

A native of Kyōto, Arikoto was a chamberlain for some years and later Vice-
Lieutenant-General of the Left Division of the Imperial Guards.

富 士 山
有 功

千たび見て　千たびめづらし　雲風に
姿さだめぬ　ふじのしば山

### Fuji-San

*Chitabi mite　Chitabi mezurashi　Kumo-kaze ni
Sugata sadamenu　Fuji no shibayama.*

### Mount Fuji

Arikoto

A thousand times at Fuji-San I look,
A thousand times I wonder that 'tis ever new;
In clouds and wind still always varying,
The whole year through.

## 大 隈 言 道

### Ōkuma Kotomichi (1798–1868)

The eldest son of a merchant at Fukuoka, Ōkuma Kotomichi gave his birthright to his younger brother and studied versification and Chinese classics at Ōsaka, where he was recognized as a poet. Later he returned to his province and taught poetry in a village. All his life he lived in poverty and was barely able to publish a collection of his verses entitled *Sōkei Shū* (草徑集) or "A Collection from a Grass Path."

## 雛　　鶏　　　　　言 道

庭つ鳥　羽うちきする　はぐくみを
もりいでて子の　あるが悲しき

### *Hina-Dori*

*Niwa-tsu-dori   Hane uchi-kisuru   Hagukumi wo*
*Mori-idete ko no   Aru ga kanashiki.*

### A Little Chicken　　　　Kotomichi

When the mother hen gathers her little ones
　　　　Under her wing,
To see one little chicken left outside
　　　Is a sorrowful thing.

Probably the poet has some social affair in mind.

## をのこ孫　　　　言 道

初春に　抱きそめたる　をのこ孫
わが手のうちの　玉ぞこの玉

### Onoko-Mago

*Hatsu-haru ni  Idaki some taru  Onoko-mago*
*Waga te no uchi no  Tama zo kono tama.*

**My Grandson**          **Kotomichi**

My grandson whom I have embraced
    For the first time at this New Year—
He is a jewel in my hand,
    A jewel dear!

### 花 と 月          言 道

貴人に　あらねばこそは　安く見れ
花といへば花　月といへば月

### Hana to Tsuki

*Umabito ni  Araneba koso wa  Yasuku mire*
*Hana to ieba hana  Tsuki to ieba tsuki.*

**Flowers and the Moon**          **Kotomichi**

Only because I was not highly born,
    I am at all times free,
Unhindered, as I will, the moon
    Or else the flowers to see.

### 月          言 道

山邊より　歸るわが身を　送り來て
あくれば門を　月も入りけり

### *Tsuki*

*Yamabe yori   Kaeru waga mi wo   Okuri kite*
*Akureba kado wo   Tsuki mo iri keri.*

### The Moon                    Kotomichi

All the way back, the moon
    Escorted me down the mountain side;
And when I opened the gate of my home,
    The moon too came inside.

### 鶯 の 一 聲                    言 道

鶯の　鳴く一聲に　忘れけり
いづこにか行く　わが身なりけむ

### *Uguisu no Hitokoe*

*Uguisu no   Naku hitokoe ni   Wasurekeri*
*Izuko ni ka yuku   Waga mi nari ken.*

### One Song of an *Uguisu*          Kotomichi

Only one song of an *uguisu*,
    And all else, forgotten, has fled away!
I wonder where I had been meaning
    To wend my way.

### わ が 心 の み                    言 道

火を消せば　ありつる物も　一つなく
わが身に殘る　心のみして

### *Waga Kokoro Nomi*

*Hi wo keseba   Aritsuru mono mo   Hitotsu naku*
*Waga mi ni nokoru   Kokoro nomi shite.*

## My Mind Alone                    Kotomichi

When I put out the light,
   None of the things that were I see!
My mind alone
   Remains with me.

## 花 間 の 鳥                    言 道

咲く花に　遊ぶを見れば　鳥だにも
はむことのみは　思はざりけり

### *Kwakan no Tori*

*Saku hana ni   Asobu wo mireba   Tori dani mo*
*Hamu koto nomi wa   Omowazari keri.*

## Birds amidst Flowers                    Kotomichi

Watching how among the flowers
   Birds are fluttering about,
Even they have other thoughts
   Than food alone, we cannot doubt.

## ま た の 世                    言 道

しな高き　事も願はず　またの世は
また我身にぞ　なりてきなまし

## *Mata no Yo*

*Shina takaki   Koto mo negawazu   Mata no yo wa*
*Mata waga mi nizo   Narite kinamashi.*

### The Next World                    Kotomichi

Not to be highly born
　　In the next world, do I aspire;
This only—to become *myself* again
　　Is my desire.

## 撫 子 の 花                    言 道

放つ矢の　行方尋ぬる　草むらに
　見出でて折れる　撫子の花

### *Nadeshiko no Hana*

*Hanatsu ya no   Yukue tazunuru   Kusamura ni*
*Mi-idete oreru   Nadeshiko no hana.*

### Pinks                    Kotomichi

I sought an arrow, gone I knew not where,
　　Which from my bow had sped;
But found among the grasses wild fringed pinks,
　　And gathered them instead.

## 明 日 の 憂                    言 道

今日は今日　あらむ限は　飲みくらし
　明日の憂ひは　明日ぞうれへむ

### Asu no Urei

*Kyō wa kyō    Aran-kagiri wa    Nomi-kurashi*
*Asu no urei wa    Asu zo ure-en.*

## To-morrow's Sorrow                   Kotomichi

I will enjoy to-day,
   Drinking what wine I have to-day;
To-morrow's sorrow
   I will endure to-morrow.

### 平 賀 元 義

#### Hiraga Motoyoshi (1799–1865)

The son of a samurai of the Okayama Clan, Motoyoshi studied Japanese
poetry by himself and became a prominent poet. During many years he led
a wandering life, and in old age returned to his native town of Okayama, where
he died in poverty.

### 河 邊 川                               元 義

わかくさの　妻の子故に　河邊川
　　しばしば渡る　嬬の子故に

### Kawabe-gawa

*Wakakusa no    Tsuma-no-ko yue ni    Kawabe-gawa*
*Shibashiba wataru    Tsuma-no-ko yue ni.*

## The River Kawabe                     Motoyoshi

Ah, for the sake of my loved one
   I cross the River Kawabe;
I cross it again and again,
For the sake of my loved one.

The Kawabe-gawa is a famous river in Bitchū Province. *Wakakusa* or "young grass" is a pillow-word belonging to *tsuma* or "wife".

*Tsuma-no-ko* means "sweetheart", not "wife's son".

## 奈義 の 神山　　　　　　　　元　義

峰はみな　雪にかくれて　雪の上に
霞棚引く　奈義の神山

### Nagi no Kami-yama

*Mine wa mina   Yuki ni kakurete   Yuki no ue ni
Kasumi tanabiku   Nagi no kami-yama.*

## The Holy Mount Nagi　　　　Motoyoshi

Lo! on the holy Mount Nagi,
The peak is all hidden in snow,
And mists are trailing
Upon the snow.

Nagi-yama stands in Katsuta County, Mimasaka Province. It is called *Kami-yama* or "God's Mountain", because there is at its foot a shrine dedicated to the God Izanagi.

## 野　村　望　東

### Nomura Bōtō (1806–1867)

The daughter of Urano Jūbei Katsuyuki, a samurai (?) of Fukuoka Clan, Moto—her real name—married Nomura Shinzaburō, a samurai of the same clan. When she was fifty-three, her husband died, whereupon she shaved her head and assumed the *nom de plume* of Bōtō Ni (望東尼*), the Chinese characters 望東

---

* Ni (尼) means a ' nun". In Old Japan a chaste woman after her husband's death often shaved her head and, in the case of a literary woman, added Ni (尼) or "Nun" to her pen name, although she did not live in a convent.

representing her name Moto. She studied Japanese versification under the poet, Ōkuma Kotomichi, and became a good poetess. She entertained deep sympathy with patriots who exerted themselves for the overthrow of the Shōgunate and the restoration of the Imperial régime, and often gave refuge to many of them in her villa in a remote village. She was banished as a political offender to Himejima, a small island, but soon afterwards was rescued from it by two patriots of her clan. In 1893 she was granted the posthumous court rank of Senior Fifth Grade.

うぐひす      望東尼

類なき　聲になくなる　鶯の
こにすむうきめ　みるよなりけり

### Uguisu

*Tagui-naki　Koe ni naku naru　Uguisu no*
*Ko ni sumu ukime　Miru yo nari keri!*

### The *Uguisu*      Bōtō-Ni

**Because of their peerless sweet notes,**
**The *uguisu* must undergo**
**The sorrow of cage-confinement.**
**Alas! with men, too, it is so.**

This verse was secretly sent to Hirano Kuni-omi, who had been thrown into prison on account of his patriotic appeal for the overthrow of the Shōgunate and the restoration of the Imperial régime.

たらひの水      望東尼

月かげの　うつるを見れば　程もなき
たらひの水も　千尋なりけり

### Tarai no Mizu

*Tsuki-kage no   Utsuru wo mireba   Hodo mo naki*
*Tarai no mizu mo   Chihiro nari keri.*

### The Water of a Tub                    Bōtō-Ni

Because the moon above
   Is clear reflected at its bottom,
Even the little water of a tub
   Is deep, a thousand fathom.

Sasaki Nobutsuna considers this verse a mystic masterpiece.

### 友 な き 人                    尼 望 東

櫻花　あまたにほへる　里にても
友なき人は　さびしからまし

### Tomo naki Hito

*Sakurabana   Amata nioeru   Sato nitemo*
*Tomo naki hito wa   Sabishikaramashi.*

### A Friendless Man                    Bōtō-Ni

Though he be in a village where
   The cherry flowers richly glow,
A man who has no friend—
   How lonely he must go!

## 籠 の 鶯　　　　　望東尼

たぐひなき　音にて鳴かすば　鶯の
籠にすむうき目　見すやあらまし

### Kago no Uguisu

*Taguinaki　Ne nite nakazuba　Uguisu no*
*Ko ni sumu ukime　Mizu ya aramashi.*

### A Caged *Uguisu*　　　　　**Boto-Ni**

**The *uguisu* in the cage**
**Would never meet**
**So hard a fate if its unrivalled notes**
**Were not so sweet.**

## 安 藤 野 雁
**Andō Nukari** (1810–1867)

Nukari was for some years an official of the Handa silver mine in Iwashiro Province, which was under the control of the Tokugawa Government.　He wrote "New Studies in the *Manyō Shū* Anthology" and left a collection of his verses.

## こほろぎの聲　　　　　野雁

白露の　玉のこぼるる　音かとも
きこゆるよるの　こほうぎの聲

### Kōroji no Koe

*Shiratsuyu no　Tama no koboruru　Oto ka tomo*
*Kikoyuru yoru no　Kōrogi no koe.*

### The Voices of Crickets　　　　Nukari

Hark! they sound as if
　　Beads of dew, all sparkling white,
Were spilling and rolling—
　　Voices of crickets in the night!

### 蟲　　　　野　雁

庭くらき　所の蟲は　ひるなれど
夜と思ひて　なきぬなりけり

### *Mushi*

*Niwa kuraki　Tokoro no mushi wa　Hiru naredo
Yoru to omoite　Nakinu narikeri.*

### Insects　　　　Nukari

In the dark spots of my garden
　　Insects are chirping, though 'tis still daylight;
'Tis likely that they think
　　It is already night.

### 橘　曙　覽
#### Tachibana Akemi (1811–1868)

A man of Fukui, Echizen Province, Akemi handed over his inheritance to his younger brother, and going up to Yedo, devoted some years to a study of Japanese classics, taking lessons in poetry from the famous poet Moto-ori Nori-naga. On the completion of his studies, he returned to his native city, where he lived by teaching verse-making. He wrote a few books on poetry, including "A Peep into the *Kokin Shū*", and left a collection of his own verses.

蟻　　　　　　曙覽

蟻と蟻　うなづきあひて　何事か
　ありげに走る　西へ東へ

## *Ari*

*Ari to ari　Unazuki-aite　Nani-goto ka
Ari-ge ni hashiru　Nishi e higashi e.*

### Ants　　　　　　Akemi

One ant nods to another ant,
And then they run and run
From east to west, from west to east,
As on some urgent business bent.

山　　中　　　　　　曙覽

樵歌　鳥のさへづり　水の音
濡れたる小草　雲かかる松

## *Sanchū*

*Kikori-uta　Tori no saezuri　Mizu no oto
Nuretaru ogusa　Kumo kakaru matsu.*

### In the Mountain　　　　　　Akemi

Some woodmen's songs;
The birds' warbling; water's sound;
Small grasses wet with dews;
A pine-tree overhung with clouds.

This is one of several well known verses consisting entirely of noun phrases. The nouns in the above verse, which appeal to the ear or to the eye, constitute a delightful picture in words.

長雨の後　　　　　曙覽

天地も　廣さ加はる　ここちして
まづあふがるる　青雲の空

### Naga-ame no Ato

*Ame-tsuchi mo　Hirosa kuwawaru　Kokochi shite*
*Mazu aogaruru　Aogumo no sora.*

### After a Long Rain　　　Akemi

**It seemed as if heaven and earth had both**
**Grown wider to my eye,**
**When, for the first time, after rains,**
**I looked up to blue sky.**

*Aogumo no sora* or, literally, "the sky of blue clouds", is a synonym of *aozora* or "the blue sky".

珍らしき書　　　　　曙覽

たのしみは　珍らしき書　人に借り
始め一ひら　ひらげたる時

### Mezurashiki Fumi

*Tanoshimi wa　Mezurashiki fumi　Hito ni kari*
*Hajime hito-hira　Hirogetaru toki.*

### A Rare Book
Akemi

When from someone else
A rare book I borrow,
And open the first page of it—
Ah, what delight doth follow!

### 我 が 樂 み
曙 覽

樂しみは 乏しきままに 人集め
酒飲め物を 食へといふ時

### Waga Tanoshimi

*Tanoshimi wa   Toboshiki mamani   Hito atsume
Sake nome mono wo   Kue to yū toki.*

### My Great Pleasure
Akemi

My greatest pleasure is to call,
Poor tho' my potluck be,
My friends together, saying, "Eat!
Yea, drink rice-wine with me!"

### た の し み
曙 覽

たのしみは 朝おきいでて 昨日まで
無かりし花の 咲ける見る時

### Tanoshimi

*Tanoshimi wa   Asa oki-idete   Kinō made
Nakarishi hana no   Sakeru miru toki.*

### A Joy                                                                 Akemi

O joy, to rise and find
By morning's ray,
A flower which was not
Here yesterday!

### 螢                                                                     曙覽

み谷川　水音くらき　岩かげに
晝もひかりて　飛ぶ螢かな

### Hotaru

*Mi-tanigawa　Mizu-oto kuraki　Iwa-kage ni
Hiru mo hikarite　Tobu hotaru kana.*

### Fireflies                                                             Akemi

Over the stream in the mountain gorge,
There where the water soundeth dark,
In the shadow of the precipice, at noontide even,
Fireflies flitting, show their shining spark.

*Mi* of *Mitanigawa* is an honorific.
*Mizu-oto kuraki* or "the sound of the water is dark" is a clever abbreviation
for "the water runs sounding in the dark shade of rocks".

### 義 貞 の 碑                                                            曙覽

にひ田塚　たたかひ負けて　うせぬてふ
文字讀みをれば　野風身にしむ

**Night in a Bamboo Grove**

By Taikwan (横山大観),
a contemporary painter
In the possession of
Mr. Mochizuki Gunshirō, Tokyo

### Yoshisada no Hi

*Nüta-zuka    Tatakai-makete    Usenu chō*
*Moji yomi oreba    Nokaze mi ni shimu.*

### The Monument to General Yoshisada          Akemi

As I perused the epitaph,
    "Here Yoshisada was in battle slain,"
Upon the warrior's monument,
    I shivered in the keen wind of the plain.

This verse was composed when the poet visited the monument to General
Nitta Yoshisada at the village of Tōmyōji (燈明寺村), Yoshida County, in Echizen
Province. The epitaph on the monument runs as follows:
    "Nitta Yoshisada died fighting on this spot".
    Nitta Yoshisada was a warrior of the 14th century, famed for his courage
and for his devotion to the Emperor Go-Daigo's cause, in opposition to the
usurping families of Hōjō and Ashikaga.

篁                                          曙　覧

賤どちの　夜もの語りの　ありさまを
篁ごしに　見するともし火

### Takamura

*Shizu dochi no    Yo-monogatari no    Arisama wo*
*Takamura goshi ni    Misuru tomoshibi.*

### Green Bamboos          Akemi

The light shining out from a thatched country cottage
Reveals, through green bamboos,
A comfortable scene, of peasants sitting round
For evening chat.

幼き娘のみまかれるに　　　　曙覽

昨日まで　わが衣手に　とりすがり
父よ父よと　言ひてしものを

### Osanaki Musume no Mimakareru ni

*Kinō made　Waga koromo-de ni　Tori-sugari*
*Chichi yo chichi yo to　Ii teshi mono wo.*

## On the Death of a Little Daughter　　Akemi

Alas! to think that only
　　Till yesterday,
She would catch at my sleeve and "Daddy,
　　Daddy!" would say!

The daughter was three years old.

### 雪　の　朝　　　　曙覽

今朝も來て　枯木の小枝　くぐるかな
雪にあさりを　うしなへる鳥

### Yuki no Ashita

*Kesa mo kite　Kareki no koeda　Kuguru kana*
*Yuki ni asari wo　Ushinaeru tori.*

## A Snowy Morning　　Akemi

The birds have come this morning again,
　　Bereft of their food by the snow,
And from twig to twig of the leafless trees
　　Flit, flitting they go.

## 河 野 鐵 兜
### Kōno Tettō (1825-1867)

A native of a village in Harima Province, Tettō became a physician at the age of twenty-one and later a samurai of the Hayashida Clan in the same province. He was widely read in Japanese and Chinese classics and an authority on botany and Buddhism. He was also skilled in music. He wrote many books on literature and history.

秋 の 月　　　　　　　鐵 兜

誰が捨ひ　殘しし珠か　伊勢の海の
清き渚の　秋の夜の月

### Aki no Tsuki

*Taga hiroi　Nokoshishi tama ka　Ise no umi no*
*Kiyoki nagisa no　Aki no yo no tsuki.*

### The Autumn Moon　　　Tettō

A jewel which someone, neglecting to pick up,
Has carelessly left here, can it be?
The moon of this glorious night of autumn,
On the beach undefiled of the Ise Sea?

The five repetitions of *no* (の), the soft possessive postposition in the original, rather adds to its melody, which cannot be reproduced in translation.
Literally—
The moon of this night of autumn
Of the pure beach of the Sea of Ise.

平 野 國 臣

**Hirano Kuni-omi** (1828–1864)

Hirano Kuni-omi was a samurai of the Fukuoka Clan and a prominent figure among the pioneers of the Restoration of 1868. He was executed by the Tokugawa Government.

The following verse was composed when he was captured by the police at Himeji, together with a robber, confined in a wicker-cage and grossly insulted by them.

日 本 魂　　　　　　國 臣

こも著ても　あじろにねても　大丈夫の
日本魂　何穢るべき

### *Yamato-Damashii*

*Komo kitemo　Ajiro ni netemo　Masurao no*
*Yamato-damashii　Nani kegaru beki.*

### The Japanese Spirit　　Kuni-omi

**Although I am in rags,**
**　Or in a wicker-cage confined,**
**Nothing whatever can defile**
**　My staunch Japanese mind.**

An *ajiro* (an abbreviation for *ajiro-kago*) is a wicker-cage in which a prisoner was carried in olden days.

京 の 獄 に て　　　　　國 臣

とらはれと　身はなりぬれど　天地に
恥づる心は　露なかりけり

### *Kyō no Hitoya nite*

*Toraware to    Mi wa narinuredo    Ame-tsuchi ni*
*Hazuru kokoro wa    Tsuyu nakarikeri.*

## In a Kyōto Prison                    Kuni-omi

**Although I am taken prisoner,**
**My conscience is clear;**
**'Fore Heaven and Earth, not a dewdrop even**
**Of shame need I feel or fear.**

吉 田 松 陰

**Yoshida Shō-in** (1830–1859)

Yoshida Shō-in was one of the most prominent pioneers of the Revolution of 1868, by which the Shōgunate was abolished and the Imperial régime was restored. He was executed by the Tokugawa Government as a political offender. A week prior to his execution, the young patriot wrote a letter of farewell to his parents and other immediate relatives, accompanied by the following verse.

辭　世                    松　陰

親を思ふ　心にまさる　親心
けふの音信　なにときくらん

### *Jisei*

*Oya wo omō    Kokoro ni masaru    Oya-gokoro*
*Kyō no otozure    Nani to kikuran.*

### The Death Poem                    Shō-in

Surpassing far my love for them,
    My parents' love for me is great—
How will they bear to-day's sad news
    Of this my fate?


よみ人しらす

**Anonymous**


## 憂きこと                    よみ人しらす

憂きことの　なほこの上に　積れかし
限りある身の　力ためさん


### *Ukikoto*

*Ukikoto no　Nao kono ue ni　Tsumore-kashi*
*Kagiri aru mi no　Chikara tamesan.*


### Troubles and Cares                    Anon.

Let my troubles and cares be piled
    And up-piled still more;
Then I will try and test
    What strength I have in store.

This well known verse is ascribed either to Yamazaki Ansai, a great authority on Chinese classics, who lived in the seventeenth century, or to Yamanaka Shikanosuke, a brave warrior who lived in the same century.

The *Ran*, a kind of Orchid, the noblest
of the "Four Gentlemen" among plants

By Chikuden (田能村竹田 1776–1835)

## Poets of the Tōkyō Period (from 1868 up to present date)

### 明 治 天 皇
### The Emperor Meiji (1852–1912)

The Emperor Meiji was the greatest of Japanese Emperors, during whose reign took place the abolition of the Shōgunate in 1868, and the victorious wars with China, 1894–5, and Russia, 1904–5.  He was a poet of outstanding merit, and the verses he composed number a hundred thousand.  It was the Emperor Meiji who initiated the beautiful custom of inviting his people to present the Emperor at New Year time with verses on a subject chosen by himself.

鳥       明治天皇

かくばかり　廣き林を　いかなれば
一つ木にのみ　鳥のとまれる

### *Tori*

*Kaku-bakari　Hiroki hayashi wo　Ika nareba*
*Hitotsu ki ni nomi　Tori no tomareru.*

### Birds      Emperor Meiji

In such a spacious wood,
I cannot see
The reason why the birds
Perch only on one tree.

大 空       明治天皇

あさみどり　澄み渡りたる　大空の
廣きをおのが　心ともがな

## Ō-zora

*Asa-midori   Sumi-watari taru   Ōzora no*
*Hiroki wo ono ga   Kokoro tomo gana.*

### The Blue Sky                              Emperor Meiji

**A vast expanse it is—**
**The clear blue sky.**
**Would that my heart were broad**
**As the vault is high.**

\*      \*      \*      \*      \*

Would that my heart were as broad as the azure vault above!
                              Trans. by Wadagaki Kenzō

し　　づ                              明治天皇

あつしとも　いはれざりけり　にえかへる
水田にたてる　しづをおもへば

### Shizu

*Atsushi tomo   Iware zari keri   Niekacru*
*Mizuta ni tateru   Shizu wo omoeba.*

### The Peasants                              Emperor Meiji

**"How hot it is!" I dare not say,**
**When I think of the peasants toiling,**
**During the heat of day,**
**In ricefields with the water boiling.**

\*      \*      \*      \*      \*

**Poem, "The Blue Sky,"—Emperor Meiji**
Handwritten by Chiba Taneaki
**Picture, "Spring Morning,"**
By Kwanzan (下村観山 1874-1931)

Complain not thou art hot: but rather turn
To yonder slushy fields, where labourers
Wade 'neath the sun, and e'en the water boils.

Trans. by Arthur Lloyd

## 四 海 同 胞　　　　　明 治 天 皇

よもの海　みなはらからと　思ふ世に
など波風の　たちさわぐらむ

### *Shikai Dōbō*

*Yomo-no-umi　Mina harakara to　Omō yo ni*
*Nado namikaze no　Tachi-sawaguran.*

## All Men Are Brothers　　Emperor Meiji

**Surely in this world men are brothers all,**
　　**One family!**
**Then why do winds and waves on all the seas**
　　**Rage stormily?**

\*　　　\*　　　\*　　　\*　　　\*

My heart's at peace with all, and fain would I
Live, as I live, in peace and brotherhood;
And yet the storm-clouds lower, the rising wind
Stirs up the waves, the elemental strife
Rages around. I do not understand
Why this should be. 'Tis plainly not our fault.

Paraphrased by Arthur Lloyd

The above verse was composed in 1904, when the Russo-Japanese War was
in progress. In December of the same year, Professor Arthur Lloyd of the
Imperial Tōkyō University published an English booklet consisting of his trans-

lations of this verse and several others by the Emperor and Empress Meiji under
the title of "Imperial Songs", and presented the book to the rulers of the prin-
cipal countries of the world; and it is said that Theodore Roosevelt, the twenty-
sixth president of the United States, was smitten with wonder and admiration
at this particular poem, which proved the Emperor to be an ardent lover of
peace.  Probably the President had supposed the Emperor Meiji to be a warlike
man like Alexander or Napoleon.

海 上 月　　　　　　　　明 治 天 皇

あたの船　うちしりぞけて　いくさびと<br>大海原の　月やみるらむ

*Kaijō no Tsuki*

*Ata no fune   Uchi-shirizokete   Ikusa-bito*<br>*Ō-unabara no   Tsuki ya miruran.*

**The Moon on the Sea**　　　**Emperor Meiji**

**The warriors who have just repulsed**<br>**The warships of the enemy,**<br>**Are now, it may be, gazing at the moon**<br>**Shining above the great plains of the sea.**

An enemy is nowadays generally called *ada*, but *ada* is a corruption of *ata*,
which pronunciation is often used by poets.

This verse was composed in 1904, on August 10 of which year the Japanese
fleet defeated the Russian fleet in the Yellow Sea.

植 物 苑　　　　　　　　明 治 天 皇

我園に　しげりあひけり　外國の<br>草木の苗も　おほしたつれば

## Shokubutsu-en

*Waga sono ni    Shigeri-ai keri    Totsukuni no*
*Kusaki no nae mo    Ō-shi-tatsureba.*

### The Botanical Garden          Emperor Meiji

**Behold! in my garden together**
**Vigorous grown and fair—**
**The seedlings of foreign trees and plants,**
**Reared and nursed with care.**

The Emperor refers to the foreign culture assimilated with Japanese culture.

\*      \*      \*      \*      \*

Lo!  In my garden all things thrive and grow.
E'en foreign trees and plants, with care bestowed
Upon their tender shoots, grow strong and green
Like those indigenous to soil and clime.

Trans. by Arthur Lloyd

我　國　　　　　明治天皇

人もわれも　道を守りて　かはらすば
この敷島の　國はうごかじ

## Waga Kuni

*Hito mo ware mo    Michi wo mamorite    Kawarazuba*
*Kono Shikishima no    Kuni wa ugokaji.*

### Our Country  Emperor Meiji

If I myself and other men the true way keep,
    And not a moment waver,
Our glorious Japan will never
    Be in danger.

仁  明治天皇

國のため　あたなす仇は　くだくとも

いつくしむべき　事な忘れそ

### Jin

*Kuni no tame　Atanasu ata wa　Kudaku tomo*
*Itsukushimu beki　Koto na wasure so.*

### Benevolence  Emperor Meiji

Though for your country's sake,
    You strike the foe,
See you do not forget
    The love you owe.

\*　　\*　　\*　　\*　　\*

The foe that strikes thee, for thy country's sake,
    Strike him with all thy might;
        But while thou strik'st,
    Forget not still to love him.

        Trans. by Arthur Lloyd

天　　　　　　明治天皇

ひさかたの　空はへだても　なかりけり
つちなる國は　さかひあれども

### Sora

*Hisakata no   Sora wa hedatemo   Nakarikeri*
*Tsuchi naru kuni wa   Sakai aredomo.*

### The Sky　　　　　Emperor Meiji

The wide blue sky no barriers has,
　　Nor any bound,
Although on earth the countries all
　　Make frontiers to divide the ground.

幼兒の言葉　　　　　明治天皇

おもふこと　うちつけにいふ　幼兒の
言葉はやがて　歌にぞありける

### Osanago no Kotoba

*Omō-koto   Uchi-tsuke ni yū   Osanago no*
*Kotoba wa yagate   Uta ni zo ari keru.*

### The Words of a Little Child　　Emperor Meiji

The truest poems here
　　We find—
In the words of a little child,
　　Who simply says what is in his mind.

窓　前　蟲　　　　　明治天皇

くさひばり　鳴きもぞやむと　秋の夜の

月なき窓も　さされざりけり

## Sōzen no Mushi

*Kusa-hibari   Nakimozo-yamu to   Aki-no-yo no
Tsuki naki mado mo   Sasare-zarikeri.*

### Insects by the Windows　　Emperor Meiji

**For fear the *kusa-hibari*
Might cease to chirrup,
I dared not shut the windows,
Though there was no autumn moon.**

The *kusa-hibari* (literally "grass-lark") is a kind of cricket, less than half an inch in length, remarkable for its sweet notes.

One chilly autumn night, when there was no moon and therefore no need to keep the paper windows open to see it, the Emperor would have shut them, but desisted lest the noise might startle some *kusa-hibari* which were chirping sweetly outside.

"Imagine a cricket about the size of an ordinary mosquito—with a pair of antennae much longer than his own body, and so fine that you can distinguish them only against the light. *Kusa-hibari*, or "Grass-Lark", is the Japanese name for him; and he is worth in the market exactly twelve cents. By day he sleeps or meditates, except while occupied with the slice of fresh egg-plant or cucumber which must be poked into his cage every morning. But always at sunset the infinitesimal sound of him awakens; then the room begins to fill with a delicate and ghostly music of indescribable sweetness—a thin, thin silvery rippling and thrilling as of tiniest electric bells. As the darkness deepens, the sound becomes sweeter—sometimes swelling till the whole house seems to vibrate with the elfish resonance,—sometimes thinning down into the faintest imaginable thread of a voice. But loud or low, it keeps a penetrating quality that is weird......All night the atomy thus sings; he ceases only when the temple bell proclaims the hour of dawn".—From *Kottō* ("Curios") by Lafcadio Hearn

## 鳥　　　　　　　明治天皇

大空に　つばさをのべて　とぶ鳥も
ねぐらに迷ふ　ときはありけり

### Tori

*Ōzora ni　Tsubasa wo nobete　Tobu tori mo*
*Negura ni mayō　Toki wa ari keri.*

### Birds　　　Emperor Meiji

Great birds up in the sky,
　　Spreading their wings to the lofty height—
They—even they—are sometimes at a loss
　　For a roosting-place at night.

## 日露戰役中　　　　明治天皇

子等はみな　いくさの庭に　いで果てて
翁やひとり　山田守るらむ

### Nichiro Sen-eki Chū

*Ko-ra wa mina　Ikusa no niwa ni　Ide hatete*
*Okina ya hitori　Yamada moruran.*

### During the Russo-Japanese War   Emperor Meiji

The young men all away
To the front have gone;
At home the old men work
In the ricefields alone.

*     *     *     *     *

The sons all, ere this fall,
At the country's call,
To the front are gone,
Leaving farm and field and all
In the hands of the aged sires alone.

Trans. by Wadagaki Kenzō

They're at the front,
Our brave young men, and now the middle-aged
Are shouldering their arms, and in the fields
Old men are gathering the abundant rice,
Low bending o'er the sheaves. All ages vie
In cheerful self-devotion to the Land.

Paraphrased by Arthur Lloyd

心                              明 治 天 皇

さし昇る　朝日の如く　爽やかに
もたまほしきは　心なりけり

### *Kokoro*

*Sashi-noboru　Asahi no gotoku　Sawayakani
Motama hoshiki wa　Kokoro narikeri.*

### My Heart                    Emperor Meiji

Like the rising sun, which shines
   Serene and bright,
Would that my heart might ever be,
   Filled with light!

\*    \*    \*    \*    \*

Would I could keep my heart as bright
  and serene as the dawning sun.

                Trans. by Wadagaki Kenzō

### 夏　述　懷                    明治天皇

まつりごと　いでてきくまは　かくばかり
　　暑き日としも　思はざりしを

### Natsu Jukkwai

Matsurigoto  Idete kiku ma wa  Kaku-bakari
　Atsuki hi to shimo  Omowa-zari shiwo.

### My Feelings in Summer                    Emperor Meiji

While I went forth
   And heard affairs of state,
I did not feel so much
   The day's great heat.

### 初春の風                    明治天皇

梅にふれ　柳にふれて　きのふけふ
　　風のこころも　春になるらし

### Hatsu-haru no Kaze

*Ume ni fure  Yanagi ni furete  Kinō-kyō*
*Kaze no kokoro mo  Haru ni naru rashi.*

### The Wind of Early Spring  Emperor Meiji

**Stirring the plum-blossom,**
**Stirring the willow,**
**The mind of the wind, yesterday and to-day,**
**Seems to be turning to spring.**

Now that the plum-blossoms and the willow leaves have appeared, genia！
spring has come round; and the erstwhile chilly wind has become a delightful
spring breeze.

### 埋　木　　明治天皇

うもれ木を　みるにつけても　思ふかな
しづめるままの　人もありやと

### Umoregi

*Umoregi wo  Miru ni tsukete mo  Omō kana*
*Shizumeru mama no  Hito mo ariya to.*

### Bogwood  Emperor Meiji

**Looking upon this bogwood, thoughts arise—**
**How there may be**
**Men, too, sunk deep, now lying**
**In obscurity.**

樹 間 花　　　　明治天皇

こずえのみ　人に知られて　櫻花
こがくれながら　散りやはつらむ

### Jukan no Hana

*Kozue nomi　Hito ni shirarete　Sakura-bana*
*Kogakure nagara　Chiri ya hatsuran.*

### Cherry-Flowers Among Trees　Emperor Meiji

Their slender boughs alone
Known unto men,
The cherry-flowers may fall,
Hidden among the trees.

寄 玉 述 懷　　　　明治天皇

きづなきは　すくなかりけり　世の中に
もてはやさるる　玉といへども

### Tama ni Yosete Omoi wo Nobu

*Kizu naki wa　Sukunakari keri　Yo no naka ni*
*Mote-hayasaruru　Tama to iedomo.*

### To Jewels　Emperor Meiji

Of the gems which receive
The world's applause,
How very few
Are free from flaws!

おのが身　　　　明治天皇

おのが身は　かへりみずして　ともすれば
人のうへのみ　いふ世なりけり

### Ono ga Mi

*Ono ga mi wa　Kaerimizu shite　Tomosureba*
*Hito no ue nomi　Yū yo nari keri.*

### One's Own Self　　Emperor Meiji

Ah! men are apt to talk
Of others' faults,
And never to reflect
Upon themselves.

朝　鳥　　　　明治天皇

朝まだき　ねぐら離れて　たつみれば
鳥もつとめは　ある世なりけり

### Asa no Tori

*Asamadaki　Negura hanarete　Tatsu mireba*
*Tori mo tsutome wa　Aru yo nari keri.*

### Morning Birds　　Emperor Meiji

Since at the early dawn
Birds rise and fly away,
Even for them, it seems, this is a world
With duties to obey.

籠 中 鳥　　　　　明治天皇

籠のうちに　さへづる鳥の　聲きけば
放たまほしく　思ひなりぬる

### Rōchū no Tori

*Kago no uchi ni　Saezuru tori no　Koe kikeba*
*Hanatama-hoshiku　Omoi narinuru.*

### A Caged Bird　　Emperor Meiji

When I hear
　A caged bird sing,
I long to set it free—
　Free to take wing.

草　　　　　明治天皇

いぶせしと　思ふなかにも　えらびなば
くすりとならむ　草もあるべし

### Kusa

*Ibuseshi to　Omō naka ni mo　Erabinaba*
*Kusuri to naran　Kusa mo arubeshi.*

### Herbs　　Emperor Meiji

Even among the wild plants
　Which you think commonplace,
If you but search, there well may be
　Some healing herbs of grace.

春　島　　　　　明治天皇

船ならで　ゆきかひすべく　見ゆるかな
霞に浮ぶ　あはぢ島山

## Haru no Shima

*Fune narade   Yuki-kai subeku   Miyuru kana
Kasumi ni ukabu   Awaji-shima yama.*

### An Island in Spring　　　Emperor Meiji

**Surely it were easy to cross over
Without a boat,
Where the Island of Awaji
In mists of spring doth float!**

This verse seems to have been composed from actual observation in April, 1903, when the Emperor stayed at Maiko, just opposite Awaji Island.

鴉　　　　　明治天皇

やどるべき　木立多かる　森にても
ねぐら爭ふ　むら鳥かな

## Karasu

*Yadoru beki   Kodachi ōkaru   Mori nite mo
Negura arasō   Mura-garasu kana.*

### Crows                    Emperor Meiji

Behold, in the wood there are many trees
   Where birds may rest for the night,
Yet how fiercely the flocks of crows with each other
   For roosting-places fight!

## 中　秋　月                    明治天皇

心にも　かかる雲なき　この秋の
　もなかの月の　かげのさやけさ

### *Chūshū no Tsuki*

*Kokoro ni mo　Kakaru kumo naki　Kono aki no
Monaka no tsuki no　Kage no sayakesa.*

### The Moon in Mid-Autumn    Emperor Meiji

Oh, the clear brilliance of the moon
In this mid-autumn,
When on my mind, too,
There rests no cloud!

This verse was composed in the autumn of 1896, when peace reigned through-
out Eastern Asia, the Sino-Japanese War having come to a close in the previous
year.

The moon in mid-autumn is the full moon of August 15 in the lunar calendar,
i. e. about September 15 in the solar calendar; in Japan it is the most beautiful
of all the full moons in the year. Needless to say, since he had nothing to
disturb his peace of mind, the Emperor particularly enjoyed the glorious moon
of that autumn.

新 年 望 山 　　　　　明 治 天 皇

新しき　年を迎へて　富士のねの
高きすがたを　仰ぎみるかな

### Shinnen Yama wo Nozomu

*Atarashiki　Toshi wo mukaete　Fuji no ne no*
*Takaki sugata wo　Aogi miru kana.*

## Gazing Up at a Mountain in the New Year

**Emperor Meiji**

**Welcoming the New Year in,**
**Most reverentially**
**I gaze up at the lofty peak**
**Of sacred Mount Fuji.**

This was composed at the New Year's Imperial Poetry Party held in January, 1876.

鶯 　　　　　明 治 天 皇

あたらしき　年のほぎごと　いふ人に
おくれぬけさの　鶯のこゑ

### Uguisu

*Atarashiki　Toshi no hogi-goto　Yū hito ni*
*Okurenu kesa no　Uguisu no koe.*

**Mount Fuji**

By Raishō (田中頼璋),
a contemporary painter

### Uguisu
**Emperor Meiji**

Listen! the *uguisu*
Utter their first songs this morning,
Not to be outdone by the men
Bringing New Year's greeting.

### いにしへのふみ
明治天皇

いにしへの　ふみ見るたびに　思ふかな
おのがをさむる　國はいかにと

### Inishie no Fumi

*Inishie no　Fumi miru tabi ni　Omō kana*
*Ono ga osamuru　Kuni wa ikani to.*

### Ancient Writings
**Emperor Meiji**

Each time I read the writings
Of ancient sages,
The thought arises,
"How is it with the land o'er which I reign?"

### 月不撰處
明治天皇

萩の戸の　露にやどれる　月影は
しづが垣根も　へだてざるらむ

### Tsuki Tokoro wo Erabazu

*Hagi-no-to no　Tsuyu ni yadoreru　Tsuki-kage wa*
*Shizu ga kakine mo　Hedatezaruran.*

### The Moon Shines Everywhere    Emperor Meiji

The autumn moonshine, which rests in splendour
On our palace garden dews to-night,
Knows no difference, but shines on the peasant's
Garden fence, too, with .equal light.

*Hagi-no-to* (萩の戸) is the name of a chamber of the Seiryōden Hall in the Imperial Palace at Kyōto. It is so named, it is said, because some *hagi* or lespedezas were planted in the garden in front of it. But this name is used here in the sense of "the Imperial Palace".

河水久澄                    明治天皇

昔より　ながれたえせぬ　五十鈴川
なほ萬代も　すまむとぞ思ふ

### *Kasui Kyūchō*

*Mukashi yori   Nagare taesenu   Isuzu-gawa
Nao yorozu-yo mo   Suman to zo omō.*

### The River Will be Clear
### to All Future Ages    Emperor Meiji

The River Isuzu, which has never ceased
To flow from time immemorial—
I surely believe, will still flow clear
To all eternity.

The Isuzu-gawa, a clear little stream flowing through the precincts of the Great Shrines of Ise, is a symbol of the eternity of the Imperial line.

**Cherry Blossoms in Moonlight**

By Bunrin (鹽川文麟 1808–1877)

鶯　　　　　　明治天皇

このごろは　かきねの柳　のきの梅
みな鶯の　やどとなりぬる

## *Uguisu*

*Kono-goro wa　Kakine no yanagi　Noki no ume*
*Mina uguisu no　Yado to narinuru.*

### The *Uguisu*　　　Emperor Meiji

**Of late the willows by the fence,**
**The plum-trees at the eaves—**
**Aye, all the trees in the garden-ground**
**Are perches for the *uguisu*.**

The *uguisu*, the messengers of spring, are sweetly singing in the green willow trees and amidst the snow-white plum-blossoms.  A fascinating scene.

## 小金井の櫻　　　明治天皇

春風の　ふきのまにまに　雪とちる
櫻の花の　おもしろきかな

### *Koganei no Sakura*

*Haru-kaze no　Fuki no mani-mani　Yuki to chiru*
*Sakura no hana no　Omoshiroki kana.*

### The Cherry-Blossoms at Koganei  Emperor Meiji

How delightful they are,
 Like flakes of snow—
The cherry petals fluttering down
 As spring breezes blow!

This verse was composed extempore when the Emperor took a long distance ride on horseback to Koganei, several miles west of Tōkyō, with a fine avenue of cherry-trees, two miles and a half in length, along the banks of a small canal which used to conduct the waters of the Tamagawa to Tōkyō.

鴨　獵　　　　明治天皇

皆人の　手ごとにもたる　網のめを
のがれかぬらむ　あはれ水鳥

### *Kamo-Ryō*

*Mina-bito no   Te-goto ni motaru   Ami no me wo
Nogare-kanuran   Aware mizutori.*

### Wild Duck Hunting  Emperor Meiji

Poor water-birds!
 To escape, befreed,
From the meshes of nets in so many hands
 Is hard indeed!

In the Hama Detached Palace (now a park) in Tōkyō, many wild ducks were kept in a large pond; and on the occasion of a wild duck hunting party, held once or twice annually, they were driven into a small canal and caught with hand-nets carried by every one present.

The above verse was a natural outburst of the Emperor's sympathy for the poor birds on such an occasion.

海 上 月　　　　明治天皇

ひさかたの　空にありながら　わたつみの
底まで照らす　秋の夜の月

### Kaijō no Tsuki

Hisakata no　Sora ni ari-nagara　Watatsumi no
Soko made terasu　Aki no yo no tsuki.

### The Moon on the Sea　　Emperor Meiji

Though it hangeth high
In the infinite sky,
The moon of autumn shineth bright,
Down into the sea-depths, through the night.

冬 　 泉　　　　明治天皇

冬ふかき　池のなかにも　ほとばしる
水ひとすぢは　こほらざりけり

### Tōsen

Fuyu fukaki　Ike no naka ni mo　Hotobashiru
Mizu hitosuji wa　Kōrazari keri.

### A Fountain in Winter　　Emperor Meiji

The fountain in the pond, alone,
　　In depths of winter, even,
Rushing up in white spray,
　　Is never frozen.

## 五 十 鈴 川　　　　明 治 天 皇

さざれ石の　巖とならむ　末までも
五十鈴の川の　水はにごらじ

### *Isuzu-Gawa*

*Sazare-ishi no　Iwao to naran　Sue made mo
Isuzu no kawa no　Mizu wa nigoraji.*

### The River Isuzu　　Emperor Meiji

To all eternity,
　　Till pebbles into solid rocks shall grow,
The waters of the Isuzu River will
　　Unsullied flow.

## 社 頭 祈 世　　　　明 治 天 皇

とこしへに　民やすかれと　いのるなる
わが世をまもれ　伊勢の大神

### *Shatō Yo wo Inoru*

*Tokoshieni　Tami yasukare to　Inoru naru
Waga yo wo mamore　Ise no Ōkami.*

### A Prayer at the Ise Shrines　　Emperor Meiji

To all eternity, in tranquillity,
　　Be my people kept—'tis this I pray,—
Guard ye my reign, O mighty Gods,
　　Gods of Ise!

## 小金井の櫻　　明治天皇

こがねゐの　里ちかけれど　この春も
人傳にきく　花ざかりかな

### Koganei no Sakura

*Koganei no　Sato chikakeredo　Kono haru mo*
*Hito-zute ni kiku　Hanazakari kana.*

### The Cherry-Blossoms at Koganei　Emperor Meiji

**Though Koganei is near,**
**Yet this spring too,**
**Of its cherry-trees in bloom**
**I know but hearsay through.**

It may well be imagined that the Emperor was too busy with his duties to visit the cherry blossoms at Koganei, for which he had a great longing.

## 雲　雀　　明治天皇

つぎつぎに　あがるをみれば　雲の上に
入りしひばりや　友をよぶらむ

### Hibari

*Tsugi-tsugi ni　Agaru wo mireba　Kumo no ue ni*
*Irishi hibari ya　Tomo wo yoburan.*

### Skylarks
Emperor Meiji

Since skylarks soar above
One after another,
It may be that those that have entered the clouds
Are calling their friends together.

### 曙　鶯
明治天皇

花の色も　まだみえそめぬ　曙に
いづくなるらむ　鶯の啼く

### Akatsuki no Uguisu

*Hana no iro mo　Mada mie somenu　Akatsuki ni*
*Izuku naruran　Uguisu no naku.*

### Uguisu at Early Dawn
Emperor Meiji

At early dawn,
Before the flowers' hues were visible—
I wonder whence they came—
Uguisu's notes were audible.

### 靜　見　花
明治天皇

よものうみ　波をさまりて　この春は
心のどかに　花を見るかな

### Shizuka ni Hana wo Miru

*Yomo no umi　Nami osamarite　Kono haru wa*
*Kokoro nodokani　Hana wo miru kana.*

**An *Uguisu* on a Plum Tree**

By Kaisen (小田海仙 1785-1862)

### I View Flowers Calmly    Emperor Meiji

On all four seas, the stormy waves
    Have sunk to rest;
This spring I can enjoy the cherry-bloom,
    With tranquil breast.

This verse was composed in the spring of 1896, when peace reigned through-out Eastern Asia, the Sino-Japanese War having come to a close in the previous year. "On all four seas the stormy waves have sunk to rest" is a figure for the prevalence of peace.

### 待　鶯    明治天皇

思ふこと　多きことしも　鶯の
聲はさすがに　またれぬるかな

### Uguisu wo Matsu

*Omōkoto   Ōki kotoshi mo   Uguisu no*
*Koe wa sasugani   Matare nuru kana.*

### Waiting for *Uguisu*    Emperor Meiji

Even in this year's spring
    Though many matters task my mind,
With great impatience I await
    The *uguisu*'s song for which I've pined.

This was composed in the spring of 1904, in January of which year the Russo-Japanese War had broken out.

紅 葉 映 日　　　　　明 治 天 皇

夕日影　てらすをみれば　をぐら山
松よりおくも　紅葉なりけり

### Kōyō Hi ni Eizu

*Yūhi-kage   Terasu wo mireba   Ogura-yama*
*Matsu yori oku mo   Momiji nari keri.*

### Maple Leaves Glow in the Sun　Emperor Meiji

The setting sun lit up Mount Ogura,
Which while I gazed upon,
Lo, there beyond the pines, as well,
The glow of maple leaves.

Mount Ogura (小倉山), a small hill in the village of Saga west of Kyōto, is noted for its beautiful maples and pine-trees, and also for the circumstance that Prince Kane-akira and Fujiwara no Teika, famous poets of the Heian Period (794–1186), had villas on its top.

春 　 山　　　　　明 治 天 皇

山はみな　緑になりて　富士のねの
ほかには雪も　みえぬ春かな

### Shun-zan

*Yama wa mina   Midori ni narite   Fuji-no-ne no*
*Hoka niwa yuki mo   Mienu haru kana.*

**The Pine Grove at Miho**
**With a Distant View of Fuji**

By Manshū (川村曼舟), a contemporary painter

### Mountains in Spring     Emperor Meiji

Ah, spring is here,
  And all the hills are green.
Now only on Mount Fuji's peak
  Can snow be seen.

### 埋　　火     明治天皇

埋火に　むかへど寒し　ふる雪の
したにうもれし　人を思へば

### *Uzumi-Bi*

*Uzumi-bi ni   Mukaedo samushi   Furu-yuki no
Shita ni umoreshi   Hito wo omoeba.*

### Buried Fire     Emperor Meiji

Though sitting beside the brazier,
  Where buried charcoal embers glow,
I suddenly turn cold, remembering the men
  Deep buried under falling snow.

This was composed in 1902.  On January 25 of the same year, an infantry detachment of 200 men belonging to the Aomori Army Division, lost their lives while marching through a heavy snowfall, being buried under the snow.

*Uzumi-bi* (埋火), literally "buried fire", means live charcoal in the ashes in a brazier.

### 鄙 の 長 路     明治天皇

國民の　おくりむかへて　行くところ
さびしさ知らぬ　鄙の長みち

### *Hina no Nagamichi*

*Kunitami no   Okuri-mukaete   Yuku-tokoro*
*Sabishisa shiranu   Hina no nagamichi.*

### Long Country Roads     Emperor Meiji

My people come to welcome me
　　And speed me on my way where'er I go,
So even on long country roads
　　No loneliness I know.

### 夏　　氷　　　　　　　明治天皇

かたはらに　おける氷の　きゆるにも
道ゆく人の　あつさをぞおもふ

### *Natsu-Gōri*

*Katawara ni   Okeru kōri no   Kiyuru ni mo*
*Michi yuku hito no   Atsusa wo zo omō.*

### Summer Ice     Emperor Meiji

Seeing how quickly the ice which was set at my side
　　Has melted away,
I cannot but think, "How terribly hot they must be—
　　The people who walk on the roads to-day!"

### 水　　　　　　　明治天皇

器には　したがひながら　岩がねも
とほすは水の　ちからなりけり

### Mizu

*Utsuwa ni wa   Shitagai nagara   Iwa-ga-ne mo*
*Tōsu wa mizu no   Chikara nari keri.*

### Water
**Emperor Meiji**

Water conforms to the shape of its vessel;
    But yet has mighty force,
Piercing even the hardest rocks
    Lying athwart its course.

### 雨 夜 思 花
明治天皇

春雨の　ふりいでざらば　花の上に
月もさすべき　夜はならましを

### Uya Hana wo Omō

*Harusame no   Furi-ide zaraba   Hana no ue ni*
*Tsuki mo sasu beki   Yowa naramashi wo.*

### Longing for Flowers in a Rainy Night
**Emperor Meiji**

If the spring rain were not falling,
    It should be a lovely night,
Moonbeams on the cherry-blossoms
    Shining white.

薄暮眺望　　　　明治天皇

家なしと　思ふかたにも　ともし火の
影みえそめて　日はくれにけり

### Hakubo Chōbō

*Ie nashi to　Omō kata ni mo　Tomoshi-bi no*
*Kage mie-somete　Hi wa kure ni keri.*

### A Distant Landscape in Dusk　Emperor Meiji

Day is darkening into night,
　　And where I thought no houses were,
Lights begin to peep
　　Here and there.

山 の お く　　　　明治天皇

山のおく　島のはてまで　尋ねみむ
世にしられざる　人もありやと

### Yama no Oku

*Yama no oku　Shima no hate made　Tazune-min*
*Yo ni shirarezaru　Hito mo ari ya to.*

### Mountain Recesses　Emperor Meiji

I fain would search the islands' farthest shores
　　And the mountains' recesses,
If by chance I might find there a hidden man—
　　Whose greatness the world scarce guesses.

よろこびの聲　　　明治天皇

おほづつの　響はたえて　四方の海
よろこびの聲　いつかきこえむ

### Yorokobi no Koe

*Ōzutsu no　Hibiki wa taete　Yomo no umi*
*Yorokobi no koe　Itsu ka kikoen.*

### Shouts of Jubilation　　　Emperor Meiji

O, when will the boom of guns
　　Have an end,
And shouts of jubilation everywhere
　　From the four seas ascend?

新　聞　紙　　　明治天皇

みな人の　見るにひぶみに　世の中の
あとなしごとは　書かすもあらなむ

### Shimbunshi

*Mina-bito no　Miru niibumi ni　Yo no naka no*
*Ato-nashi goto wa　Kakazu mo aranan.*

### Newspapers　　　Emperor Meiji

Would that baseless reports
About the world's doings
Were not written in the daily press,
Which all men read!

蝶 　　　　　　　　　　　　　明治天皇

咲きつづく　花より花に　あくがれて
蝶も夢みる　ひまやなからむ

## Chō

*Saki-tsuzuku   Hana yori hana ni   Akugarete*
*Chō mo yume-miru   Hima ya nakaran.*

### Butterflies　　　　　　　Emperor Meiji

Attracted from flower to flower,
　　The butterflies, even, it seems,
Can find no time at all
　　For quiet dreams.

春　　旅 　　　　　　　　　明治天皇

とほからぬ　旅にいでても　みてしがな
鶯なきて　さくらちるころ

## Haru no Tabi

*Tōkaranu   Tabi ni idetemo   Miteshi gana*
*Uguisu nakite   Sakura chiru koro.*

### An Excursion in Spring　　Emperor Meiji

Oh, that I might but journey out
　　To some fair spot not far from town,
When the *uguisu* is in song
　　And cherry flowers flutter down!

The Emperor's position forbade him to make pleasure expeditions at will, lest doing so might interfere with the people's life.

こがらし　　　　　明治天皇

大空の　星のはやしも　動くかと
思ふばかりに　こがらしの吹く

### Kogarashi

Ozora no   Hoshi no hayashi mo   Ugoku ka to
Omō bakari ni   Kogarashi no fuku.

### The Winter Gale　　　Emperor Meiji

The starry forests of the sky
Seem to rock and quail
In the furious blast
Of the winter gale.

待　花　　　　　明治天皇

吹かばかつ　散りなむ花を　まちどほに
思ふぞ人の　こころなりける

### Hana wo Matsu

Fukaba katsu   Chirinan hana wo   Machidō ni
Omō zo hito no   Kokoro nari keru.

### Waiting for Cherry-Blossoms　　Emperor Meiji

It is but human nature to await
　Impatiently the cherry-flowers,
Although we know that when they open, all too soon
　They will drift down in showers.

### 巖 上 松　　　明治天皇

あらし吹く　世にも動くな　人ごころ
　いはほに根ざす　松のごとくに

#### Ganjō no Matsu

*Arashi fuku　Yo ni mo ugokuna　Hito-gokoro*
　*Iwao ni nezasu　Matsu no go!okuni.*

### Pine-Trees on Rocks　　Emperor Meiji

Although a storm-wind rages through the world,
　My people, brace your hearts against its shocks,
Unshaken as the pine-trees are,
　Deep-rooted in the rocks.

### 高　　嶺　　　明治天皇

おほぞらに　そびえて見ゆる　たかねにも
　登ればのぼる　道はありけり

#### Takane

*Ōzora ni　Sobiete miyuru　Takane nimo*
　*Noboreba noboru　Michi wa arikeri.*

### The High Peak        Emperor Meiji

E'en up a mountain peak which seems
　　To reach the skies, we dare to say,
For him whose will is set on climbing it,
　　There *is* a way.

### こ が ら し        明治天皇

むら鳥も　やどらむかたや　なかるらむ
　　林ゆすりて　こがらしのふく

### *Kogarashi*

*Mura-dori mo　Yadoran kata ya　Nakaruran*
　　*Hayashi yusurite　Kogarashi no fuku.*

### The Winter Gale        Emperor Meiji

Haply the flocks of birds
　　Cannot find safe roosts to-night;
Shaking and swaying the wood,
　　The winter gale blows at its height.

### 海 邊 蟲        明治天皇

浪のおと　遠ざかり行く　ひきしほに
　　むしのねたかし　濱の松原

### *Kaihen no Mushi*

*Nami no oto　Tōzakari yuku　Hiki-shio ni*
*Mushi no ne takashi　Hama no matsubara.*

### Insects on the Seashore     Emperor Meiji

Insect songs grow louder in the pine grove,
  The sea beside,
As the murmur of waves grows fainter,
  With the ebbing tide.

### 籠　中　蟲     明治天皇

ところせき　ふせごの内に　鳴くむしは
えらばれたるや　恨なるらむ

### *Rōchū no Mushi*

*Tokoro-seki  Fusego no uchi ni  Naku mushi wa
  Erabaretaru ya  Urami naruran.*

### The Insects in Cages     Emperor Meiji

Hark! in their small cages, the insects sing
  With plaintive voice;
Are they not lamenting that hard fate
  Which caused to fall on them the hunters' choice?

### 思　往　事     明治天皇

いにしへは　夢とすぐれど　まことある
臣のことばは　耳にのこれり

### *Ōji wo Omō*

*Inishie wa  Yume to suguredo  Makoto aru
  Omi no kotoba wa  Mimi ni nokoreri.*

**Spring on a Stream**
(willow tree and ferryboat)

By Seihō (竹内栖鳳), a contemporary painter

### Longing for Bygone Days       Emperor Meiji

Alas! like dreams have passed away
    The olden· days and years;
But my devoted Ministers' words are left
    To ring on in my ears.

### 舟中落花       明治天皇

ちる花を　のせてかへりぬ　渡舟
むかひの岸に　人はおろして

### *Shūchū Rakkwa*

*Chiru-hana wo   Nosete kaerinu   Watashi-bune*
*Mukai no kishi ni   Hito wa oroshite.*

### Fallen Flowers in a Ferryboat       Emperor Meiji

The ferryboat has returned
    With fallen flowers aboard,
Although it has left its passengers
    On the opposite bank of the ford.

よみ人しらす
**Anonymous**

### 船　人　　　よみ人しらす

波風の　静かなる日も　船人は
かぢにこころを　ゆるさざらなむ

## Funabito

*Nami-kaze no   Shizuka naru hi mo   Funabito wa*
*Kaji ni kokoro wo   Yurusazaranan.*

### The Sailor                                   Anon.

**Even on peaceful days**
**With quiet waves and wind,**
**The sailor off the helm**
**Should never take his mind.**

This didactic verse is often ascribed to the Emperor Meiji, but in reality its author is unknown.

### 昭 憲 皇 太 后
**The Empress Dowager Shōken** (1849–1913)

The consort of the Emperor Meiji, she was a gracious and gifted lady. She studied versification under Konoe Tadahiro, Hatta Tomonori and Takasaki Masakaze, and became a prominent poetess.

### 民 の 心                                   昭憲皇太后

浅しとて　堰けば溢るる　川水の
心は民の　こころなりけり

## Tami no Kokoro

*Asashi tote   Sekeba afururu   Kawa-mizu no*
*Kokoro wa tami no   Kokoro nari keri.*

### The People's Mind
**Empress Dowager Shōken**

Altho' the stream be shallow,
   Yet it will overflow,
If all its waters are dammed up—
   The people's mind is even so.

This verse seems to refer to Government repression.

\*         \*         \*         \*         \*

The still and silent water of a stream,
Shallow as it may be, does swell and rise
And flows o'er the land if abruptly stemmed:
Likewise with the most peaceful people.

Trans. by Wadagaki Kenzō

### 眞 の 寶          昭憲皇太后

夜ひかる　玉もなにせむ　身をてらす
　　ふみこそ人の　寶なりけれ

### Makoto no Takara

*Yoru hikaru   Tama mo nanisen   Mi wo terasu*
*Fumi koso hito no   Takara nari kere.*

### The True Treasure
**Empress Dowager Shōken**

Even the gem which shines away
   The darkness of the night is naught;
A book enlightening the mind—
   This is true treasure, to be sought.

This verse refers to the traditional Chinese *Yakō-no-Tama* or "Night-Shining Jewel", which is said to have shone the darkness of night away.

✻  ✻  ✻  ✻  ✻

The jewel in a Lady's Coronet
Gleams in her hair, and sparkles in the gloom,
And yet 'tis naught—a sparkle, not a light.
The book whose page enlightens the dark mind
Is the true treasure.   Trans. by Arthur Lloyd

## 綾 に し き      昭憲皇太后

綾にしき　とりかさねても　おもふかな
さむさおほはむ　袖もなき身を

### *Aya Nishiki*

*Aya nishiki Tori kasanetemo Omō kana
Samusa ōwan Sode mo naki mi wo.*

### Silk and Brocade

**Empress Dowager Shōken**

**Although I am clad in silk and brocade,
Beyond the power of the biting cold,
Yet when I think of the poor in their rags,
I shiver, heavy with grief untold.**

✻  ✻  ✻  ✻  ✻

The winter, with its rigours, touches not
Our bodies, clad in vestments warm and rich;
But when we think upon the shivering poor
That freeze in their thin rags, the cruel tooth
Of pitiless winter bites our inmost heart.

      Trans. by Arthur Lloyd

御　軍　　　　　　　　　昭憲皇太后

戰へば　勝つが常なる　御軍も
なほ如何にかと　思ふ時あり

### Mi-Ikusa

*Tatakaeba　Katsu ga tsune naru　Mi-ikusa mo*
*Nao ikani ka to　Omō toki ari.*

### The Imperial Army

**Empress Dowager Shōken**

The Imperial army, whenever it fights,
　Is always victorious;
And yet there are times when for its welfare
　My heart is anxious.

This was composed in 1904 during the Russo-Japanese War.

春　　　　　　　　　　　昭憲皇太后

かり宮の　春いかならむ　御園生の
梅はのこらず　花咲きにけり

### Haru

*Kari-miya no　Haru ikanaran　Mi-sono-o no*
*Ume wa nokorazu　Hana saki ni keri.*

### Spring     Empress Dowager Shōken

I wonder what this spring is like
At the temporary Court!
The plum-trees in the Royal gardens here
Are all in full bloom.

This was composed in 1895 when the Sino-Japanese War was in progress,
and the Emperor Meiji shared privation with the officers and men at the Im-
perial Headquarters at Hiroshima. It may well be imagined how anxious the
Empress, who remained at Tōkyō, felt about the Emperor.

### 草 花 盛     昭憲皇太后

御馬には　何をかふらむ　秋の野の
草はみなが ら　花さきにけり

### *Sōkwa Sakari-nari*

*Mi-uma niwa　Nani wo kōran　Aki no no no*
*Kusa wa minagara　Hana saki ni keri.*

### The Grasses in Full Bloom
#### Empress Dowager Shōken

I wonder what grasses may be
The Imperial horse's fodder!
The grasses of the autumn lea
Are all now in flower.

### 道     昭憲皇太后

かへりみて　心にとはば　見ゆべきを
ただしき道に　何まよふらむ

### Michi

*Kaerimite    Kokoro ni towaba    Miyu-beki wo*
*Tadashiki michi ni    Nani mayōran.*

## The Road of Right

**Empress Dowager Shōken**

In your search for the road of right,
    Why need you go astray,
When you may look within and ask
    Your heart for the way?

螢

昭憲皇太后

寂しさも　しばし忘れて　みるものは
みまへに馴れし　螢なりけり

### Hotaru

*Sabishisa mo    Shibashi wasurete    Miru-mono wa*
*Mimae ni nareshi    Hotaru nari-keri.*

## Fireflis　　**Empress Dowager Shōken**

Forgetting loneliness awhile,
    In ecstasy
I gazed upon the fireflies
    Which glowed before His Majesty.

On June 16, 1880, the Emperor Meiji visited Hachi-ōji, a small town some
twenty-five miles west of Tōkyō, where he stayed for the night. The townsmen
presented the Emperor with numerous fireflies for his entertainment. The

Emperor graciously sent some of the fireflies to Tōkyō for the Empress, who, out of gratitude and joy, composed the above verse.

## 市　月　　　　　　昭憲皇太后

かりそめの　露の上にも　やどるらむ
植木の市の　秋の夜の月

### Ichi no Tsuki

*Karisome no　Tsuyu no ue nimo　Yadoruran*
*Ueki no ichi no　Aki no yo no tsuki.*

## The Moon on a Street Fair

**Empress Dowager Shōken**

It may be the autumn moon
Is reflected bright
In the passing dew on the plants for sale,
This market night.

Night markets of pot-plants and bushes and beautiful flowers are often held along the pavements in Tōkyō and other cities and towns. Needless to say, the above verse is an imaginary description of such a street fair.

## 月 前 千 鳥　　　　　昭憲皇太后

月清み　藻にすむ蟲や　あさるらむ
海べにむれて　千鳥なくなり

### Getsuzen no Chidori

*Tsuki kiyomi　Mo ni sumu mushi ya　Asaruran*
*Umibe ni murete　Chidori naku nari.*

### Plovers in the Moonlight

**Empress Dowager Shōken**

A flock of plovers are crying
Along the shore; in the clear moonbeams
They search, it may be, for creatures
That dwell in the seaweeds.

### 晴 天 雲 雀　　　　昭憲皇太后

なごりなく　霞は晴れて　朝ひばり
あがる限も　みゆる空かな

### Seiten no Hibari

*Nagori naku   Kasumi wa hare te   Asa-hibari*
*Agaru-kagiri mo   Miyuru sora kana.*

### Skylarks in the Blue Sky

**Empress Dowager Shōken**

The mists have passed and left no trace;
So translucently clear is the sky
That the morning larks, in their soaring flight,
Are plain to the lifted eye.

### 筆 寫 人 心　　　　昭憲皇太后

とる筆の　あとはづかしと　思ふかな
心のうつる　ものとききては

### Fude Jinshin wo Utsusu

*Toru fude no    Ato hazukashi to    Omō kana*
*Kokoro no utsuru    Monoto kikitewa.*


### Handwriting Reveals the Character

**Empress Dowager Shōken**

About my writing now
   Greatly ashamed I feel,
Because I hear that handwriting is said
   The mind to reveal.


### 湖 上 舟

昭憲皇太后

玉くしげ　箱根のうみを　ゆく舟に
うつれる富士の　影動くなり


### Kojō no Fune

*Tama-kushige    Hakone no umi wo    Yuku fune ni*
*Utsureru Fuji no    Kage ugoku nari.*


### A Boat in a Lake

**Empress Dowager Shōken**

The snow-capt Fuji upside down
   Reflected in Hakone Lake—
Behold! it sways and gleams
   In a passing rowboat's wake.

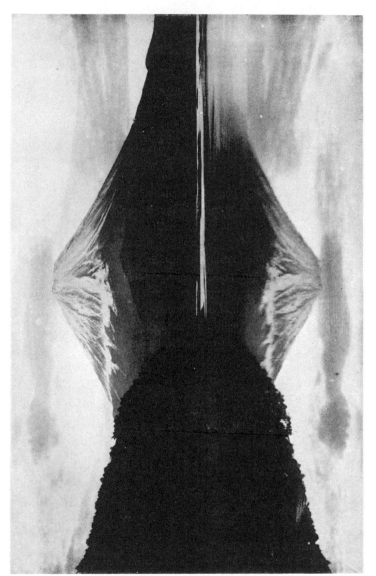

**Mount Fuji with Inverted Reflection**

(Photograph)

*Tama-kushige* is the pillow-word belonging to *hako* or "box".

Hakone-no-Umi or the Lake of Hakone, whose proper name is Ashi-no-ko ("Lake of Reeds"), is a beautiful lake, 13 miles in circumference and 2,386 feet above sea-level. It is famous for the inverted reflection of Mount Fuji("Sakasa-Fuji") which may be seen on a clear day, often at daybreak.

## 長　命　　　　昭憲皇太后

かりそめの　ことは思はで　くらすこそ
　　世に長らへむ　薬なるらめ

### Chōmei

*Karisome no　Koto wa omowade　Kurasu koso*
*Yo ni nagaraen　Kusuri narurame.*

### Long Life　　Empress Dowager Shōken

To think not of trifling things,
　And to keep the mind from care—
This is the medicine rare
Which long life in this world brings.

## 撫　子　　　　昭憲皇太后

いとほしく　思はるるかな　刈りてほす
　　夏野の草に　まじる撫子

### Nadeshiko

*Ito-oshiku　Omowaruru kana　Karite hosu*
*Natsuno no kusa ni　Majiru nadeshiko.*

### Fringed Pinks

Empress Dowager Shōken

Oh! sad to see, among the grasses mown
And spread to dry
Upon the summer meadowland,
Some fringed pinks lie!

The *nadeshiko* or "fringed pink" is a small and lovely flower.

朝　蟬　　　　昭憲皇太后

實になれる　桃の林の　葉がくれに
あした涼しく　蟬のなくなり

### *Asa-Zemi*

*Mi ni nareru　Momo no hayashi no　Hagakure ni
Ashita suzushiku　Semi no naku nari.*

### Morning Cicadas

Empress Dowager Shōken

Hidden amidst the orchard leaves,
Where peach trees fruitage bear—
Hark! cicadas are singing cool
In the morning air.

波のさわぎ　　　　昭憲皇太后

夢さめて　みふねの上を　思ふかな
舞子の濱の　波のさわぎに

**A Singing Cicada**

By Suiun (小室翠雲), a contemporay painter

## Nami no Sawagi

*Yume samete   Mifune no ue wo   Omō kana*
*Maiko no hama no   Nami no sawagi ni.*

### High Waves Roar

**Empress Dowager Shōken**

At midnight, waking from my dreams,
And hearing off Maiko Bay the high waves roar,
How anxiously I think about my lord,
Aboard the man-of-war!

## 田家夏月

昭憲皇太后

草とりし　晝の暑さも　わするらむ
門田の月に　すすむさと人

## Denka no Kagetsu

*Kusa torishi   Hiru no atsusa mo   Wasururan*
*Kadota no tsuki ni   Suzumu sato-bito.*

### The Summer Moon in the Country

**Empress Dowager Shōken**

They may have quite forgotten now
How they toiled, weeding in the heat of noon—
Those villagers who cool themselves by the ricefield,
In the light of the moon.

水 郷 春 曙          昭憲皇太后

波の上に　月はしらみて　ほのぼのと
柳みえゆく　川づらのさと

## Suikyō no Shunsho

*Nami no ue ni　Tsuki wa shiramite　Hono-bono to*
*Yanagi mie-yuku　Kawazura no sato.*

## Spring Dawn in a Village on the Stream

**Empress Dowager Shōken**

Upon the ripples running slow
The pallid moonbeams gleam,
With willow leaves that dimly show
Here in the village on the stream.

野 徑 夏 草          昭憲皇太后

草ふかき　夏野の原も　人のゆく
道ひとすぢは　うづもれずして

## Yakei Kasō

*Kusa fukaki　Natsu-no no hara mo　Hito no yuku*
*Michi hito-suji wa　Uzumorezu shite.*

## Summary Grasses on the Path across a Plain

Summer Grasses on the Path across a Plain
Empress Dowager Shōken

Even upon the summer plain,
With grasses deeply overgrown,
One line of path on which men walk
Remains unburied—one alone.

太 田 垣 蓮 月

### Ōtagaki Rengetsu (1790–1875)

The daughter of Ōtagaki Kōko, a samurai in the service of the Chion-in Temple in Kyōto, Sei (her lay name) married his adopted son, to whom she bore four children. They all died young, and her husband also died when she was about thirty years old. Thereupon Sei shaved her head and assumed the name of Rengetsu-Ni* which literally signifies "Lotus Moon Nun". She studied verse-making under Chigusa Arikoto and later became an excellent poetess. When she was about forty, her father died. Then she earned a living by making chinaware, particularly tea cups and pots, inscribed with her verses in her own hand, which soon won a high reputation throughout the Empire. She left a collection of her own verses.

鶯

蓮 月 尼

おりたちて　朝菜洗へば　加茂川の
岸のやなぎに　鶯のなく

### Uguisu

*Ori-tachite　Asana araeba　Kamogawa no*
*Kishi no yanagi ni　Uguisu no naku.*

---

*Ni (尼) means a "nun". In Old Japan a chaste woman, after her husband's death, often shaved her head and, in the case of a literary woman, added 尼 ("Nun") after her pen name, although she did not live in a convent.

### The *Uguisu* Rengetsu

Stepping down to the Kamo River,
I washed my morning greens,
When sweetly rang out an *uguisu*'s notes
From a willow on the shore.

## 花 の 下 蓮 月 尼

宿かさぬ　人のつらさを　なさけにて
朧月夜の　花の下臥

### *Hana no Shita*

*Yado kasanu　Hito no tsurasa wo　Nasake nite*
*Oboro-zuki-yo no　Hana no shita-bushi.*

### Beneath Cherry Blossoms Rengetsu

A man who lodging did refuse me
　　Proved to be kind: I had sweet sleep
Beneath a cherry-tree in bloom
　　Bathed in the hazy moonbeams deep.

This verse is generally considered a masterpiece; but the translator does not altogether approve it, because evidently it is not based on a real experience and it is too artificial.

## 松 の こ ゑ 蓮 月 尼

山ざとは　松のこゑのみ　聞きなれて
風吹かぬ日は　さびしかりけり

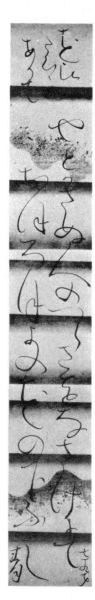

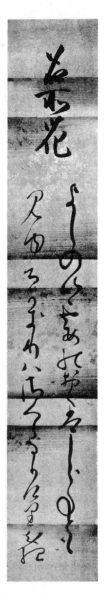

**"Beneath Cherry Blossoms"**
**—Rengetsu**

In the poetess' own handwriting

**"The Cherry Blossoms on Mount Yoshino"—Tomonori**

In the poet's own handwriting

## *Matsu no Koe*

*Yamazato wa   Matsu no koe nomi   Kiki narete*
*Kaze fukanu hi wa   Sabishikari keri.*

## The Voices of Pine Trees          Rengetsu

In this mountain village, I have grown accustomed
To listen to the voices only of the trees,
So when the pines are silent, then I am lonely,
On days when there blows no breeze.

### 大 國 隆 正
#### Ōkuni Takamasa (1792-1871)

Born a samurai of the Tsuwano Clan in Iwami Province, Takamasa became
an authority on Japanese and Chinese classics, and founded a sect of Shintō
called *Honkyō Hongaku* (本教本學) or "True Religion and True Doctrines".
He wrote numerous books on Shintō, current politics and literature, including
notes on one hundred long poems of the *Manyō Shū* anthology.

### 志                                隆 正

立てそむる　志だに　たゆますば
龍のあぎとの　玉もとるべし

### *Kokorozashi*

*Tate somuru   Kokorozashi dani   Tayumazuba*
*Tatsu no agito no   Tama mo torubeshi.*

## Aim in Life  Takamasa

If you stick to the aim you had at first,
  Nor in your efforts ever pause,
You may even hope at last to obtain
  The gem beneath the dragon's jaws.

"The gem beneath the dragon's jaws", of course, symbolizes a wellnigh impossible task.

### 八 田 知 紀
### Hatta Tomonori (1799-1874)

Hatta Tomonori was a samurai of the Kagoshima Clan.  While residing in Kyōto as an official of his clan, he studied Japanese poetry under the instruction of the famous poet, Kagawa Kageki.  After the Restoration of 1868, he became an official of the Imperial Household Department, and for some time had the honour of revising the verses of the poet-Emperor Meiji.  He wrote many books on Japanese literature and a few accounts of short journeys.

## 芳野山の櫻  知 紀

芳野山　霞のおくは　知らねども
見ゆるかぎりは　櫻なりけり

### Yoshino-Yama no Sakura

*Yoshino-yama    Kasumi no oku wa    Shiranedomo*
*Miyuru kagiri wa    Sakura nari keri.*

## The Cherry-Blossoms on Mount Yoshino  Tomonori

I know not on Mount Yoshino
  What there may be beyond the haze;
But far as eye can reach,
  'Tis cherry-bloom that meets my gaze.

**A Dragon**

By Sansetsu (狩野山雪 1589–1651)

The verse means: I don't know what is to be found—perhaps another expanse of cherry-blossoms—behind the beautiful veil of haze wrapping a part of the hills; but all around as far as eye can reach, the pale-pink cherry-blossoms are gleaming over the hills and down in the vales.

This verse is a masterpiece in that it is exceedingly rhythmical and a natural, artless description of the beautiful scene. It is so famous that it is included in primary school readers.

Yoshino-Yama or Mount Yoshino in Yamato Province is not a single mountain but a few hills, covered with cherry-trees. There is a hamlet on one part of these hills, consisting of several Buddhist and Shintō temples and many inns and shops for the accommodation of visitors to the cherry-blossoms and the temples. The Yoshino hills are the most famous of all places noted for the flower. They are also celebrated for historic associations. It was there that the Emperor Go-Daigo (reigned 1319–1339) and his son, the Emperor Go-Murakami (reigned 1339–1368), of the Southern Court, resided in exile, so to speak, and a battle was fought between the Imperial army and the rebel troops, which resulted in a defeat of the former.

A legion of Japanese and Chinese-style poems have been written on the cherry-blossoms and the tragic fortunes of the Imperial cause. Among the numberless *tanka* on the cherry-flowers, the above by Tomonori is the best known; and among the numerous *haiku* on the same theme, the following one, by Teishitsu (1609–1673), is the most famous.

これはこれは　とばかり花の　吉野山

*Korewa korewa　To bakari hana no　Yoshino-yama.*

I could but say "Oh! Oh!"
On flower-clad Mount Yoshino.

The poet was overwhelmingly smitten by the beauty of the cherry-blossoms which wrapt the hills and dales of Yoshino, so that he could only exlaim "*Kore wa! Kore wa!*" or "Oh! Oh!"

\*　　\*　　\*　　\*　　\*

Hail to the sacred mount of yore renowned,
A veil of haze doth hide thy hallowed ground,
Yet far, afar—as far as eye can reach,
'Tis naught but cherry-blossoms all around!

Trans. by Wadagaki Kenzō

## 燕　　　　　　　　　　知　紀

春來れば　必す歸る　燕かな
人の心は　賴まれぬ世に

### Tsubame

*Hara kureba　Kanarazu kaeru　Tsubame kana*
*Hito no kokoro wa　Tanomarenu yo ni.*

### The Swallow　　　Tomonori

**The swallow is sure to return**
**When spring comes round;**
**While men's minds are too oft**
**Unreliable found.**

## 嵐 山 の 櫻　　　　　知　紀

うつせみの　わが世のかぎり　見るべきは
あらしの山の　櫻なりけり

### Arashiyama no Sakura

*Utsusemi no　Waga yo no kagiri　Miru-beki wa*
*Arashi no yama no　Sakura nari keri.*

### The Cherry-Flowers on Mount Arashi    Tomonori

The flowers I must, above all,
Gaze upon lovingly still,
As long as I live in this world,
Are the cherries on Arashi Hill.

*Utsusemi*, literally "the body existing in this world", is a pillow-word belonging to *yo*, "the world" or "life".

The poet's verse on "The Cherry-flowers on Mount Yoshino" is generally considered his best, but he himself judged this the best of his poems on the subject. The translator, however, prefers the verse on Mount Yoshino.

### 櫻 の 花    知 紀

旅人の　袖にもつれて　行く蝶は
梢はなれし　櫻なりけり

### *Sakura-no-Hana*

*Tabibito no　Sode ni motsurete　Yuku chō wa
Kozue hanareshi　Sakura nari keri.*

### Cherry-flowers    Tomonori

Lo! on the traveller's sleeves
Some butterflies are flickering;
Nay, 'tis only cherry-flowers
From the branch down fluttering.

This verse, it is evident, was suggested by the following *haiku* by Arakida Moritake (荒木田守武), which is familiar to every cultured Japanese:

落花枝に　歸ると見れば　胡蝶かな

*Rakkwa eda ni   Kaeru to mireba   Kochō kana.*

> It seemed to my eye
> > A fallen flower flew back to the branch;
> > Lo! 'twas a butterfly.

It is the translator's judgment that Tomonori's verse, which describes just the opposite effect, is more natural and more beautiful.

### 井 上 文 雄

### Inoue Fumio (1800–1871)

A physician to Lord Tayasu, and a prominent poet, Fumio wrote several works on Japanese literature and left a collection of his verses.

## 心 の 鬼　　　　　　文 雄

おのづから　心の鬼に　かちてこそ
よに恐るべき　事なかりけれ

### *Kokoro no Oni*

*Onozukara   Kokoro no oni ni   Kachite koso*
*Yo ni osoru-beki   Koto nakari-kere.*

### The Devil in the Mind　　　Fumio

When you have once subdued
> The devil in your mind,
In all the world
> You will no terror find.

## 夕 立 の 雨　　　　　　文 雄

あら川に　瀬の音のこして　水上の
秩父にかへる　夕立の雨

## *Yūdachi no Ame*

*Arakawa ni   Se no to nokoshite   Minakami no*
*Chichibu ni kaeru   Yūdachi no ame.*

### The Summer Shower                    Fumio

Leaving its sound in the shallows
    Of the Arakawa River,
To the Chichibu Mountains up the stream
    Has returned the summer shower.

## 千　鳥                    文　雄

落ちはてし　夕日の名殘　ほのかなる
波の面白く　立つ千鳥かな

### *Chidori*

*Ochi-hateshi   Yūhi no nagori   Honoka naru*
*Nami no mo shiroku   Tatsu chidori kana.*

### Plovers                    Fumio

On the waves where yet
    Glows faint light
From the sun that has gone down—
    Plovers floating white!

## 與　謝　野　尙　絅
### Yosano Shōkei (1813–1888)

A priest of the western branch of the Hongwanji Temple, who participated
in the Restoration of 1868; the father of Yosano Hiroshi, a leading poet of
the present era.

燕　　　　　　　　　　　　尚　綱

うつばりに　黄なる嘴　五つ鳴く
雛に痩せて出で入る　親燕あはれ

## *Tsubame*

*Utsubari ni　Kinaru kuchibashi　Itsutsu naku*
*Hina ni yasete ide-iru　Oyatsubame aware.*

## Swallows　　　　　　　　　　Shōken

Behold, five yellow little bills
Wide open, on the beam;
Poor parent-swallows, coming, going—
Their crying young have made them lean!

勝　安　芳
### Katsu Yasuyoshi (1823–1899)

Better known by his other name Katsu Awa (勝安房) and his pen name
Kaishū (海舟).

Born the son of a retainer of the Tokugawa Shōgun, Yasuyoshi served the
Shōgun's government successively as a Dutch translator, Governor of Men-of-
War and Commander-in-Chief of the Army. In March, 1868, a great Imperial
army marched on Yedo (the present Tōkyō) and the Shōgun's capital and castle
were on the eve of destruction, when Yasuyoshi, Commander-in-Chief, rising
to the occasion, surrendered the Capital to the Imperialists. Soon afterward
took place the abolition of the Shōgunate and the restoration of the Imperial
régime. Under the new government, Yasuyoshi was appointed Minister of the
Navy and Privy Councillor, and was created a Count. He was proficient in
fencing, gunnery and the art of navigation; he was also a good Japanese and
Chinese poet, and wrote several books on the Japanese army and navy and
on literature.

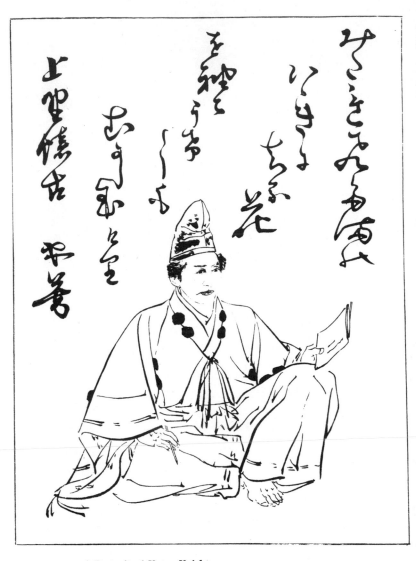

**A Portrait of Katsu Kaishu**

By Kōgyō (寺崎廣業 1866-1919)
The poem, '' Recollections of the Battle of
Ueno ''—Kaishū
Handwritten by the poet

## 上野懷古                                 海 舟

みだれ飛ぶ　たまのひびきに　ちる花を
袖にうけしも　むかしなりけり

### *Ueno Kaiko*

*Midare tobu   Tama no hibiki ni   Chiru hana wo*
*Sode ni ukeshi mo   Mukashi nari keri.*

### Recollections of the Battle of Ueno        Kaishū

**Ah, it was long ago**
**That cherry blossoms in profusion**
**Came fluttering down upon my sleeves,**
**Scattered by the sound of shots**
**That rained in wild confusion.**

The Battle of Ueno (the present day Ueno Park in Tōkyō) took place on May 15, 1868, between the Imperialists and those men of the Ex-Shōgun's troops who were discontented with the surrender of the Capital and the abolition of the Shōgunate.   As a matter of fact, the poet-statesman took no part in the battle, but he imagines himself to be among those Ex-Shōgun's troops.

The poet, on one hand, sadly recollects the olden troublous times, while, on the other, he rejoices over peace reigning in his country.

*Tama no hibiki ni chiru hana* or "the flowers scattered by the sound of shots" is a customary phrase, a beautiful extension of the simple form "scattered by shots".

## 錨　索                                 海 舟

かけとめん　ちびきのいかり　つなをなみ
ただよふ船の　行方しらずも

## *Ikari-Zuna*

*Kake-tomen   Chibiki no ikari   Tsuma wo nami*
*Tadayō fune no   Yukue shirazu mo.*

### The Anchor-Rope                    Kaishū

**Its heavy anchor-rope**
**Broken away,**
**The great ship is drifting.**
**Ah! whither will it stray?**

*Kake-tomen* means "for mooring". *Chibiki* means "hauled by a thousand men".

### 税 所 敦 子
#### Saisho Atsu-ko (1825–1900)

A native of Kyōto, Atsu-ko married Saisho Atsuyuki, a Satsuma samurai, who died when she was twenty-eight. Later she became a court lady and served the Empress and the Empress Dowager in connection with literary affairs. From her girlhood she was proficient in versification, and she left a collection of her verses.

### 鶯                                            敦 子

なほざりに　をらせじとてか　鶯の
梅の下枝を　はなれざるらむ

### *Uguisu*

*Naozari ni   Oraseji tote ka   Uguisu no*
*Ume no shizu-e wo   Hanarezaruran.*

**"The Autumn Moon"—Tettō**

Handwritten by the poet
(See Page 531)

**"An *Uguisu*"—Atsuko**

In the poetess' own handwriting
The picture by Tangetsu (樋口探月
1821–1896)

### *Uguisu* Atsu-ko

To ensure, perhaps, that no plum-branches
Carelessly broken off shall be,
The *uguisu* refuses to leave her post
On the lower branches of the tree.

### 春　雨 敦　子

花の上に　眠るこてふの　夢にだに
こよひの雨は　しらすやあるらむ

### *Harusame*

*Hana no ue ni　Nemuru kochō no　Yume ni dani
Koyoi no ame wa　Shirazu ya aruran.*

### Spring Rain Atsu-ko

The fragile butterflies,
Sleeping upon the flowers,
May nothing know, e'en in their dreams,
Of this night's gentle showers.

In Japan gentle spring rain is a joy belonging to that season; and the
spring rain referred to in this verse is so soft that even the butterflies sleep-
ing on the flowers may not be conscious of it.

### 若　菜 敦　子

かはぎしの　若菜つむとて　少女子が
かざしの花を　ながしつるかな

## *Wakana*

*Kawagishi no   Wakana tsumu tote   Otomego ga*
*Kazashi no hana wo   Nagashi tsuru kana.*

### Young Green Shoots                    **Atsu-ko**

A maiden, gathering young green shoots
That grew at the river-side—
Alas!—let flowers that decked her hair
Drop down into the tide.

## 菊 の 香                          敦 子

君がため　をらんと思ひし　菊の香を
はやくも風の　ささげつるかな

### *Kiku no Ka*

*Kimi ga tame   Oran to omoishi   Kiku no ka wo*
*Hayakumo kaze no   Sasagetsuru kana.*

### The Fragrance of Chrysanthemums        **Atsu-ko**

The chrysanthemums that I meant to pluck
For His Imperial Majesty—
The wind has presented
Their fragrance already.

## 散 る 花                          敦 子

大君の　みけしの袖に　ちる花は
風をうしとも　思はざるらむ

## Chiru Hana

*Ōkimi no   Mikeshi no sode ni   Chiru hana wa*
*Kaze wo ushi tomo   Omowazaruran.*

### Falling Flowers                    Atsu-ko

I think the petals that flutter down
On His Majesty's sleeve,
Have no bitter feelings against the wind,
Which gave them leave.

## 松 の 影                    敦 子

くるるまで　降りしみゆきの　上にいま
月やさすらむ　松のかげみゆ

## Matsu no Kage

*Kururu made   Furishi miyuki no   Ueni ima*
*Tsuki ya sasuran   Matsu no kage miyu.*

### The Shadows of Pine-Trees         Atsu-ko

Upon the snow that fell till twilight came,
The moon must now be shining bright;
For see! the shadows of the pines
Have sprung to sight.

## 木 村 正 辭

### Kimura Masakoto (1827–1913)

Masakoto was a professor of Japanese literature at the Literature College, Imperial Tōkyō University, and a member of the Imperial Academy. He wrote three books on the *Manyō Shū* Anthology.

## よしの山　　　正 辭

よしの山　こと木は花に　うづもれて
さくらのほかの　ものなかりけり

### *Yoshino-Yama*

*Yoshino-Yama　Kotoki wa hana ni　Uzumorete*
*Sakura no hoka no　Mono nakari keri.*

### Monnt Yoshino　　Masakoto

Upon Mount Yoshino
Nothing but cherry bloom I see,
Those flowers burying, where they blow,
Every other tree.

## 佐 々 木 弘 綱

### Sasaki Hirotsuna (1828–1891)

A native of Ishi-Yakushi, a village in Ise Province, Hirotsuna studied poetry under Ashiro Hironori. At the age of twenty-four, he wrote *Uta-Kotoba Tōkagami* or "A Telescope of Poetical Diction", and afterwards a number of literary books. For some years he was a lecturer on poetry at the Imperial Tōkyō University.

病おもかりしとき　　　　　弘綱

命あらば　嬉しからまし　もしなくば

それもすべなし　神にまかせむ

*Yamai Omokarishi Toki*

*Inochi araba   Ureshikaramashi   Moshi nakuba*

*Soremo sube-nashi   Kami ni makasen.*

### When Seriously Ill　　　　　Hirotsuna

**If I may longer live,**

**I shall be much rejoiced;**

**If not, t'will do no good to grieve.**

**Unto the gods all this I leave.**

### 黑　田　清　綱
**Kuroda Kiyotsuna** (1830–1917)

The son of a samurai of the Satsuma Clan, Kiyotsuna evinced poetical talent in his childhood and studied poetry under Hatta Tomonori, among whose pupils he was most prominent. After holding several important Government offices in succession, he was in his last years a Viscount, a Privy Councillor, and Chief of the Imperial Bureau of Poetry.

### 山　吹　　　　　清綱

あゆはしる　うへになびきて　咲きにけり

吉野の川の　山吹の花

### Yamabuki

*Ayu hashiru   Ue ni nabikite   Saki ni keri*
*Yoshino no kawa no   Yamabuki no hana.*

## Globeflowers                     Kiyotsuna

Lo! swaying in the breeze,
  The globeflowers bright and yellow,
Over the River Yoshino
  Where *ayu* dart in the shallow.

### 小　出　粲
**Koide Tsubara** (1833–1908)

Tsubara, who was proficient in military arts and versification, was an
official of the Imperial Bureau of Poetry.

# 櫻                                     粲

うかれつる　むかしの春の　ともはただ
　櫻ばかりに　なりにけるかな

### Sakura

*Ukare-tsuru   Mukashi no haru no   Tomo wa tada*
*Sakura bakari ni   Nari ni keru kana.*

## Cherry Flowers                   Tsubara

Of all the gay friends who made merry
  With me in long by-gone spring hours,
Alas! there survive alone
  The cherry flowers.

**An Avenue of Pine Trees**

By Taikwan (橫山大觀),
a contemporary painter

## 伊 東 祐 命
### Itō Sukenobu (1834–1889)

Born a samurai of the Tsuruta Clan (鶴田藩), Sukenobu became a prominent poet; and after the Restoration he was an important official of the Imperial Bureau of Poetry.

## 松 の 下 道 祐 命

やどからん　さとをなはての　末にみて
月にいそがぬ　松のした道

### *Matsu no Shitamichi*

*Yado karan   Sato wo nawate no   Sue ni mite*
*Tsuki ni isoganu   Matsu no shitamichi.*

### The Road under Pine Trees Sukenobu

**Seeing, at the further end of the little ricefield path,**
**The hamlet where I meant to pass the night,**
**I made no haste upon the road, under the pine trees,**
**In the clear moonlight.**

*Nawate* is a path through a ricefield.

## 高 崎 正 風
### Takasaki Masakaze (1837–1913)

The son of a leading samurai of the Satsuma Clan, Masakaze studied versification under the famous poet, Hatta Tomonori. Afterwards he became a prominent poet himself. He played a part in the Meiji Restoration. In 1871 he was appointed Senior Councillor of State; and soon after, he visited Europe and America to study political conditions. In 1876 he was made an official of the Imperial Bureau of Poetry and ten years later, he was promoted to be chief of the bureau. The following year, he was created a Baron. In his last years he was a Privy Councillor. He left a collection of his verses numbering four thousand.

戀 　　　　　正 風

たらちねの　親にむかひて　云ひがたき
心はかつて　なかりしものを

*Koi*

*Tarachine no　Oya ni mukaite　Iigataki*
*Kokoro wa katsute　Nakarishi mono wo.*

**Love** 　　Masakaze

**Oh, never before have I known, among**
**All my heart's sentiments,**
**One that was hard for me to confide**
**To my own parents.**

The confession of a young man who loves for the first time. *Tarachine* is a pillow-word of "mother" or "parents".

上杉謙信の大度 　　　正 風

贈りけん　鹽の色にも　見ゆるかな
こしぢの雪の　きよき心は

*Uesugi Kenshin no Taido*

*Okuri ken　Shio no iro ni mo　Miyuru kana*
*Koshiji no yuki no　Kiyoki kokoro wa.*

### The Generosity of General Kenshin    Masakaze

**The colour of the salt he sent
So generously to his foe—
It shows the purity of heart
Of snow in Echigo.**

This verse is a eulogy on a noble deed of Uesugi Kenshin (1530–1578), Lord of Echigo, a brave warrior. The Province of Kai, which was governed by his many years' enemy, Takeda Shingen, another hero, being situated among mountains, used to import salt from the seacoast provinces of Suruga and Sagami; but the lords of these provinces, mortal enemies of Shingen, prohibited the export of salt into Kai. In consequence, the people there suffered greatly for want of it. Uesugi Kenshin, learning this circumstance, thought that it was unworthy of samurai to resort to such base means, even against an enemy, and generously sent a large quantity of salt to Shingen, to the latter's boundless gratitude.

The verse means, that the heart of General Kenshin which is pure as the snow of his fief, Echigo, may be seen in the pure whiteness of the salt that he sent to Shingen.

Echigo, a northern province, abounds in snow. Koshiji is an old name of the Hokuroku-Dō which consists of Echigo and six other northern provinces, but here it means Echigo.

## 松 の 上 の 月    正　風

むら鴉　ねぐら爭ふ　聲たえて
月こそのぼれ　山松のうへに

### *Matsu no Ue no Tsuki*

*Mura-garasu　Negura arasō　Koe taete
Tsuki koso nobore　Yama-matsu no ue ni.*

### The Moon above Pine Trees Masakaze

The cawings of a flock of crows
Fighting for roosts, to silence die;
Above the pine trees of the peak
The moon—the moon is rising high.

### 山 縣 有 朋
#### Yamagata Aritomo (1838–1922)

Aritomo was one of the most prominent statesmen and warriors who participated in the overthrow of the Tokugawa Shōgunate and the restoration of the Imperial régime. He organized a Cabinet twice; and in his last years, he was a field-marshal and a Prince, and the most important *Genrō* (an elder statesman more powerful than a Prime Minister). He was proficient in writing Chinese and Japanese verse.

### も み ぢ 有 朋

ふもとのみ　もみぢさやかに　見ゆるかな
しぐるる雲に　峰はかくれて

#### Momiji

*Fumoto nomi　Momiji sayakani　Miyuru kana
Shigururu kumo ni　Mine wa kakurete.*

### Maple Leaves Aritomo

Only the maple leaves, glowing
At the mountain foot, I descry,
For its peak, in lowering clouds,
Is wholly lost to the eye.

**"Cherry Flowers"—Tsubara**

In the poet's own handwriting

**"A Patch of Flowers"—Aritomo**

In the poet's own handwriting

## ひとむらの花                    有 朋

もりかげの　花はひとむら　みえながら
山はしづかに　くれはてにけり

### Hitomura no Hana

*Mori-kage no   Hana wa hitomura   Mienagara*
*Yama wa shizukani   Kure-hate ni keri.*

### A Patch of Flowers                    Aritomo

**A patch of cherry flowers in the wood**
**Remains still glimmering in sight;**
**Altho' the mountain quietly**
**Has darkened into night.**

### 毛 利 元 徳
**Mōri Motonori** (1840–1896)

The Lord of the Hagi Clan, Nagato Province, Motonori played an important rôle in the overthrow of the Tokugawa Shōgunate and the restoration of the Imperial régime.

## 降 る 雪                    元 徳

ふる雪に　人のゆきゝは　絶えぬれど
きみにつかふる　みちはありけり

### Furu Yuki

*Furu yuki ni   Hito no yukiki wa Taenuredo*
*Kimi ni tsukōru Michi wa ari keri.*

### Falling Snow
Motonori

**Lo, by the falling snow the way is blocked**
**For going or for coming here;**
**Nevertheless, the road to serve our Prince**
**Is still, as ever, clear.**

This verse was composed on a snowy morning, when Motonori repaired to the Imperial Palace.

*Michi* is a pivot-word meaning both the "road" and the "way".

### 乃 木 希 典
**Nogi Maresuke** (1849–1912)

Born of a samurai family, Nogi Maresuke became a soldier and distinguished himself in the war against China in 1894-5 and in the Russo-Japanese War of 1904-5. In recognition of his brilliant service, General Nogi was created a Count. On September 13, 1912, on the day of the funeral of the Emperor Meiji, General Nogi, with his wife, committed suicide with the desire to follow his sovereign-master to the other world. General Nogi was a good poet.

### 令　名
希 典

武士は　玉も黄金も　なにかせむ
いのちにかへて　名こそをしけれ

### *Reimei*

*Mononofu wa    Tama mo kogane mo    Nanika sen*
*Inochi ni kaete    Na koso oshikere.*

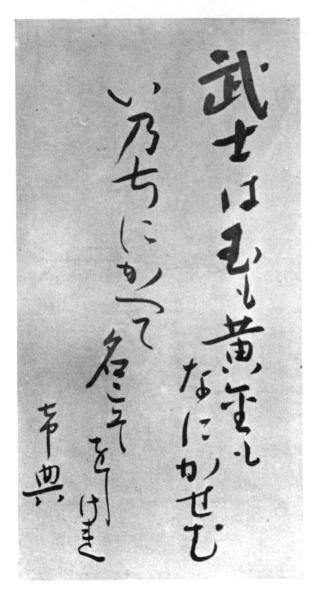

**"A Good Name"**—Nogi Maresuke

In the poet-warrior's own handwriting
In the possession of Mr. Hirafuku Ichirō

## A Good Name

Maresuke

What can a warrior have to do
    With gems and yellow gold?
More dear than life, a stainless name
    To him is wealth untold.

### 末 松 謙 澄

**Suematsu Kenchō** (1855–1920)

The son of a samurai of the Fukuoka Clan, Kenchō studied Chinese classics and English in his youth. In 1879 he sailed over to England and studied at Cambridge. While staying there he translated into English the first volumes of "The Tale of Genji", the oldest of Japanese novels. In 1889 he was Minister of Agriculture and Communications. In his last years he was a Privy Councillor and a Viscount. He wrote a few literary books.

## 瀧 の 音

謙 澄

ゆきゆきて つかれし駒を しばしとて
とむる木かげに すめる瀧の音

### Taki no Oto

*Yuki-yukite   Tsukareshi koma wo   Shibashi tote*
*Tomuru kokage ni   Sumeru taki no to.*

## The Sound of a Waterfall

Kenchō

I rode and rode, mile after mile;
    Then for a while, in green trees' shade,
I rested my wearied horse within sound
    Of a cool cascade.

音 is pronounced *oto, to,* or *ne.*

森 鷗 外

**Mori Ōgwai** (1860–1922)

The son of a physician at Tsuwano, Iwami Province, Ōgwai studied medicine at the Tōkyō Medical School, on graduation from which he was appointed a military surgeon.   Then he sailed over to Germany, where he continued his studies at four universities.   In 1907 he rose to the post of Army Surgeon-General and received the degree of Doctor of Medicine.

But Ōgwai was more famous for his literary activity.   He lectured on aesthetics at Keiō University and Tōkyō Fine Arts School.   He also contributed a great deal to the introduction of European literatures, particularly German literature.   In 1909 he received the degree of Doctor of Literature.

健 な 足       鷗 外

何一つ　よくは見ざりき　生を踏む

わが足あまり　健なれば

*Sukoyaka na Ashi*

*Nani hitotsu   Yoku wa mizariki   Sei wo fumu*

*Waga ashi amari   Sukoyaka nareba.*

**Vigorous Feet**       **Ōgwai**

Not a single thing
Have I closely observed;
My feet on life's way
Are too vigorous.

## 落 合 直 文
### Ochi-ai Naobumi (1861-1903)

The second son of Ayugai Morifusa, a leading samurai of the Sendai Clan, Naobumi was adopted by Ochi-ai Naosuke, a man of Musashi Province, who played a part in the Meiji Restoration.  Naobumi, a prodigy of learning, studied Japanese classics and history in the school attached to the Ise Shrines.  Later he went up to Tōkyō, where he took lessons in Chinese classics from Naitō Chisō and Mishima Chūshū, famous authorities on the subject.  At the same time he attended a special course in Japanese classics at the Tōkyō Imperial University.  After the completion of his studies, he taught at the First High School, the Kokugakuin University and two or three other schools.  Meanwhile his fame as a poet had steadily risen.  In 1893 he established the *Asaka-sha*, a society for the composition of poetry of a new style.  Among its members—his pupils—were Yosano Hiroshi, Kaneko Kun-en, Kubo Inokichi and Onoe Shibafune, all of whom were destined later to shine in the galaxy of contemporary poets.  Constitutionally delicate, Naobumi died in 1903 at the comparatively early age of forty-two.  He wrote many books on poetry and left a collection of his own verses.  He may be called the founder of the present day New School of poetry.

つくづくし                    直 文

つくづくし　手にもちながら　寝たる子の
ゆめは春野に　なほ遊ぶらむ

### Tsukuzukushi

*Tsukuzukushi  Te ni mochi nagara  Netaru ko no*
*Yume wa haru-no ni  Nao asoburan.*

### Horsetails                    Naobumi

Fast asleep, the little child,
　Clutching horsetails in its hand,
Still in the spring field is playing,
　In dreamland.

# 死 　　　　直 文

父君よ　けさはいかにと　手をつきて
とふ子をみれば　死なれざりけり

## Shi

*Chichi-gimi yo　Kesa wa ikani to　Te wo tsukite*
*Tō ko wo mireba　Shinarezari keri.*

## Death 　　　　Naobumi

Not to death can I resign me,
　　When I see my loved child asking,
Bowing—both hands on the mat,
　　"Father, how are you this morning?"

# 我 が 歌 　　　　直 文

我が歌を　哀れと思ふ　人ひとり
見出でて後に　死なむとぞ思ふ

## Waga Uta

*Waga uta wo　Aware to omō　Hito hitori*
*Mi-idete nochini　Shinan tozo omō.*

## My Poems 　　　　Naobumi

It is my ardent wish
　　A single man to find,
Who thinks my poems beautiful—
　　Then die in peace of mind.

病 牀 吟　　　　直 文

我が墓を　訪ひこむ人は　誰れ誰れと
寝られぬままに　數へつるかな

### Byōshō Gin

*Waga haka wo   Toi-kon hito wa   Tare-tare to
Nerarenu mamani   Kazoetsuru kana.*

## When Ill in Bed　　　Naobumi

At midnight when I lay
　Awake in my sickroom,
I counted who and who of all my friends
　Would pay a visit to my tomb.

我 も 神 な り　　　　直 文

さ夜中に　ひとり目覺めて　つくづくと
歌おもふ時は　我も神なり

### Ware mo Kami nari

*Sa-yonaka ni   Hitori mezamete   Tsuku-zukuto
Uta omō toki wa   Ware mo kami nari.*

## I am a God　　　Naobumi

When I wake up alone
At dead of night,
And muse on verse-making,
Even I am a god.

## 富 士 山　　　　　　　直文

この宿は　寝ながら富士の　見えにけり
死なばここにて　死なむとぞ思ふ

### *Fuji-San*

*Kono yado wa　Ne-nagara Fuji no　Mie ni keri*
*Shinaba koko nite　Shinan to zo omō.*

### Mount Fuji　　　　**Naobumi**

Ah! in this inn I can see Mount Fuji
While lying down in bed;
Would that when my last moments come,
I might here in this house lie dead.

A natural outburst of the poet's pious admiration for the peerless mountain

## 菫とたんぽぽ　　　　　　直　文

咲きつづく　菫たんぽぽ　なつかしみ
もと來し道を　またもどりけり

### *Sumire to Tanpopo*

*Saki tsuzuku　Sumire tanpopo　Natsukashimi*
*Moto kishi michi wo　Mata modori keri.*

### Violets and Dandelions                    Naobumi

Bewitched by dandelions
    And violets in continuous bloom,
I retraced my steps again
    On the road by which I had come.

## 大 口 鯛 二
### Ōguchi Taiji (1864–1920)

A native of Nagoya, Taiji studied versification under Takasaki Masakaze, later was appointed an official of the Imperial Poetry Bureau, and left a collection of his verses.

## 孝                          鯛 二

わが子には　とあれかかれと　のぞみつつ
　親にはえこそ　盡さざりけれ

### *Kō*

*Waga ko niwa   Toare kakare to   Nozomi-tsutsu*
*Oya niwa ekoso   Tsukusa-zari kere.*

### Filial Piety                          Taiji

This or that, for my sake, now I bid my children,
    And expect obedience, too;
But alas, alas! for my own parents
    Little did I try to do!

## 雛　鳥 鯛　二

もとよりの　こがひの鳥は　空かける
翼ありとも　しらでおゆらむ

### *Hina-Dori*

*Motoyori no　Kogai no tori wa　Sora kakeru*
*Tsubasa aritomo　Shirade oyuran.*

## A Young Bird Taiji

A bird that from the first is captive-reared,
May live, grow old and die,
And never know that it has wings with which
To soar into the sky.

## 大　西　祝
### Ōnishi Shuku (1864–1900)

Born the son of a samurai in Okayama, Shuku studied at Dōshisha, the famous Christian school at Kyōto, and later studied philosophy at the Imperial Tōkyō University and in Germany. He lectured on philosophy at Tōkyō Senmon Gakkō, which has developed into Waseda University. He wrote a few books, including a history of philosophy.

## 嵐 祝

むら雲を　拂ひし風の　いかなれば
又むら雲を　さそひ來にけん

### *Arashi*

*Murakumo wo　Haraishi kaze no　Ikanareba*
*Mata murakumo wo　Sasoi-ki ni ken.*

## The Tempest
Shuku

**The wind which swept away
One bank of clouds—
Why has it brought again
Yet another?**

Simon Peter likens false teachers to "clouds that are carried with a tempest" (Second Epistle of Peter 11 : 17); and this verse probably implies that even a man who has been baptized is often subject to temptation.

### 伊 藤 左 千 夫
#### Itō Sachi-o (1864–1911)

Itō Sachi-o was born in the town of Narutō, Chiba Prefecture. He studied poetry under Masa-oka Shiki, a famous poet. Later he established the poetry magazine, *Araragi* or "The Yew". He was a prolific writer of verses, essays, and novels.

## 牛 飼 の 歌
左 千 夫

牛飼が　歌よむ時に　世のなかの
新しき歌　大いにおこる

### *Ushikai no Uta*

*Ushikai ga　Uta yomu toki ni　Yo no naka no
Atarashiki uta　Ōini okoru.*

## Cowherds' Poetry
Sachi-o

**When cowherds come to strive
Poems to write,
New styles of poetry
Will rise and thrive.**

我が幼兒　　　　左千夫

いとけなき　兒等の睦びや　しが父の
貧しきも知らず　聲樂しかり

## Waga Yōji

*Itokenaki   Kora no mutsubi ya   Shiga chichi no*
*Mazushiki mo shirazu   Koe tanoshikari.*

## My Children　　　　Sachi-o

**My little children play**
**And chatter merrily,**
**Quite unconscious of**
**Their father's poverty.**

千 葉 胤 明
**Chiba Tane-aki** (1864-　　)

Tane-aki is an official of the Imperial Bureau of Poetry.

のぼるひ　　　　胤　明

のぼるひに　八潮路とほく　照りはえて
島かと見えし　雲ものこらず

## Noboru-Hi

*Noboru-hi ni   Yashi-oji tōku   Teri-haete*
*Shima ka to mieshi   Kumo mo nokorazu.*

## The Rising Sun          Tane-aki

In splendour shines the rising sun
Far on the sea for miles;
And none of all the clouds remain,
Which looked like isles.

### 正 岡 子 規

**Masa-oka Shiki** (1866–1902)

Masa-oka Shiki was born at Matsuyama, Iyo Province, the son of a samurai of lower rank. In his boyhood he was a prodigy of learning. In 1890, when he was twenty-four years old, he entered the Literature College of the Imperial Tōkyō University; but he was very irregular in attendance, and devoted most of his time to the study and composition of *haiku*, seventeen-syllable verses. Soon after he began to contribute *haiku* to the *Nippon*, then a leading Tōkyō newspaper; and later, withdrawing from the college, he joined the staff of the journal. In 1894 when the Sino-Japanese War broke out, he went over to China as a war correspondent of his paper; but three months later, on account of ill health, he came back to Tōkyō. From this time to 1902 he was confined to bed throughout; but while lying ill, he incessantly composed *haiku*, *tanka* and wrote book after book on poetry and literature in general. He was one of the four greatest *haiku* poets who have ever lived, but his rank as a *tanka* poet is lower.

### 松 の 露          子 規

庭中の　松の葉におく　白露の
今か落ちむと　見れども落ちず

#### *Matsu no Tsuyu*

*Niwa-naka no　Matsu no ha ni oku　Shira-tsuyu no
Ima ka ochinto　Miredomo ochizu.*

### The Dews on Pine Leaves Shiki

The white dews on the needles
Of a pine-tree in the garden
Were wellnigh dripping down,
Yet did not fall.

### 天 の 川 子 規

寝しづまる　里のともしび　皆消えて
天の川白し　竹藪のうへに

#### *Ama-no-Gawa*

*Ne-shizumaru　Sato no toboshibi　Mina ki-ete
Ama-no-gawa shiroshi　Take-yabu no ueni.*

### The Milky Way Shiki

The lights are all gone out
In the village wrapt in sleep;
The Milky Way gleams white
Over the bamboo grove.

### 夕 顔 子 規

夕顔の　棚つくらむと　思へども
秋まちがてぬ　わがいのちかも

#### *Yūgao*

*Yūgao no　Tana tsukuran to　Omoe-domo
Aki machi-gatenu　Waga inochi kamo.*

## The Evening-Glories     Shiki

**I will make a trellis**
**For evening-glories to climb—**
**But oh! my life can hardly last**
**Till autumn-time.**

*Yūgao*, literally, "evening-face", resembles the morning glory both in its vines and flowers, and blooms in the evening; and since the morning-glory which blooms in the morning is called *asagao* or "morning-face", it is well to call *yūgao* "evening-glory".

One day in early summer, through the windows of his sickroom, the poet observed that the shoots of some *yūgao* had appeared and the climbing plants would soon grow up. He thought that he must get a trellis made for them. But the next moment he remembered that he was seriously ill and wondered whether he could live on till autumn when the plants would be ready to bloom.

### 金 子 元 臣

**Kaneko Moto-omi** (1868–    )

Moto-omi is a professor of Japanese literature at the Kokugakuin University and an official of the Imperial Bureau of Poetry. He has written "Notes on the *Kokin Shū* Anthology" and some other valuable literary books.

### 麥 の 笛     元 臣

麥の笛　吹けどもならす　あげまきの
むかしのこゝろ　われや忘れし

### *Mugi no Fue*

*Mugi no fue   Fuke-domo narazu   Agemaki no*
*Mukashi no kokoro   Ware ya wasureshi.*

### Whistles of Barley Stalks      Moto-omi

I blow thro' whistles of straw,
  But not a sound can I raise;
Is it that I have quite forgotten
  The innocent mind of my childhood's days?

Young boys, walking by fields of barley, often pluck barley stalks, make whistles of them and blow them skilfully.

菫                    元 臣

思ふ子の　春のこゝろを　満たしめん
箱根すみれの　あるかぎり摘み

### *Sumire*

*Omō ko no   Haru no kokoro wo   Mitashimen*
*Hakone sumire no   Aru-kagiri tsumi.*

### Violets      Moto-omi

I will gather here at Hakone,
  All the violets growing wild,
That the spring mood I may satisfy
  Of my beloved child.

入 江 爲 守

**Iri-e Tamemori** (1868–   )

Viscount Iri-e is a member of the House of Peers, Chief of the Empress Dowager's Court and President of the Imperial Bureau of Poetry.

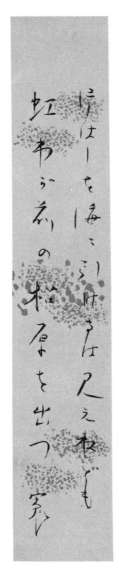

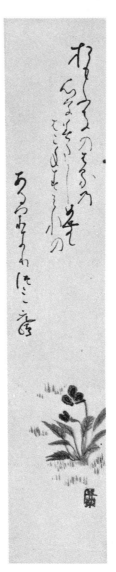

**"A Rainbow"—Hiroshi**

In the poet's handwriting

**"Violets"—Moto-omi**

In the poet's handwriting

**The Picture**

By Kumasaka Keizō (熊抜圭三),
An authority on Chinese classics

## 大 波　　　　　爲 守

苫屋にも　よせむいきほひ　見えながら
磯をかぎりに　かへる波かな

### Ōnami

*Tomaya nimo　Yosen ikioi　Mie-nagara*
*Iso wo kagiri ni　Kaeru nami kana.*

### Billows　　　　　**Tamemori**

**The billows are so wild,**
　　**They threaten to march on my hut;**
　　**But stopping short at the beach,**
**They roll back mild.**

## 石 槫 千 亦
### Ishikure Chimata (1869–　)

A native of a village in Ehime Prefecture, Chimata took part in the establishment of the *Teikoku Suinan Kyūsai Kwai* or the Imperial Life-Saving Association, of which he is now a managing director. He studied versification under Sasaki Nobutsuna and has published two collections of his own verses.

## 御 大 典　　　　　千 亦

ひむがしの　海を照らして　さしのぼる
朝日の如き　わが大君かも

### Go-Taiten

*Himugashi no　Umi wo terashite　Sashi-noboru*
*Asahi no gotoki　Waga Ōkimi kamo.*

### The Coronation of the Emperor
Chimata

Our gracious Emperor—
Ah! like the morning sun,
Rising in splendour,
Upon the eastern ocean shining!

### 航　海　中
千　亦

翼張りて　鷗とびゆく　をち方に
又はじめての　島見出でつ

### Kōkai-Chū

*Tsubasa harite  Kamome tobi-yuku  Ochikata ni*
*Mata hajimete no  Shima mi-idetsu.*

### During a Voyage
Chimata

Where far ahead
With outspread wings a seagull flies,
Another first-seen island now
Delights my eyes.

### 北　海
千　亦

しらけ立つ　波はろばろと　大海に
一つの船も　見えずさびしき

### Hokkai

*Shirake-tatsu  Nami haro-baro to  Ō-umi ni*
*Hitotsu no fune mo  Miezu sabishiki.*

### The Northern Sea          Chimata

White waves roll far ahead;
No ship there is on the great sea.
Loneliness overwhelmeth me!

亡妻を憶ふ          千 亦

汝しあらば 汝しあらばと いふことの
いひ古りたれど 日に新らしき

*Bōsai wo Omō*

*Nare shi araba   Nare shi araba to   Yū koto no
Ii-furitare do   Hi ni atarashiki.*

### Longing for My Departed Wife          Chimata

Again and again I exclaim,
"Oh, if only thou wert alive!"
Yet each time the old phrase soundeth new
As sad feelings revive.

### 佐 々 木 信 綱
#### Sasaki Nobutsuna (1872      )

Sasaki Nobutsuna was born the son of Sasaki Hirotsuna, a Japanese classical scholar, in a village of Mi-e Prefecture. In his boyhood he took lessons
in poetry from his father. Since finishing the special course for Japanese classics at the Imperial Tōkyō University in 1888, he has been engaged principally
in writing literary books. About 1895-6 there arose a movement for poetical
renovation, in which he participated with enthusiasm. In 1898 he started the
poetry magazine, *Kokoro no Hana*, or "The Flower of the Heart", which conti-

nues up to date. In 1905 he was appointed a lecturer on the history of Japanese poetry at his Alma Mater, in which position he still remains. In 1911 he received the degree of Doctor of Literature, and in 1917 was awarded a prize by the Imperial Academy. About this time he worked as one of the committee for compiling collections of the verses of the Emperor Meiji and the Empress-Consort Meiji, who has the posthumous title of the Empress Dowager Shōken.

He is one of the most prominent contemporary poets and an authority on the *Manyō Shū*. He has published a few collections of his own verses and written numerous books, including critical notes on the *Manyō Shū, Kokin Shū* and *Shin Kokin Shū* and "A History of Japanese Poetry".

## 水 の 音　　　　　　信 綱

天地の　かくろへごとを　わが胸に
ささやく如き　水の音かな

### *Mizu no Oto*

*Ame-tsuchi no　Kakuroe-goto wo　Waga mune ni*
*Sasayaku gotoki　Mizu no oto kana.*

### The Sound of the Water　　　Nobutsuna

Hark! the water sounds as though
It whispers to my bosom
The mysteries of Heaven and Earth
Impossible to fathom.

## まことの我　　　　　信 綱

變りゆく　昨日の我が身　今日のわれ
いづれまことの　我にかあるらむ

### Makoto no Ware

*Kawari-yuku   Kinō no waga mi   Kyō no ware*
*Izure makoto no   Ware ni ka aruran.*

## The True I                    Nobutsuna

I change from day to day;
    The I of yesterday
Was different from the I to-day.
    Which is the true I, who can say?

### 我 が 心                     信 綱

我が心　われを殺して　喜びぬ
さもあさましき　我が心かな

### Waga Kokoro

*Waga kokoro   Ware wo koroshite   Yorokobinu*
*Samo asamashiki   Waga kokoro kana.*

## My Mind                     Nobutsuna

My mind has murdered me
    And is rejoicing o'er the deed.
How mean and wretched is
    My mind, indeed!

### 笛                     信 綱

人は世は　吾をすてたり　しかはあれど
吾に笛あり　この笛あるを

## *Fu-e*

*Hito wa yo wa    Ware wo sutetari    Shika wa aredo*
*Ware ni fu-e ari    Kono fu-e aru wo.*

### A Flute                            **Nobutsuna**

By man I am forsaken and the world,
  But though of all bereft,
There is my flute—
  This flute, at least, is left.

### 洞 庭 湖                          信 綱

わが世に　よき幸得たり　洞庭の
湖の月夜を　よき風にわたる

### *Dōtei-Ko*

*Waga yo ni    Yoki sachi etari    Dōtei no*
*Umi no tsuki-yo wo    Yoki-kaze ni wataru.*

### Lake Tung-Ting                    **Nobutsuna**

A blessing great in my life I enjoyed;
  One refreshing breezy night
I sailed across Lake Tung-Ting,
  In bright moonlight.

Tung-Ting Hu is the largest and most beautiful lake in China (upwards of 260 miles in circumference), of whose beauty numberless Chinese poets from ancient times, including Li Pai (李白), Tu Hu (杜甫) and Hên Hao Jan (孟浩然), have sung. It is celebrated particularly for its view of the autunm moon.

薄 の 葉　　　　　信　綱

見つつあれば　ありなし風に　ゆれゆるる
薄の葉かな　わが心かな

### Susuki no Ha

*Mitsutsu areba　Ari-nashi kaze ni　Yure yururu*
*Susuki no ha kana　Waga kokoro kana.*

### Pampas Grass Leaves　　　Nobutsuna

Behold the leaves of pampas grass!
At slightest stir of wind,
They tremble, sway and wave;
Alas, like my own mind.

富士に登りて　　　　　信　綱

もゆる火の　もえたつ上に　天ぎらひ
み雪ふりけむ　神代をし思ふ

### Fuji ni Noborite

*Moyuru hi no　Moetatsu ueni　Amagirai*
*Miyuki furiken　Kamiyo wo shi omō.*

### When Climbing Mount Fuji　　　Nobutsuna

I think of the Age of the Gods
When on the sacred Fuji
Virgin snow fell thick
Upon fire* burning with fury.

---

* Mount Fuji was an active volcano in ancient times.

## 山中の村　　　　　　信　綱

鳥の聲　水の響に　夜はあけて
神代に似たり　山中の村

### Yamanaka no Mura

*Tori no koe　Mizu no hibiki ni　Yo wa akete*
*Kamiyo ni nitari　Yamanaka no mura.*

### The Mountain Village　　Nobutsuna

To the murmuring sound of water
　　And the birds' clear morning song,
Day has dawned.　The mountain village seems
　　As if unto the Age of Gods it might belong!

## わ　が　歌　　　　　　信　綱

わが歌ぞ　わが命なる　わが歌ぞ
わが涙なる　わが血汐なる

### Waga Uta

*Waga uta zo　Waga inochi naru　Waga uta zo*
*Waga namida naru　Waga chishio naru.*

### My Verses　　Nobutsuna

My verses are my life;
　　My verses are my tears;
They are my blood,
　　My hopes and fears.

わ が 目　　　　　信 綱

かなしきは　自らわれを　知れること
わが目さやかに　我を見ること

### Waga Me

*Kanashiki wa   Mizukara ware wo   Shireru koto*
*Waga me sayakani   Ware wo miru koto.*

### My Eyes　　　Nobutsuna

I know myself—
  It saddens me
That mine own eyes clearly
  Self can see.

わ が み ち　　　　　信 綱

道の上に　殘さむ跡は　ありもあらすも
われ虔みて　わがみちゆかむ

### Waga Michi

*Michi no ue ni   Nokosan ato wa   Ari mo arazu mo*
*Ware tsutsushimite   Waga michi yukan.*

### My Chosen Way　　　Nobutsuna

My footprints on the road
  May be effaced—or stay;
Howe'er it be, I still will go
  Most humbly on my chosen way.

Evidently "My chosen way" means the cause of Japanese poetry.  But the verse is beautiful if understood in a wider sense.

## 春 の 朝 風　　　　　信　綱

そしる人　あたなす人も　にくからず
たもとにかろし　春の朝風

### Haru no Asa-Kaze

*Soshiru hito   Ata-nasu hito mo   Nikukarazu*
*Tamoto ni karoshi   Haru no asa-kaze.*

### The Morning Breeze of Spring　　　**Nobutsuna**

**I hate not the men who do me wrong,**
**Who slander me despitefully—**
**Now when the morning breeze of spring**
**Is caressing my long sleeves lightly.**

The influence of sweet spring upon the poet's heart is delightfully depicted.

## 春　　風　　　　　信　綱

ねがはくは　われ春風に　身をなして
憂ある人の　門を訪はばや

### Haru-Kaze

*Negawakuwa   Ware haru-kaze ni   Mi wo nashite*
*Urei aru hito no   Kado wo towabaya.*

### The Spring Breeze Nobutsuna

Would that I could become
The soft spring breeze,
And call at the doors
Of men whom sorrows freeze.

### 花　か　げ　　　　　　　　　　信　綱

一とせの　はるのさかりの　花かげに
酔ひて眠るを　誰かとがむる

### *Hana-Kage*

*Hito-tose no   Haru no sakari no   Hana-kage ni*
*Eite nemuru wo   Tare ka togamuru.*

### Under the Flowers Nobutsuna

Who blames a man for drunken sleep
Under the cherry flowers,
In height of spring, which once a year
Visits this world of ours?

### 與　謝　野　寛
**Yosano Hiroshi** (1873–1935)

Born in Kyōto the son of a Buddhist priest, Hiroshi had no academic career, but studied Japanese literature under Ochi-ai Naobumi and Mori Ōgwai for two or three years, and then Chinese classics and French literature by himself. He had such poetical gifts that he was a good poet in the early twenties. In 1900, with some friends, he organized the "New Poetry Society" and started a movement for poetical renovation, publishing his verses and views on poetry in a poetry magazine entitled *Myōjō* or "The Morning Star", edited by himself. His verses which were novel both in diction and thought, were unfavourably criticized; but before long his new school came to dominate the poetical world. In 1911–14 Hiroshi visited Europe, staying most of the time in Paris. He was a professor of Japanese literature at Keiō University, and the editor of a poetry magazine called *Tōhaku* or "The Camellia". In 1933 a complete collection of his verses was published.

## 歌　人　　　　寛

こころ燃え　歌へる人に　冬は無し
光る師走の　椿のごとし

### *Kajin*

*Kokoro moe　Utaeru hito ni　Fuyu wa nashi*
*Hikaru shiwasu no　Tsubaki no gotoshi.*

## A Poet　　　Hiroshi

**A man who verses writes,**
**With burning heart, no winter knows—**
**Like the camellia flower which in**
**December glows.**

## 隕　石　　　　寛

誰知らん　光る刹那を　持ちしとは
博物館の　片隅の石

### *Inseki*

*Tare shiran　Hikaru setsuna wo　Mochishi towa*
*Hakubutsukan no　Katasumi no ishi.*

### A Meteorite
Hiroshi

Who knows?
It had its moment of splendour—
This stone, lying in a corner
Of the museum.

An ugly blackish stone lies in a corner of the museum. Visitors look at it with indifference, unaware that it is a meteorite which was once a bright, beautiful shooting star. The meteorite symbolizes a man of talent who once flourished, but has fallen into oblivion. Probably the poet alludes to himself.

虹
寛

片はしを　海に引けるは　見えねども
虹わが前の　松原を出づ

### Niji

*Kata-hashi wo　Umi ni hikeru wa　Miene-domo*
*Niji waga mae no　Matsubara wo izu.*

### A Rainbow
Hiroshi

Although invisible
Its one end, trailing in the sea,
The rainbow has emerged
From that pine grove in front of me.

大堰川にて
寛

竹筏　あをきが上に　さくら散り
油のごとき　嵯峨の春雨

## Ōi-Gawa nite

*Take-ikada   Aoki ga ue ni   Sakura chiri*
*Abura no gotoki   Saga no harusame.*


### At the Ōigawa                    Hiroshi

**Upon a raft of green bamboos**
**Are dropping cherry flowers;**
**And oil-like rain of Saga falls**
**In calm spring showers.**

The Ōigawa is a beautiful river flowing under Mount Arashi, noted fo
cherry flowers, west of Kyōto. Saga is the extensive village about the river.


## 海 の 風                    寛

海の風　初めて人を　見るごとき
よろこびをして　わが袖を吹く


### Umi no Kaze

*Umi no kaze   Hajimete hito wo   Miru gotoki*
*Yorokobi wo shite   Waga sode wo fuku.*


### The Sea-Wind                    Hiroshi

**The sea-wind blows upon my sleeves**
**With such delight**
**As if it were the first time that**
**A man had met its sight.**

## 蝶 ひ と つ　　　　　　寛

蝶ひとつ　黄なるぞ來る　夕ぐれの
木のもと歩み　ものを思へば

### *Chō Hitotsu*

*Chō hitotsu　Ki naru zo kitaru　Yūgure no
Ko no moto ayumi　Mono wo omoeba.*

### A Butterfly　　　　　　**Hiroshi**

A single butterfly—yellow—came flying
　　On fluttering wings,
As under the trees, in evening twilight,
　　I wandered, thinking of things.

## 挽　　歌　　　　　　寛

君なきか　若狭の登美子　しら玉の
あたら君さへ　碎けはつるか

### *Banka*

*Kimi nakika　Wakasa no Tomi-ko　Shiratama no
Atara kimi sae　Kudake-hatsuru ka.*

### A Dirge　　　　　　**Hiroshi**

Art thou indeed no more,
　　Tomi-ko of Wakasa?
Thou, the precious jewel white,
　　Shattered in thy splendour?

Tomi-ko, a native of Wakasa Province, was a beautiful young woman, a pupil of the poet.

## 別 れ 路 寛

そや理想　こや運命の　別れ路に
白き菫を　あはれと泣く身

### *Wakare-Ji*

*Soya risō   Koya unmei no   Wakareji ni*
*Shiroki sumire wo   Aware to naku mi.*

### The Crossroads Hiroshi

There my ideal, here my destiny—
I stand at the crossroads between them.
The little white violet wakens my pity,
And I weep.

The poet stands at the crossroads between his ideal and his destiny, and the latter almost overcomes him. He sympathises with the white violet, which seems to be a symbol of humility and resignation, and his tears flow.

## 草 寛

野に生ふる　草にも物を　言はせばや
涙もあらむ　歌もあるらむ

### *Kusa*

*No ni ōru   Kusa ni mo mono wo   Iwasebaya*
*Namida mo aran   Uta mo aruran.*

### Grasses
Hiroshi

If grasses growing in the field
Should be allowed expression free,
There would be tears of sorrow shed,
There would be songs of glee.

### 薔　薇
寛

君とわれ　中の隔てに　薔薇を置く
餘るなさけを　花に遣らんと

### *Bara*

*Kimi to ware　Naka no hedate ni　Bara wo oku
Amaru nasake wo　Hana ni yaran to.*

### A Rose
Hiroshi

'Twixt you and me
I placed a rose,
That the flower might share
In love's overflows.

### 太　陽
寛

太陽よ　おなじ所に　留まれと
云ふに等しき　願ひするかな

### *Taiyō*

*Taiyō yo　Onaji tokoro ni　Todomare to
Yū ni hitoshiki　Negai suru .kana.*

### The Sun                                          Hiroshi

"Oh, mighty sun, remain
  For ever in one spot of sky!"
Ah, I have a desire
  Like this, wellnigh.

### 虹                                                寛

天の門　ひとつ開けて　前にあり
美しきかな　山に立つ虹

#### *Niji*

*Ten no mon　Hitotsu hirakete　Maeni ari
Utsukushiki kana　Yama ni tatsu niji.*

### The Rainbow                                      Hiroshi

One of the gates of heaven
  Is open before us, now;
How beautiful it is!—
  The rainbow on the mountain's brow.

### 帆 か け 舟                                        寛

夕燒の　皆朱の海に　百合咲くと
ほのかに白く　船一つ來る

#### *Hokake-Bune*

*Yūyake no　Kaishu no umi ni　Yuri saku to
Honokani shiroku　Fune hitotsu kuru.*

"A Crimson Butterfly"—Aki-ko     "My Heart"—Hiroshi

In the poetess' handwriting     In the poet's handwriting

### A Sailing Ship

Hiroshi

See! where the ocean is bathed
In vermilion of sunset glow,
A lily has bloomed faintly white—
Nay! a ship comes sailing slow!

### 我　心

寛

ねがはくば　若き木花　咲耶姫
我心をも　花にしたまへ

### *Waga Kokoro*

*Negawakuba　Wakaki Kono-Hana-　Saku-ya-Hime*
*Waga kokoro wo mo　Hana ni shitamae.*

### My Heart

Hiroshi

Oh, I pray thee,
Young Goddess Blooming-Like-Flowers,
Make my heart beautiful,
Flower-like.

Kono-Hana-Saku-ya-Hime　(木花咲耶姫)　or　Princess　"Blooming-Like-the-Flowers-of-the-Trees", an exceedingly beautiful goddess, was the daughter of the Deity Ōyama-zumi and the consort of the Deity Ninigi-no-Mikoto.

### 武　島　羽　衣

**Takejima Hagoromo** (1873–　　)

Hagoromo is an official of the Imperial Bureau of Poetry and a professor of Japanese literature at the Women's University.

石 羽 衣

蹴らるれば　蹴らるるまゝに　ころがりて
物言はぬ石　撫でてやりたき

### Ishi

*Kerarureba   Keraruru mamani   Korogarite*
*Mono-iwanu ishi   Nadete yaritaki.*

## A Stone Hagoromo

**When it is kicked,**
> **Never giving a moan**
**It silently rolls—**
> **I could fondle that stone!**

今　日 羽 衣

きのふてふ　紀念も悲し　あすといふ
頼みもはかな　けふに生きなむ

### Kyō

*Kinō chō   Katami mo kanashi   Asu to yū*
*Tanomi mo hakana   Kyō ni ikinan.*

## To-day Hagoromo

**Ah, sorrowful the memories**
> **Of yesterday!**
**To-morrow is uncertainty.**
**I would then that my life should be**
> **Lived in to-day.**

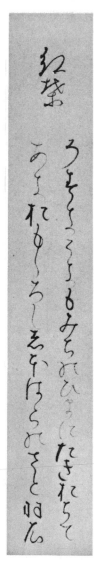

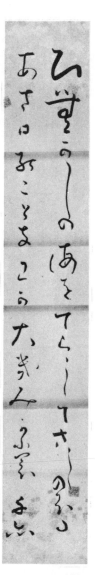

**" Shiobara "—Hagoromo**

In the poet's own handwriting

**" The Coronation of the Emperor "—Chimata**

In the poet's own handwriting.

## 歌　　　　　　　　羽　衣

日ごと日ごと　わが行く道は　歌の道
神も踏むてふ　美しき道

### Uta

*Higoto-higoto   Waga yuku michi wa   Uta no michi
Kami mo fumu chō   Utsukushiki michi.*

### Poetry　　　　　　Hagoromo

The way by which I go,
　　Day after day,
Is the way of song, the beautiful way,
　　The road by which the gods, too, go, they say.

＊　　＊　　＊　　＊　　＊

"Poetry is itself a thing of God'.　　　Philip James Bailey

## 鹽　原　　　　　　羽　衣

うすき濃き　紅葉のひまに　瀧おちて
秋おもしろき　鹽原の里

### Shiobara

*Usuki koki   Momiji no hima ni   Taki ochite
Aki omoshiroki   Shiobara no sato.*

Shiobara                              **Hagoromo**

**Cascades falling in the breaks between**
**Light or deep red maple foliage—**
**Autumn here is picturesque, indeed,**
**In Shiobara Village.**

熊　谷　武　雄

**Kumagai Takeo** (1873–　 ）

Takeo is engaged in farming, his ancestral occupation, at his native village of Niitsuki, Motoyoshi County, in Rikuzen Province, and during his leisure hours he reads and writes. He has published two collections of his own verses.

低　氣　壓                              武　雄

低氣壓は ゛土佐沖に　ありといふ
しまらくは半開の　さくらの枝のしづけさ

*Teiki-atsu*

*Teiki-atsu wa　Tosa-oki ni　Ari to yū*
*Shimaraku wa hankai no　Sakura no eda no shizukesa.*

An Atmospheric Depression          **Takeo**

**Off Tosa there is a depression—**
**So it is said.**
**The cherry-boughs, with half-unfolded flowers—**
**For a little while,**
**How still they are!**

捕 鯨 船　　　　　　　武　雄

捕鯨船　いまだ歸らず　荒海の
天うつ波に　月おし照れり

## Hogeisen

*Hogeisen　Imada kaerazu　Ara-umi no*
*Sora-utsu nami ni　Tsuki oshitereri.*

### Whalers　　　　　　　Takeo

The whalers had not yet returned;
The moon shone high
Upon the waves of the wild sea,
Dashing against the sky.

This was composed when the poet visited Kinkwazan Island in the Province of Rikuzen. The sea off the island is noted for whaling.

五 十 嵐 力
**Igarashi Chikara** (1874–　　)

Chikara is a professor of Japanese literature at Waseda University and the author of the famous book, *Kokka no Taisei oyobi Hattatsu* or "The Origin and Development of Japanese Poetry".

妙 義 山　　　　　　　力

杉のごと　山は立ちたつ　山のごと
杉は立ちたつ　おもしろや妙義

### Myōgi-San

*Sugi no goto   Yama wa tachi-tatsu   Yama no goto*
*Sugi wa tachi-tatsu   Omoshiro ya Myōgi.*

### The Myōgi Mountains                    Chikara

**The mountains tower like cedar trees,**
**  The cedar trees like mountains stand;**
**These mountains of Myōgi are**
**  Fantastically grand.**

The Myōgi Mountains in the southwest of Kōzuke Province are well known for their fantastic shapes.

The *sugi* or "Japan cedar" is a tall pointed tree, and the Myōgi Mountains have jagged rock spires.

### 春 の 夜 の 雨                    力

天とつち　戀のひめごと　さゝやくと
かそけきかなや　春の夜の雨

### Haru no Yo no Ame

*Ame to tsuchi   Koi no himegoto   Sasayaku to*
*Kasokeki kanaya   Haru no yo no ame.*

### Rain on a Spring Night                    Chikara

**How gently falls**
**  The fine night rain in spring!**
**As though the Heaven and the Earth**
**  Love-secrets were whispering.**

うつくしき金魚の死　　　　　力

うつくしき　金魚死にたり　美しき
花に咲けとて　牡丹につちかふ

## Utsukushiki Kingyo no Shi

*Utsukushiki　Kingyo shinitari　Utsukushiki*
*Hana ni sake tote　Botan ni tsuchikō.*

## The Death of a Beautiful Goldfish　　　Chikara

A beautiful goldfish has died, and I,
That so it may blossom forth
Into a beautiful flower, bestow it
On peony roots, to enrich the earth.

久 保 猪 之 吉
**Kubo Inokichi** (1874–　　)

A native of Nihonmatsu, Fukushima Precture, Inokichi graduated from the Medical College, Imperial Tōkyō University. He continued his studies in Germany for four years. He is now a professor at Fukuoka Medical College.

葡　　萄　　　　　猪 之 吉

妹は　軒の葡萄を　指さして
熟せむ日まで　とどまれといふ

## Budō

*Imōto wa　Noki no budō wo　Yubisashite*
*Jukusen hi made　Todomare to yū.*

### Grapes
Inokichi

**Pointing at the green grapes**
**Growing close to the eaves,**
**My little sister said, "Please stay**
**Until they ripen!"**

The poet has come back to his old father's home after a long absence. The whole family has given him a hearty welcome. It is still a happy home, as it was of old. His little sister, hanging on to his sleeve, and pointing at the grapes growing near the eaves, still green, says, "Dear brother, please stay on till they get ripe. They are very nice, indeed"! The innocent girl does not realize that the poet, who is a professor at Fukuoka Medical College, cannot stay so long.

### 鮎
猪之吉

草鞋して　渉る淺瀬の　水きよみ
さばしる鮎の　かずもよむべし

### *Ayu*

*Waraji shite　Wataru asase no　Mizu kiyomi*
*Sabashiru ayu no　Kazu mo yomu beshi.*

### *Ayu*
Inokichi

**Straw sandals wearing,**
**I waded in the river shallows;**
**The water was so clear that I could read**
**The number of the *ayu*, darting like arrows.**

What a refreshing scene! The *ayu* is a kind of trout, the most valuable of Japanese river fishes.

## 島 木 赤 彦

### Shimaki Akahiko (1876–1925)

A native of Kami-Suwa in Shinano Province, Akahiko graduated from the Nagano Normal School and for a few years was a school inspector in Suwa County. He studied poetry under Itō Sachi-o. Later he went up to Tōkyō, where he joined the editorial staff of the *Araragi*, a magazine devoted to poetry, and taught Japanese and Chinese classics at a girls' school. He wrote several books on poetry, including "An Appreciation and Criticism of the *Manyō Shū*", and left a collection of his own verses. The poet's real name is Kubota Toshihiko (久保田俊彦), Shimaki Akahiko being his pen name.

## 小　雀　　　　　　赤　彦

畫はあそび　夜はねむれり　只一つ
籠にかはるる　小雀あはれ

### *Kogarame*

*Hiru wa asobi　Yoru wa nemureri　Tada hitotsu
Kago ni kawaruru　Kogarame aware.*

### A Marsh-Tit　　　Akahiko

The marsh-tit in a cage
Is a pitiful sight!
Alone it plays by day,
And sleeps by night.

The Chinese characters 小雀 may be read either way: *kosuzume* ("small sparrow") or *kogara* or *kogarame* ("marsh-tit"); and here they are used in the latter sense.

## 上高地溫泉にて　　　　　赤　彦

森深く　鳥鳴きやみて　たそがるる
木の間の水の　ほの明りかも

### Kami-Kōchi Onsen Nite

*Mori fukaku   Tori naki-yamite   Tasogaruru*
*Ko no ma no mizu no   Hono-akari kamo.*

## At the Hot Springs of Kami-Kōchi          Akahiko

In the depths of the wood
    The birds have ceased to cry;
Through trees, in the growing dusk,
    Gleaming water I espy.

### 我 が 魂          赤彦

魂は　いづれの空に　ゆくならむ
　　我に用なき　ことを思へり

### Waga Tamashii

*Tamashii wa   Izure no sora ni   Yuku-naran*
*Ware ni yō-naki   Koto wo omoeri.*

## My Soul          Akahiko

I wonder to what sky
    My soul has gone!
Things so remote from me
    I think upon.

### 青葉の丘          赤彦

静やかに　雲行きぬれば　圓らなる
　　青葉の丘の　動くおもひすも

### *Aoba no Oka*

*Shizuyakani   Kumo yukinureba   Marora naru*
*Aoba no oka no   Ugoku omoisu mo.*

### The Hill Covered with Green Leaves   Akahiko

Quietly, quietly
Passed away the clouds.
One might have thought the green-clad rounded hill
Had gently moved the other way from out its shrouds.

### 子 等 の 聲   赤 彦

隣室に　書よむ子等の　聲きけば
心に沁みて　生きたかりけり

### *Kora no Koe*

*Rinshitsu ni   Fumi yomu kora no   Koe kikeba*
*Kokoro ni shimite   Ikitakari-keri.*

### The Voices of My Children   Akahiko

When I hear my children's voices
Reading in the room hard by,
How my heart cries out with longing
To live and not to die!

### 吾 が 悲   赤川彦

人に告ぐる　悲しみならす　秋草に
息を白じろと　吐きにけるかも

### Waga Kanashimi

*Hito ni tsuguru   Kanashimi narazu   Akikusa ni*
*Iki wo shirojiro to   Haki ni keru kamo.*

## My Sorrow                              Akahiko

To man I cannot tell the grief
Which in my heart all hidden lies,
But to the autumn grasses I
Have breathed it white in sighs.

"White" refers to the white cloud of the breath in the cold autumn air.
My sorrow is too deep for any mortal to understand. Therefore I have
heaved profound sighs to the autumn grasses. The autumn, which is loneliness
itself, will understand it and relieve me of it.

## 富 士 山                              赤 彦

土肥の海　榜き出でて見れば　白雪を
天に懸けたり　富士の高根は

### Fujisan

*Tohi no umi   Kogi-idete mireba   Shirayuki wo*
*Ame ni kaketari   Fuji no takane wa.*

## Mount Fuji                              Akahiko

Rowing my boat on the sea
Off Tohi, I descry
The lofty summit of Fuji,
Draping white snow in the sky.

Tohi is a harbour in the Province of Izu.

### 金 子 薫 園

**Kaneko Kun-en** (1876–    )

A native of Tōkyō, Kun-en has had no academic career.  He studied versification under Ochi-ai Naobumi.  In 1918 he established a poetry magazine entitled "The Light", which continues up to date.  He has published ten collections of his verses and several books on poetry.

### 桃 の 花　　　　　薫 園

桃の花　君に似るとは　いひかねて
ただ美しと　めでてやみしか

#### *Momo-no-Hana*

*Momo no hana　Kimi ni niru towa　Iikanete*
*Tada utsukushi to　Medete yamishika.*

#### Peach-Blossoms　　　　Kun-en

Lacking courage enough to say,
　"These peach-blossoms are just like thee!"
I simply exclaimed, and then was silent,
　"How beautiful!" admiringly.

### 水 車　　　　　薫 園

牛の行く　白川道の　水車
かたりことりと　いとまあるかな

### *Mizuguruma*

*Ushi no yuku   Shirakawa-michi no   Mizuguruma*
*Katari kotori to   Itoma aru kana.*

### A Waterwheel                                    **Kun-en**

On Shirakawa Road,
   Where cows walk lazily along,
A waterwheel turns leisurely,
   With *katari kotori* for its song.

A quiet country scene naturalistically portrayed.

### 富 士                                    薫 園

親しく　呼びかけたきほど　夕ばえの
富士は　大きくあたたかき

### *Fuji*

*Shitashiku   Yobikaketaki hodo   Yūbae no*
*Fuji wa   Ōkiku atatakaki.*

### Fuji                                    **Kun-en**

So large and warm it is—
Fuji bathed in the gold of the setting sun!
I would gladly send out
A friendly call to the mountain.

In this verse which consists of twenty-eight syllables, the poet shows his recent tendency to write irregular verse.

風　　　　　　　　　　薫　園

橡青葉　一枚一枚　ゆれゐしが
やがて樹をゆする　風となりけり

### Kaze

*Tochi aoba　Ichimai ichimai　Yureishi ga*
*Yagate ki wo yusuru　Kaze to nari keri.*

### The Wind　　　　　　　Kun-en

One green horse-chestnut leaf after another
　　Swayed in the breeze;
But it soon was a wind which had such power—
　　It shook whole trees.

我　が　心　　　　　　　薫　園

兒等の欲し　といふ品物を　買ひやりて
　　我心春の　ごとくのどけし

### Waga Kokoro

*Kora no hoshi　To yū shinamono wo　Kai-yarite*
*Waga kokoro haru no　Gotoku nodokeshi.*

### My Heart　　　　　　　Kun-en

For my children, when I bought
　　What they asked for—everything—
Then my heart at last was tranquil,
　　Like a day in spring.

## 夏 の 柳 薫 園

てりかへす　夏の柳の　陽の青さ
わが白浴衣　よらば染むべし

### Natsu no Yanagi

*Teri-kaesu　Natsu no yanagi no　Hi no aosa*
*Waga shiro yukata　Yoraba somubeshi.*

### The Summer Willow Kun-en

How green the sunbeams
Reflected from the summer willow!
My cool white robes might be dyed in the tint,
If the rays should touch them.

## 日 蓮 上 人 薫 園

大いなる　力をおぼゆ　この松の
蔭は日蓮が　法を説きしところ

### Nichiren Shōnin

*Ōinaru　Chikara wo oboyu　Kono matsu no*
*Kage wa Nichiren ga　Hō wo tokishi tokoro.*

### Saint Nichiren Kun-en

Great power do I feel,
　　This pine-tree below;
For on this spot Saint Nichiren
　　In old days preached the "law".

*Kono matsu* or "this pine-tree" refers to a great old pine-tree at Kamakura, under which Saint Nichiren practised so-called *tsuji-seppō* or, "street-preaching". Nichiren (1222–1282) was the founder of the Nichiren Sect of Buddhism, one of the most popular sects. In his last years he preached zealously in the street at Kamakura, the capital at that time of the Hōjō *Shikken* or "Regent".

## 尾 上 柴 舟

### Onoe Shibafune or Saishū (1876–   )

A graduate of Tōkyō Imperial University and a professor of Japanese classics in Tōkyō Women's Higher Normal School. Two or three collections of his verses have been published. The poet has a number of pupils who form a poetical society called "Saishū Society". He is famous also as a calligrapher. He is one of the most prominent contemporary poets.

## 小　鳥　　　　柴 舟

飛びうつり　一木の枝に　かゝはらぬ
庭の小鳥も　われにまされる

### Kotori

*Tobi-utsuri   Hitoki no eda ni   Kakawaranu*
*Niwa no kotori mo   Ware ni masareru.*

### A Small Bird　　　　Shibafune

A little bird in my garden,
　　Flitting from tree to tree,
In its perfect freedom,
　　Surpasses me.

## 夕靄 柴舟

夕靄は　蒼く木立を　つつみたり
思へば今日は　やすかりしかな

### *Yū-Moya*

*Yū-moya wa　Aoku kodachi wo　Tsutsumi-tari*
*Omoeba kyō wa　Yasukarishi kana.*

### The Evening Haze　Shibafune

The evening haze has wrapt
　The trees in blue.
Ah! what a peaceful time I've had
　This whole day through.

A feeling of thankfulness at the close of a peaceful spring day.

## おなじ木 柴舟

おなじ地に　おなじ木ならび　今日もまた
おなじ葉と葉と　あひ觸れて鳴る

### *Onaji Ki*

*Onaji chi ni　Onaji ki narabi　Kyō mo mata*
*Onaji ha to ha to　Ai-furete naru.*

**The Dale in Spring**

By Gyokudō (川合玉堂),
a contemporary painter

**" The Dale in Springtime"**
—**Shibafune**

In the poet's own handwriting

### The Same Trees                    Shibafune

Behold! on the same ground
　　To-day, too, the same trees stand tame;
The same leaves one another touch,
　　And rustle, just the same.

This verse suggests that men, too, repeat the same things everyday.


### 春 の 谷                    柴 舟

春の谷　あかるき雨の　中にして
鶯なけり　山のしづけさ


### *Haru no Tani*

*Haru no tani　Akaruki ame no　Nakani shite*
*Uguisu nakeri　Yama no shizukesa.*


### The Dale in Springtime        Shibafune

How still the mountain is!
　　Down in the dale in spring,
Through bright, soft rain,
　　*Uguisu* sing.


### 牡 丹 の 花                    柴 舟

吸ふかぎり　春日を吸ひて　吐く息の
人の面うつ　牡丹の花は

### Botan no Hana

*Sū-kagiri   Harubi wo suite   Haku iki no*
*Hito no tsura utsu   Botan no hana wa.*

## Peony Flowers                    Shibafune

How it meets the faces of men—
    The breath of the peony flowers,
Which have been inhaling the bright spring sun
    With all their powers!

## 蛙                                柴 舟

一つ呼べば　一つ應へて　つひにみな
　月の夜蛙　なき立ちにけり

### Kawazu

*Hitotsu yobeba   Hitotsu kotaete   Tsuini mina*
*Tsuki no yo-kawazu   Naki tachini keri.*

## Frogs                              Shibafune

One calling loud,
    Another instantly replied,
Till all the frogs under the moon
    In chorus cried.

## 初　夏                             柴 舟

初夏の　日をさまざまに　照りかへし
　輕く林の　葉の躍るかな

**Peony Flowers and Kingfisher**

By Rosetsu (長澤蘆雪 1755-1799)

### Shoka

*Hatsu-natsu no   Hi wo sama-zama ni   Teri-kaeshi*
*Karuku hayashi no   Ha no odoru kana.*

**Early Summer**                                    **Shibafune**

Reflecting in different ways
    The early summer sun,
The leaves of the wood
    Dance lightly, full of fun.

早　　春                          柴　舟

雉子のこゑ　鳥の囀り　葉のそよぎ
世は物音に　滿ちはじめたり

### Sōshun

*Kiji no koe   Tori no saezuri   Ha no soyogi*
*Yo wa mono-oto ni   Michi-hajime tari.*

**Early Spring**                                    **Shibafune**

Hark! the pheasant's cries;
    The twitter of birds manifold;
The rustling of foliage; many sounds
    Have begun to fill the world.

A delightful description of early spring.

## 古葉と新葉　　　　　　　　　柴舟

落ちて行く　ふる葉のうれひ　よそにして
新葉ぞをどる　初夏の森

### Furu-Ba to Nii-Ba

*Ochite yuku　Furu-ba no urei　Yoso ni shite*
*Nii-ba zo odoru　Hatsu-natsu no mori.*

### Old and New Leaves　　　　　Shibafune

Heedless of the sorrow
Of old leaves falling,
New leaves in the wood are
In early summer dancing.

## 瑣細のことば　　　　　　　　柴舟

思はざる　ことばの末に　あはれわれ
人の憎みを　もとめてありけり

### Sasai no Kotoba

*Omowazaru　Kotoba no sue ni　Aware ware*
*Hito no nikumi wo　Motomete arikeri.*

### Trifling Words　　　　　　　Shibafune

A few light words
Spoken unguardedly—
Ah, woe is me!—
Have brought hatred upon me.

朝　日　　　　　　　柴　舟

木も草も　我に等しき　喜びに
ひたるか朝の　日にをどりをり

## Asahi

*Ki mo kusa mo　Ware ni hitoshiki　Yorokobi ni
Hitaruka asa no　Hi ni odori ori.*

### The Morning Sun　　　　Shibafune

**It may be the grasses and trees
Are steeped in the same joy and fun
As I ; for, behold, they dance
In the bright morning sun !**

太　田　水　穂
**Ōta Mizuho** (1876–　　)

A native of a village in Nagano Prefecture, Ōta Mizuho graduated from a Normal School, and for some years taught in a primary school and in a Higher Girls' School.　Later he went up to Tōkyō, where he wrote essays and novels.　In 1911 he started a poetry magazine, *Chō-on* or "The Sound of the Tide", which continues up to date.　He has written several books on literature and published a few collections of his own verses.

故　　郷　　　　　　　水　穂

豆の葉の　露に月あり　野は晝の
明るさにして　盆唄のこゑ

### Kokyō

*Mame no ha no   Tsuyu ni tsuki ari   No wa hiru no*
*Akarusa ni shite   Bon-uta no koe.*

## At My Old Home

Mizuho

Upon the dews of the bean leaves,
There is a brilliant moon.
The field is light as at high noon.
*Bon*-dance* songs sound afar.

椿 の 蕾

水 穂

玉割れて　春の吐息の　いちどきに
聲ともならむ　紅の眞椿

### Tsubaki no Tsubomi

*Tama warete   Haru no toiki no   Ichidokini*
*Koe to mo naran   Ake no matsubaki.*

## The Camellia Bud

Mizuho

The scarlet camellia bud !
When the jewel bursts open, maybe
The breath of spring will escape,
Finding voice suddenly.

---

*Bon odori* or "*Bon* dances" are popular open air dances performed in memory of the dead on the nights of July 13, 14 and 15. *Bon* is an abbreviation for "urabon", derived from the Sanskrit "Ullambana" which, literally, means "Hung upside-down", and is the name of a Buddhist festival held to relieve the dead from their pain in being hung head downwards in Hell.

**Camellia Flowers**

By Tekison (字田秋郷), a contemporary painter

The above impressionistic fantasy is characteristic of the poet.

*Tama warete* or, literally, "The jewel has split" is a beautiful figure for "the bud bursts open".

## 一ひらの雲　　　　水 穂

雲一ひら　月の光りを　さへぎるは

白鷺よりも　さやけかりけり

### Hito-hira no Kumo

*Kumo-hitohira　Tsuki no hikari wo　Saegiru wa*

*Shirasagi yori mo　Sayake kari keri.*

### A Wreath of Cloud　　　Mizuho

Behold! a wisp of cloud
　Intercepts the moonlight.
'Tis brighter than a heron
　With plumage white.

## 夜　の　池　　　　水 穂

くろぐろと　暮れはてにける　ひところ

鯉の動かす　水みゆるなり

### Yoru no Ike

*Kuro-guro to　Kure-hate ni keru　Hito-tokoro*

*Koi no ugokasu　Mizu miyuru nari.*

### A Pond in the Night　　　　Mizuho

Behold! the pond is wrapt
In pitch-dark night;
But in one spot the water, moved by carp,
Gleams faintly white.

平　福　百　穂

**Hirafuku Hyakusui** (1876–1933)

The son of Suian, a celebrated painter, Hyakusui studied Japanese painting of the Maruyama School. He became an instructor in painting at his Alma Mater, the Tōkyō School of Fine Arts, and a member of the Imperial Academy of Fine Arts. He was a prominent figure in the galaxy of contemporary painters and a poet of the *Araragi* School.

### 垂　　氷　　　　　百　穂

窓にうつる　垂氷の影の　一ならび
今宵の月夜　あきらけくこそ

### Taruhi

*Mado ni utsuru　Taruhi no kage no　Hito-narabi*
*Koyoi no tsukiyo　Akirakeku koso.*

### Icicles　　　　Hyakusui

A row of icicles
　Against the window glitters bright;
Undoubtedly the moon
　Is shining brilliantly to-night.

**Carp**

By Jippo (荒木十畝), a contemporary painter

## 窪 田 空 穂

### Kubota Utsubo (1877–    )

Born in a village near Matsumoto, Shinano Province, Kubota Utsubo finished the course of the Matsumoto Middle School and later graduated from the Tōkyō Semmno Gakkō, the predecessor of Waseda University. After leading a journalist's life for several years, he is now a professor at the Literature College of Waseda University. He is one of the most prominent contemporary poets. He has published several collections of his own verses, some notes on Japanese classics and a collection of his essays. His most recent work is "Critical Notes on *Shin Kokin Shū*".

泉　　　　　　　　　　空　穂

湧きいづる　泉の水の　盛りあがり
くづるとすれや　なほ盛りあがる

### *Izumi*

*Waki-izuru　Izumi no mizu no　Mori-agari*
*Kuzuru to sure-ya　Nao mori-agaru.*

### The Fountain　　　　　　　Utsubo

Behold! the fountain, springing up,
　Rises high, then would collapse,
When immediately again
　It rises, higher still perhaps.

\*　　\*　　\*　　\*　　\*

Glorious fountain!
　Let my heart be
Fresh, changeful, constant,
　Upward like thee!　　　　　James Russell Lowell

瀧　　　　　　　　　　空　穂

落ちよ瀧　日のかげ白く　照らすらん
眞夏しばしの　ほどにあらすや

## Taki

*Ochiyo taki　Hi no kage shiroku　Terasuran*
*Manatsu shibashi no　Hodo ni arazuya.*

### The Waterfall　　　　　　Utsubo

O, waterfall, flow down abundantly,
　　For soon will pass away the light
Of this midsummer sun which shines on thee,
　　Dazzling and white.

This verse suggests that the heyday of youth is brief.

母 の 死 に ま せ る 頃 を　　　　空　穂

誰定めて　一世といひし　我はしも
また會はむ世の　母にありと思ふ

### Haha no Shinimaseru Koro wo

*Tare kimete　Hitoyo to üshi　Ware wa shimo*
*Mata awan yo no　Haha ni ari to omō.*

### When My Mother Passed Away　　　Utsubo

Who positively stated,
"Men have one life alone"?
I feel there is another world,
Where I can see my mother once again.

**A Waterfall**

By Bunrin (鹽川文麟 1808-1877)

入學試驗　　　　　空　穗

死ぬるまで　競爭すべき　此世ぞと
下げ髪の子を　あはれみ見送る

### Nyūgaku Shiken

*Shinuru made　Kyōsō subeki　Kono yo zo to*
*Sage-gami no ko wo　Awaremi mi-okuru.*

## An Entrance Examination　　　Utsubo

"Ah! in this world all must compete,
　Each with other, till they die!"
So saying, I saw off my daughter—
　Long hair hanging down her shoulder—
　　With a pitying sigh.

This verse is prefaced by the following words: "On my eldest daughter going to a girls' school for an entrance examination".

白　鷺　　　　　空　穗

### I

ペリカンと　共に飼はるる　網の中の　小さき白鷺—
其嘴の　細き伸して　網の目の　外には出しつ
壺の泥鰌　盗みて食ひぬ　人見ぬ今を

### II

ペリカンの　食はむ泥鰌を　盗み取る　小さき白鷺
其みの毛　ゆるがしつつも　細き嘴に　捉ふるみれば
いや更に　盗めとぞ思ふ　ペリカンの泥鰌

## *Shira-Sagi*

### I

*Perikan to   Tomoni kawaruru   Ami no naka no   Chisaki shira-sagi—*
*Sono hashi no   Hosoki nobashite   Ami no me no   Soto niwa dashitsu*
*Tsubo no dojō   Nusumite kuinu   Hito minu ima wo.*

### II

*Perikan no   Kuwan dojō wo   Nusumi-toru   Chisaki shira-sagi*
*Sono mi no ke Yurugashi tsutsu mo   Hosoki hashi ni   Torōru mireba*
*Iya-sara ni   Nusume tozo omō   Perikan no dojō.*

## A White Heron                        Utsubo

### I

A heron small and white,
Kept in the netting with some pelicans,
Stretched out its slender bill athwart the net,
And stole and ate the loaches in a pot,
Intended for the pelicans,
When no one saw.

### II

The small white heron which purloined
The loaches for the pelicans—
When I observed it catch the fish
With its long bill, its feathers swaying,
I wished that it would steal yet more
Of those fish for the pelicans.

These lines were composed when the poet visited the Hana-Yashiki in Asa-
kusa Park, Tōkyō—a place of entertainment, consisting of some small mena-
geries, shows of comical dolls, a variety-hall, playgrounds for children and so
forth.

These seemingly humorous poems imply a deep sympathy for the weaker against the stronger.

## 我が嬰兒　　　　空　穂

おもちや買ふ　錢のありやと　問ひし子の
問はずなりけり　なしと思ふらし

### *Waga Eiji*

*Omocha kau  Zeni no ari ya to  Toishi ko no*
*Towazu nari-keri  Nashi to omou-rashi.*

### My Little Son　　　　Utsubo

"Daddy, have you any money to buy toys?"
So he used to ask—my little son—
But lately he has ceased to question me;
He seems to think that I have none.

## 亡　き　子　　　　空　穂

はるばるに　弔ひに來て　わが舅
亡き子がことは　云はでかへりき

### *Naki Ko*

*Haru-baru ni  Tomurai ni kite  Waga shūto*
*Naki ko ga koto wa  Iwade kaeriki.*

### The Dead Child                                    Utsubo

My father-in-law, to condole with us,
Came a long, long way,
And left, but yet of the little dead child
Never a word did he say.

The old man was too full of grief to say even a word of his dead grandson.

### 畫　寝                                    空　穗

畫寝より　目覺めたる子は　母をよび
應へする聞きて　また眠りけり

### Hirune

*Hirune yori   Mezametaru ko wa   Haha wo yobi*
*Iraesuru kikite   Mata nemuri keri.*

### Noonday Sleep                                    Utsubo

Awaking from noonday sleep,
The child called for its mother,
And hearing her voice reply,
Has fallen asleep again.

### 岡　麓
#### Oka Fumoto (1877-    )

Fumoto was born in Tōkyō, the son of a physician of the Chinese school.
He studied Chinese and Japanese classics under Takarada Michibumi (寶田道
文), a Shintō priest, and later became a pupil of Masaoka Shiki, the poet. He
now teaches Japanese literature at a girls' school, and regularly contributes
verses to the magazine, *Araragi*, or "The Yew".

孫                                     麓

ねそびれし　孫を抱きて　望の夜の
月を見にけり　光くまもなき

### Mago

*Nesobireshi　Mago wo idakite　Mochi no yo no*
*Tsuki wo mini keri　Kage kuma mo naki.*

## My Grandchild                    **Fumoto**

**Holding in my arms**
**My grandchild, who was sleepless,**
**I gazed at the full moon shining**
**In unshadowed brightness.**

*Mochi* (望) is the fifteenth of the lunar month, the night of the full moon.
This verse shows the poet's love of his grandchild and of the moon.

山 と 稲 田                          麓

あの山も　ここの稲田も　わが家の
ものなりしといふ　よそごとのごとく

### Yama to Inada

*Ano yama mo　Koko no inada mo　Waga ie no*
*Mono narishi to yū　Yosogoto no gotoku.*

### A Mountain and a Ricefield      Fumoto

"That mountain and this ricefield, too,
Belonged once to my family",
I said with an indifferent air,
As had it no concern with me.

Supply, "to my son-in-law, Masahiko" after "I said". The poet had lost all his hereditary property in the country in some business undertakings which had proved failures.

### 木 曾 川      麓

木曾川の　水のひびきと　思ふにぞ
衾かつぎて　ききふけりける

### Kisogawa

*Kisogawa no　Mizu no hibiki to　Omō ni zo*
*Fusuma katsugite　Kiki-fukeri keru.*

### The Kiso River      Fumoto

Thrilled by the thought that the sound was
The Kiso's low murmur, at night,
Under my coverlet snuggling
I listened till late with delight.

The Kiso-gawa, which runs for 135 miles through the Nakasendō, ranks as one of the Three Great Rivers of Japan, the other two being the Tone-gawa and the Shinano-gawa; but it is incomparably the most beautiful.

## 與 謝 野 晶 子

### Yosano Aki-ko (1878–    )

Born in 1878, the daughter of a merchant, Ōtori by name, at the city of Sakai, Izumi Province, Aki-ko finished the course of the Sakai Girls' High School in 1894. Seven years later she went up to Tōkyō and became a pupil of Yosano Hiroshi, the poet, whom she married soon afterwards. In 1900 she joined the just started "New Poetry Society" and assisted her husband in a movement for poetical reform. In 1912 she visited Paris, staying there only half a year. She is a voluminous writer, responsible for some twenty collections of her verses, numerous novels, essays and fairy tales. She taught for two or three years at the Bunkwa Gaku-in, a women's college. The greatest of contemporary poetesses, Aki-ko is among the few leading poets of the present day.

花　　　野　　　　　　　晶　子

何となく　君に待たるる　ここちして
出でし花野の　夕月夜かな

### Hana-no

*Nanto-naku　Kimi ni mataruru　Kokochishite*
*Ideshi hana-no no　Yūzuki-yo kana.*

### The Flowery Field　　　　　　Aki-ko

know not why, I fancied that he might
Be waiting for me,
So out I came into this flowery field,
And found a glorious moonlit night!

流　　　星　　　　　　　晶　子

み空より　牟はつづく　明き道
牟はくらき　流星の道

## *Ryūsei*

*Misora yori   Nakaba wa tsuzuku   Akaki michi*
*Nakaba wa kuraki   Ryūsei no michi.*

### A Meteor                                        Aki-ko

Coursing from the distant sky,
    Its first half bright,
Its latter half in darkness lost—
    A meteor's flight.

This symbolic verse seems to suggest something in human life. It may allude to the careers of most poets.

### 厩                                        晶 子

初秋や　朝顔さける　厩には
ちさき馬あり　驢あり牛あり

### *Umaya*

*Hatsu-aki ya   Asagao sakeru   Umaya ni wa*
*Chisaki uma ari   Ro ari ushi ari.*

### The Stable                                        Aki-ko

It is early autumn.
    In the stable o'ergrown with morning-glories,
Asses there are,
    Calves and ponies.

A good subject for a water-colour painter.

## 銀　杏　　　　　晶　子

金色の　小さき鳥の　かたちして
銀杏ちるなり　丘の夕日に

### *Ichō*

*Konjiki no　Chiisaki tori no　Katachi shite
Ichō chiru nari　Oka no yūhi ni.*

### A Maiden-Hair Tree　　　Aki-ko

In the evening sun on the hill,
The leaves of a maiden-hair tree
Are fluttering down,
Like little golden birds.

## 白　蓮　　　　　晶　子

水を出でて　白蓮さきぬ　曙の
うすら赤地の　世界の中に

### *Byaku-Ren*

*Mizu wo idete　Byakuren sakinu　Akatsuki no
Usura-aka ji no　Sekai no naka ni.*

### White Lotus-Flowers　　　Aki-ko

White lotus-flowers have bloomed,
　　Out of the water born,
Into the rose-red world
　　Of early morn.

## 薔 薇 　　　　晶 子

我上に　春留まれと　聞きつるや
俄に薔薇の　手にくづれきぬ

### *Bara*

*Waga ue ni　Haru todomare to　Kiki tsuru ya
Niwakani bara no　Te ni kuzure kinu.*

### A Rose　　　　Aki-ko

**As though it thought to hear me say
" Spring, stay with me, "
A rose to pieces fell and dropped
On my hand, suddenly.**

As the poetess came to a rose-bush, suddenly its petals fell on her hand, as if it might have fancied that she had said, "Beautiful Spring, please stay for ever, dwelling upon my mind and body, so that I may remain always young and happy".

## 櫻 　　　　晶 子

この世をば　誰もめでたき　我世ぞと
思はぬは無き　花の下かな

### *Sakura*

*Kono yo woba　Taremo medetaki　Waga yo zo to
Omowanu wa naki　Hana no moto kana.*

### The Cherry Flowers                                Aki-ko

Under the cherry flowers
We feel, each one,
"This is a beautiful world,
And mine own!"

### 小　　鳥                                           晶　子

小鳥きて　少女のやうに　身を洗ふ
秋の木蔭の　水たまりかな

#### *Kotori*

*Kotori kite　Otome no yōni　Mi wo arō
Aki no kokage no　Mizu-tamari kana.*

### A Little Bird                                     Aki-ko

Lo! to a pool,
Under an autumn tree,
A little bird came and washed,
Like a young girl.

### 眼                                                 晶　子

みづからの　行くべき方を　知れるより
悲しきは無し　目ある禍

#### *Me*

*Mizukara no　Yuku-beki kata wo　Shireru yori
Kanashiki wa nashi　Me aru wazawai.*

## An Eye                                   Aki-ko

Nothing is sadder than knowing
 The course by which one is bound to go ;
Oh, the misfortune of having an eye
 To see all so !

Since the poetess has an eye to see herself, she foresees her future course. Therefore she cannot try bold adventures.  She thinks that her self-knowledge and power of foresight are her misfortunes.

## 戀                                       晶 子

戀といふ　不死の大鳥　羽ばたきは
せねど鳴かねど　疑ふなゆめ

## *Koi*

*Koi to yū　Fushi no ōtori　Habataki wa*
*Senedo nakanedo　Utagōna yume.*

## Love                                     Aki-ko

Doubt not our love—
A phoenix bird,
Which neither cries nor flaps its wings,
Yet is alive.

The paraphrase by the poetess:

The love between my husband and me still continues and is as strong as ever.  It looks so calm that strangers may imagine it has already cooled down. But it is immortal like the phoenix, which is motionless, yet alive.

春　　　　　　　　　　　晶　子

美くしき　素足の春の　來りけり
ちらほらと咲く　水仙の花

### Haru

*Utsukushiki   Suashi no haru no   Kitari keri*
*Chira-hora to saku   Suisen no hana.*

### Spring　　　　　　　　Aki-ko

**See, Spring has come,**
**With her lovely bare feet!**
**Here and there are blooming**
**The jonquils sweet.**

Beautiful Spring has come walking barefooted.  Here a white jonquil is in bloom, there another.  They are the bare feet of the Goddess of Spring.

初　秋　の　空　　　　　　晶　子

幾とせを　仰がでありし　ここちしぬ
翡翠のいろの　初秋のそら

### Hatsu-Aki no Sora

*Ikutose wo   Aogade arishi   Kokochi shinu*
*Hisui no iro no   Hatsu-aki no sora.*

### The Sky of Early Autumn — Aki-ko

As if for many years I had not seen it,
Upon the sky I gaze—
The sky of early autumn tints
Of chrysoprase.

### のぼる陽 — 晶子

地はひとつ　大白蓮の　花と見ぬ
雲のなかより　陽ののぼる時

### Noboru Hi

*Chi wa hitotsu　Dai-byakuren no　Hana to minu*
*Kumo no naka yori　Hi no noboru toki.*

### The Rising Sun — Aki-ko

When rose the sun from out the clouds,
Beneath its light
Lay earth, one open lotus-flower,
Immense and white.

### 紅の蝶 — 晶子

大空の　日と我が上に　行き還り
遊ぶと見ゆる　くれなゐの蝶

### Kurenai no Chō

*Ōzora no　Hi to waga ue ni　Yuki-kaeri*
*Asobu to miyuru　Kurenai no chō.*

### A Crimson Butterfly          Aki-ko

Dancing toward the sun
In the infinite sky,
Or hither and thither over my head—
Oh, crimson butterfly!

The paraphrase by the poetess:
"Beautiful crimson butterfly, art thou not flitting delightfully between the sun and me? Thou wert born out of the sun's heart, also out of my heart. Therefore thou hast the colour of fire and that of burning love".

### 花 菱 草          晶 子

夕べには　もとの蕾に　かへるなり
花菱草に　なるよしもがな

### Hanabishisō

Yūbe niwa　Moto no tsubomi ni　Kaeru nari
Hanabishisō ni　Naru yoshi mo gana.

### The Hanabishisō          Aki-ko

Lo! in the evening
It becomes a bud once more.
Would that I could become
A hanabishisō-flower.

The hanabishisō (花菱草), according to Japanese botanical dictionaries, is what is called "eschscholtzia" in the United States. The eschscholtzia is a genus of papaveraceous plants, found throughout the western coast of the United States. They have finely divided leaves and showy yellow or orange-coloured flowers which close up every evening, and are often cultivated as garden annuals, being known as California poppies. (N. L., after Dr. J. F. V. Eschscholtz, 1793–1831, a German botanist). These were introduced into Japan some years ago, and are known either as *eshorusia* or *hanabishisō*.

塔        晶 子

塔の身は　木隠れてのみ　在り難し
山邊に立ちて　風に吹かるる

### Tō

*Tō no mi wa　Kogakurete nomi　Ari gatashi*
*Yamabe ni tachite　Kaze ni fukaruru.*

## A Pagoda      Aki-ko

**It is not a pagoda's lot**
**Always to have the shelter kind**
**Of trees; but towering tall on the mountain,**
**It must cope with the winter wind.**

This symbolic verse suggests that a man of high ideals, often, for their realization, ventures upon unusual courses ahead of the times, and runs the risk of public censure.

山 川 登 美 子

**Yamakawa Tomi-ko** (1879–1909)

A native of a village in the suburbs of Ōhama, Wakasa Province, Yamakawa Tomi-ko graduated from a Girls' High School at Ōsaka, and later studied for a year at the Japan Women's University in Tōkyō. At twenty-one she married but, two years later her husband died. She published a collection of her own verses entitled *Koi-Goromo* or "A Lover's Clothes".

**A Pagoda**

By Shūho (池上秀畝), a contemporary painter

熱　病　　　　　　　登美子

たのもしき　病の熱よ　まぼろしに
父を仄見て　喚ばぬ日もなし

## Netsubyō

*Tanomoshiki　Yamai no netsu yo　Maboroshi ni*
*Chichi wo hono-mite　Yobanu hi mo nashi.*

### Fever　　　　　　　Tomiko

Ah! thanks to my high fever,
Not a single day passes
But I see in vision my father,
In delirium, and call to him.

長　塚　節
**Nagatsuka Takashi** (1879–1917)

Takashi was the son of a farmer in Ibaraki Prefecture.  In his boyhood he was a prodigy of learning, but on account of delicate health, he was obliged to discontinue his Middle School course in his early teens.  At the age of twenty, he became a pupil of the famous poet, Masaoka Shiki.  The appearance, in the *Osaka Asahi*, of his maiden work, "Soil", a novel which realistically depicts the dark side of tenant-farmers' life in his district, gained him sudden fame as a novelist. He wrote a number of poems, some novels and several essays.

月　の　光　　　　　　節

硝子戸を　透して幗に　月さしぬ
あはれといひて　起きて見にけり

### Tsuki no Hikari

*Garasu-do wo   Tōshite kaya ni   Tsuki sashinu*
*Aware to iite   Okite mini keri.*

## The Moonbeams                    **Takashi**

The moonbeams streamed in through the panes
On my mosquito-net.
Exclaiming, " Oh, how beautiful! "
I rose and gazed.

## 病 中 吟                    節

生きも死にも　天のまにまにと　平らけく
思ひたりしは　常の時なりき

### Byōchū-Gin

*Iki mo shi ni mo   Ame no mani mani to   Tairakeku*
*Omoitarishi wa   Tsune no toki nariki.*

## Written during Illness                    **Takashi**

It was when I had good health,
That I thought in an easy mood,
I would leave it to Heaven whether
I should live on long or meet death soon.

### 齋 藤 瀏
**Saitō Ryū (1879–     )**

A native of Matsumoto, Shinano Province, Ryū is a Major-General. He participated in the Russo-Japanese War. He has published two collections of his own verses.

雲　雀　　　　　　　　　劉

なく聲と　なりて雲雀は　大空の
　　光の中に　消えにけるかも

### Hibari

*Naku-koe to　Narite hibari wa　Ōzora no*
*Hikari no naka ni　Kie ni keru kamo.*

### A Lark　　　　　　　　Ryū

Only now a singing voice,
　　The lark has vanished out of sight,
Into the distant heavens—
　　Into the light.

わ が 双 眼 鏡　　　　　　　劉

わが双眼鏡に　入れりと知らぬ　敵の兵の
　　愛しきかもよ　飯はみて居り

### Waga Megane

*Waga sōgankyō ni　Ireri to shiranu　Teki no hei no*
*Kanashiki kamo yo　Meshi hamite ori.*

### My Field-Glasses　　　　Ryū

Quite unaware that they are within range
Of my field-glasses,
Some enemy soldiers are eating lunch.
How lovable they look!

水 野 葉 舟

**Mizuno Yōshū** (1881–    )

Born in Tōkyō in 1881, Yōshū finished the course in politics and economics at Waseda University; but afterwards drifted into literature. He is both a novelist and a poet.

蟲

葉 舟

聽けよ君　畑のくまなる　庭の蟲も
力のかぎり　唱ひて老ゆる

## Mushi

*Kikeyo kimi   Hata no kuma naru   Niwa no mushi mo*
*Chikara no kagiri   Utaite oyuru.*

## Insects

Yōshū

Listen, friend, even the insects,
In corners of the field,
Sing to the utmost of their strength
Till they grow old.

齋 藤 茂 吉

**Saitō Mokichi** (1882–    )

A native of Yamagata Prefecture, Mokichi graduated from the Medical College, Imperial Tōkyō University, and later continued his studies for four years in Germany and Austria. He is now president of the Aoyama Insane Asylum. He studied poetry under Itō Sachio and is now a prominent poet and a regular contributor to the poetry magazine, *Araragi* or "The Yew". He has published some collections of his verses, a few books on poetry and "The Life of Hitomaro", and is better known as a poet than as a physician.

遠田の蛙　　　　　　　茂　吉

死に近き　母に添寝の　しんしんと
遠田のかはづ　天に聞ゆる

### Tōda no Kawazu

*Shi ni chikaki　Haha ni soine no　Shinshinto*
*Tōda no kawazu　Ten ni kikoyuru.*

### The Frogs in Distant Ricefields　　　Mokichi

Watching my mother, who was nearing death,
　As I rested on the couch, close by,
The voices of frogs, from far-away ricefields,
　In the stillness of night rose up to the sky.

狂　人　　　　　　　　茂　吉

むらぎもの　心はりつめ　しましくは
幻覺を持つ　をとこに對す

### Kyōjin

*Muragimo no　Kokoro haritsume　Shimashiku wa*
*Genkaku wo motsu　Otoko ni taisu.*

### A Lunatic　　　Mokichi

My mind intensely strained,
　I sat a little space
Before a man possessed by strange
　Hallucinations—face to face.

This is a poem characteristic of an alienist.

A lunatic haunted by hallucinations sits, for examination, trembling with wild delirium, in front of the poet-physician who, for an instant, feels a terrible tension of mind, at the sight.

挽　歌　　　　　茂吉

壁に來て　草かげらふは　すがり居り
透きとほりたる　羽のかなしさ

### Banka

*Kabe ni kite   Kusa-kagerō wa   Sugari-ori*
*Sukitōritaru   Hane no kanashisa.*

## A Dirge　　　　　Mokichi

**A lacewing has lighted upon the wall—**
**A fragile thing!**
**And, oh, the pathos of its delicate**
**Transparent wing!**

This verse is an elegy on Akutagawa Ryūnosuke, a prominent novelist, who usually suffered from delicate health and killed himself at a comparatively early age, during a nervous breakdown.

老　齡　　　　　茂吉

やうやくに　老いづきにけり　さびしさや
命にかけて　せしものもなし

### Rōrei

*Yōyaku ni   Oizukini ni keri   Sabishisa ya*
*Inochi ni kakete   Seshi mono mo nashi.*

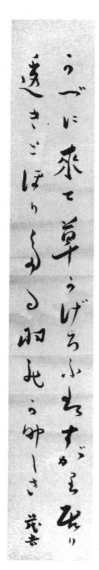

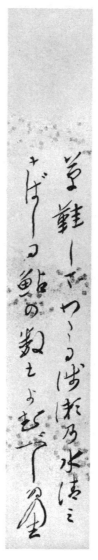

"A Dirge"—Mokichi

In the poet's own handwriting

"*Ayu*"—Inokichi

In the poet's own handwriting

### Old Age
Mokichi

At last old age is near, and oh,
  Most lonely doth me make;
For never yet have I ventured ought
  With life at stake.

### をさなご
茂吉

をさなごは　疊のうへに　立ちて居り
　　この穉兒は　立ちそめにけり

### Osanago

*Osanago wa　Tatami no ue ni　Tachite ori*
*Kono osanago wa　Tachi-some ni keri.*

### A Baby
Mokichi

The baby was standing
  Upon the *tatami*;
Ay, for the very first time
It was standing!

The *tatami* are the mats covering the floor of a Japanese room, on which we sit without using chairs.

The poet first sees his baby standing on the *tatami*, and the next moment, to his surprise and joy, realizes that it is standing for the very first time.

### 夕　鳥
茂吉

啼くこゑは　悲しけれども　夕鳥は
　木に眠るなり　われは寢なくに

## *Yū-tori*

*Naku koe wa   Kanashi kere domo   Yū-tori wa*
*Ki ni nemuru nari   Ware wa nenaku ni.*

### Evening Birds                     Mokichi

The evening birds utter sad notes,
   Yet slumber deep
They can enjoy up in the trees.
   Alas! I cannot sleep.

## 母 の 火 葬                     茂 吉

はふり火を　守りこよひは　更けにけり
今夜の天の　いつくしきかも

### *Haha no Kwasō*

*Hafuri-bi wo   Mamori koyoi wa   Fuke ni keri*
*Koyoi no sora no   Itsukushiki kamo.*

### My Mother's Cremation            Mokichi

While watching the cremation fire,
   The night has reached its height.
How solemn is the sky
   To-night!

## 電 車 に て                     茂 吉

いらだたしもよ　朝の電車に　乗りあへる
ひとのことごと　罪なきごとし

## Densha Nite

*Iradatashi mo yo   Asa no densha ni   Nori-aeru*
*Hito no kotogoto   Tsumi naki   gotoshi.*

### In a Tram-Car                    Mokichi

**How irritating 'tis,**
**To see my fellow-passengers**
**In this morning's tram-car,**
**All looking as if they were perfectly faultless!**

### 川　田　順
**Kawada Jun** (1882–　)

A native of Tōkyō, Jun studied in the Literature and the Law College, Tōkyō Imperial University; and on graduating from the latter college, he became a clerk of the Sumitomo Joint Stock Company, of which he is now a director. He studied versification under Sasaki Nobutsuna and is a regular contributor to the poetry magazine, *Kokoro no Hana* or "The Flower of the Heart". He has published several collections of his own verses.

### 後　の　世　　　　　　　順

後の世を　頼むもはかな　斯かる人
斯かる花蔭　なくば如何にせむ

## Nochi-no-Yo

*Nochi-no-yo wo   Tanomu mo hakana   Kakaru hito*
*Kakaru hana-kage   Nakuba ikani sen.*

### The Future Life
Jun

Can we two be sure of the future life?
What if, in that other world of ours,
We should not be found just as we are now,
And there were not such beautiful flowers?

Reflections of an imaginary couple of passionate lovers, who are in no situation to wed, and are almost inclined, in their disappointment, to commit "love suicide".

### 鶴
順

水ぎはに　片脚立の　鶴の鳥
しづかなるかも　影は搖れつつ

### *Tsuru*

*Mizu-giwa ni  Kata-ashi dachi no  Tsuru no tori
Shizukanaru kamo  Kage wa yure-tsutsu.*

### The Crane
Jun

The crane on one leg at the waterside—
How still it stays!
But in the ripples
Its reflection sways.

### 動物園の鶴
順

飛び立たむ　ものならなくに　おほらかに
羽根ひろげたる　鶴のかなしも

**"My Joy"—Jun**

Handwritten by the poet

**"At the Foot of Mount Fuji"
—Kano-ko**

Handwritten by the poetess

### *Dōbutsu-en no Tsuru*

*Tobi-tatan   Mono nara naku ni   Orakami*
*Hane hirogetaru   Tsuru no kanashimo.*

### A Crane in Zoological Gradens          Jun

Although it could not fly away,
    Yet gaily and with all its might,
The crane extended both its wings.
    How pitiful a sight!

### わ が 喜 び          順

日出づれば　先づ啼く鳥の　よろこびと
　君を見出でし　わが喜びと

### *Waga Yorokobi*

*Hi izureba   Mazu naku tori no   Yorokobi to*
*Kimi wo mi-ideshi   Waga yorokobi to.*

### My Joy          Jun

    The joy of birds that sing
      At the rising of the sun,
    And my joy at finding thee!—
      They are one.

## 花田比露思

### Hanada Hiroshi (1882-    )

A graduate of the Law College, Tōkyō Imperial University, Hiroshi was for some years on the editorial staff of the *Yomi-uri* and two other newspapers, and is now a professor in the Ōsaka College of Commerce. He edits the *Akebi*, a poetry magazine.

### 蟲                                    比露思

秋の夜の　永夜もすがら　庭隈に
鳴けりし蟲は　死ににけらしな

### *Mushi*

*Aki no yo no   Naga-yomosugara   Niwa-kuma ni*
*Nakerishi mushi wa   Shini ni kerashi na.*

### Insects                              Hiroshi

Those insects which would sing
The long night through, all autumn-tide,
In the corners of my garden—
Alas! they must have died.

### いにしへびとの歌              比露思

さぶしきは　いにしへびとの　歌を讀み
及び難しと　嘆かゆるとき

### *Inishie-Bito no Uta*

*Sabushisa wa   Inishie-bito no   Uta wo yomi*
*Oyobi-gatashi to   Nagekayuru toki.*

### Poems of Ancient Masters     Hiroshi

Oh, my discouraged heart!
Poems of masters of the olden days
Reading, and sorrowing that it is so hard
To emulate their lays!

### 曇 る 日     比 露 思

曇る日は　わが歌くもり　晴るる日は
わが歌晴れむ　そを我と見よ

### *Kumoru Hi*

*Kumoru hi wa　Waga uta kumori　Haruru hi wa
Waga uta haren　So wo ware to miyo.*

### Cloudy Days     Hiroshi

On cloudy days my verse
Will clouded be ;
Sunny when skies are clear ;
So thus in what I write, see me.

### 高 塩 背 山

**Takashio Haizan (1882–    )**

Haizan is a Shintō priest and a schoolmaster at his native town, Kitsure-gawa-Machi, in Tochiki Prefecture.  He is on the editorial staff of the *Nukari*, a poetry magazine.

## 白　鳩　　　　　　　　　背　山

はや見えず　なりぬと思ひし　白鳩の
はろかに光る　朝日をうけて

### *Shirahato*

*Haya miezu　Narinu to omoishi　Shirahato no
Haroka ni hikaru　Asahi wo ukete.*

## A White Dove　　　　　　Haizan

A white dove soaring in the sky
　　Had flown, it seemed, beyond our sight,
When it gleamed again, far, far away,
　　Catching the sunrise light.

### 相　馬　御　風
#### Sōma Gyofū (1883-　　　)

A native of Itoigawa, a town in Niigata Prefecture, Gyofū graduated from
the Literature College, Waseda University, and for several years was on the
editorial staff of "Waseda Literature", and a lecturer of his Alma Mater. Later
he returned to his native town, where he still lives. He is a prominent poet
and presides over the *Moku-in Kwai*, a poetry society. He has published a
collection of his own verses and many books on Japanese literature.

## 白　き　雲　　　　　　御　風

大空を　しづかに白き　雲はゆく
しづかにわれも　生くべくありけり

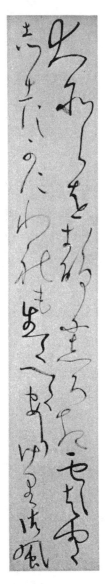

"The Fountain"—Utsubo

Handwritten by the poet

"White Clouds"—Gyofū

Handwritten by the poet

### Shiroki Kumo

*Ōzora wo   Shizukani shiroki   Kumo wa yuku*
*Shizukani ware mo   Iku beku ari keri.*

## White Clouds                                    Gyofū

**Across the great blue sky**
**White clouds pass quietly.**
**I too would live my life**
**In such tranquillity.**

## 小瓶の花                                         御 風

うなづきて　かたらふがごとし　朝夕に
一つ小瓶の　水に咲く花

### Kogame no Hana

*Unazukite   Katarō ga gotoshi   Asayū ni*
*Hitotsu kogame no   Mizu ni saku hana.*

## Flowers in a Small Vase                         Gyofū

**They seem to nod to one another**
**And whisper face to face,**
**Morn and eve— the flowers blooming**
**In th' water of this little vase.**

## 足　　跡                                          御 風

しめやかに　濡れたる朝の　砂濱に
一すぢながく　つづく足跡

## *Ashi-ato*

*Shimeyakani   Nuretaru asa no   Suna-hama ni*
*Hitosuji nagaku   Tsuzuku ashi-ato.*

### Footprints                                    Gyofū

Walking the shore,
  Upon the soft wet morning sand,
I noticed how behind me footprints lay
  In one continuous line along the strand.

This verse symbolizes the poet himself, leaving faint footprints, destined to be soon effaced, on the illimitable plain of human life.

## 嘘                                    御 風

嘘をいふ　ことをおぼえし　子の顔を
しみじみながめ　泣き居ぬ妻は

## *Uso*

*Uso wo yū   Koto wo oboeshi   Ko no kao wo*
*Shimijimi nagame   Naki-inu tsuma wa.*

### Lies                                    Gyofū

My wife was weeping,
  Her tearful eyes
Bent on the face of her child
  Who had learnt to tell lies.

## 霰 御風

地におちて　群れつ躍りつ　ころがりて
やがて消えゆく　玉霰はや

### Arare

*Chi ni ochite  Muretsu odoritsu  Korogarite*
*Yagate kie-yuku  Tama-arare haya.*

### Hail  Gyofū

Alas! the beads of hail!
They fall upon the ground,
They crowd, they roll, they bound,
And then they melt away.

Evidently "the beads of hail" are a symbol of the lives of men.

## 白 牡 丹 御風

わが焚きし　香のけむりの　ほのけきに
まぎれず薫る　白牡丹の花

### Haku-Botan

*Waga takishi  Kō no kemuri no  Honokeki ni*
*Magirezu kaoru  Haku-botan no hana.*

### White Peonies  Gyofū

Undrowned by the faintly fragrant smoke
Of the incense I have burned,
The white peony flowers
Send out their perfume.

## 前 田 夕 暮

**Maeda Yūgure** (1883–    )

Born in a village in Sagami Province, Yūgure led a wandering life in his youth. At the age of twenty-one he went up to Tōkyō and became a pupil of Onoe Shibafune, the poet. Seven years later, he started a magazine, "Poetry", which continues up to date. He has published several collections of his own verses.

## 青 き 樹 　　　夕 暮

樹に風鳴り　樹に日は近く　かがやけり
われ青き樹に　ならばやと思ふ

### *Aoki Ki*

*Ki ni kaze nari　Ki ni hi wa chikaku　Kagayakeri*
*Ware aoki ki ni　Naraba ya to omō.*

### A Green Tree 　　　Yūgure

A light wind whispers through the trees;
The sun shines brightly on the trees.
O how I wish I could become
A green tree in the sun and breeze!

## 向 日 葵 　　　夕 暮

向日葵は　金の油を　身にあびて
ゆらりと高し　日のちひささよ

### *Himawari*

*Himawari wa　Kin no abura wo　Mi ni abite*
*Yurarito takashi　Hi no chiisa sayo.*

### The Sunflower

Yūgure

The sunflower grandly sways,
Towering tall,
Bathed in an oil of gold.
The sun itself looks small.

This verse, paraphrased, runs as follows:

The sunflower swaying grandly,
Towering tall,
Bathed, as it were, in oil of gold—
Why, it makes the real sun look small!

### 四　月

夕　暮

木に花咲き　君わが妻と　ならむ日の
四月なかなか　遠くもあるかな

### *Shigatsu*

*Ki ni hanasaki　Kimi waga tsuma to　Naran hi no*
*Shigatsu nakanaka　Tōku mo aru kana.*

### April

Yūgure

Ah! April when the trees will bloom,
And you will be my wife—
How far, how very far ahead
That day seems in my life!

我が悲しみ　　　　　夕　暮

雪の上に　空がうつりて　うす青し
わが悲しみは　靜かに燃える

### Waga Kanashimi

*Yuki no ue ni　Sora ga utsurite　Usu-aoshi*
*Waga kanashimi wa　Shizukani moeru.*

### My Sorrow　　　　　Yūgure

On the virgin snow
　　The sky is reflected,
　　Faintly blue,
And calmly burns my sorrow.

監　　獄　　　　　夕　暮

囚人等　おのが棲家の　監獄の
屋根つくろへり　五月の夕日

### Kangoku

*Shūjin-ra　Onoga sumika no　Kangoku no*
*Yane tsukuroeri　Gogatsu no yūhi.*

### A Prison-House　　　　　Yūgure

Some convicts at work are repairing
　　The roof of their dwelling-place—yea,
Of their own prison-house —
　　In the evening sunlight of May.

高 村 光 太 郎

**Takamura Kōtarō** (1883–    )

Born at Tōkyō in 1883, Kōtarō finished the course in sculpture at the Tōkyō School of Fine Arts in 1902.   Soon afterwards he travelled through Europe and America.   He is now better known as a poet than a sculptor.   He has published a collection of his verses.   His most recent work is a brief life of Auguste Rodin.

海 上 に て                           光 太 郎

海にして　太古の民の　おどろきを
我ふたたびす　大空のもと

### Kaijō nite

*Umi ni shite　Taiko no tami no　Odoroki wo*
*Ware futatabisu　Ōzora no moto.*

### On the Sea                           Kōtarō

**I have experienced again,**
**Under the wide sky on the sea,**
**The wonder which was felt by men**
**In days of great antiquity.**

お　ほ　海                           光 太 郎

おほ海の　まろきが中に　船ありて
夜をみ晝をみ　こころおそれぬ

### Ōumi

*Ōumi no　Maroki ga naka ni　Fune arite*
*Yo wo mi hiru wo mi　Kokoro osorenu.*

## The Ocean
Kōtarō

The ship was sailing fast
Upon the great round sea ;
I saw the night, I saw the day,
And fear o'erwhelmèd me.

吉 植 庄 亮

### Yoshi-ue Shōsuke or Shōryō (1884-    )

Born in a village of Chiba Prefecture, Shōsuke began to write verse at the age of seventeen, and became a pupil of Kaneko Kun-en, the poet. He studied at Tōkyō Imperial University.  For three years he was a writer for the *Chū-ō*, a Tōkyō newspaper.  Ten years ago he returned to his village and has been leading a farmer's life up to the present time.

青 き 日 輪
庄 亮

筮の　中に仰げば　螢より
青き日輪　見えにけるかな

### *Aoki Nichirin*

*Takamura no　Naka ni aogeba　Hotaru yori*
*Aoki nichirin　Mie ni keru kana.*

## A Pale Sun
Shōsuke

In the grove of bamboos
I look up and espy
A sun more pale
Than a firefly.

いささかの傷　　　　　　庄　亮

いささかの　傷には土を　なすりつけて
百姓われの　恙もあらず

## Isasaka no Kizu

*Isasaka no　Kizu niwa tsuchi wo　Nasuri-tsukete*
*Hyakushō ware no　Tsuzuka mo arazu.*

### Little Wounds　　　　　　Shōsuke

On little wounds a little soil I rub,
　　Nor feel alarm ;
A farmer, I, and strong,
　　So take no harm.

A farmer's simple and healthful life.

菠薐草　　　　　　庄　亮

われ遂に　百姓となりて　憂なし
菠薐草は　霜におごれり

## Hōrensō

*Ware tsuini　Hyakushō to narite　Urei nashi*
*Hōrensō wa　Shimo ni ogoreri.*

### Spinaches　　　　　　Shōsuke

At last, a farmer become,
　　I am perfectly free from care.
My spinaches grow luxuriantly,
　　In spite of the freezing air.

牡　丹　　　　　庄 亮

牡丹花の　花心に面向ひ　大き虻
光り舞ひすみて　ゐるは靜けし

### Botan

*Botan-kwa no   Kwashin ni omo-mukai   Ōki na abu*
*Hikari mai sumite   Iru wa shizukeshi.*

## A Peony　　　　　Shōsuke

Just over against the heart of a peony,
A large horsefly is flitting round,
Bathed in the brilliant light of the sun.
Oh, deep tranquillity!

A quiet scene in spring.

橘　純　一
**Tachibana Jun-ichi** (1884–　　)

Jun-ichi is a professor of Japanese literature at Tōkyō College of Commerce.

兄　弟　　　　　純 一

何事か　いひあらそひし　兄おとと
枕ならべて　安くいねたり

### Ani-Otōto

*Nanigoto ka   Ii-arasoishi   Ani-otōto*
*Makura narabete   Yasuku inetari.*

**Peony and Bee**

By the late Hyakusui (故平福百穂)

### Two Brothers                Jun-ichi

The two little brothers
Who quarrelled o'er something or other,
Have peacefully fallen asleep,
With their pillows laid side by side

### 隅　田　川                純　一

隅田川　岸の柳は　とく暮れて
花や渡りの　しるべなるらむ

#### Sumida-Gawa

*Sumida-gawa　Kishi no yanagi wa　Toku kurete
Hana ya watari no　Shirube naruran.*

### The Sumida River            Jun-ichi

On Sumida's river shore,
　　Night has fallen where the willows grow,
But cherry-blossoms, for the ferryman,
　　A shining landmark are, I know.

### 若　山　牧　水
#### Wakayama Bokusui (1885-1928)

A native of a village in Miyazaki Prefecture, Bokusui graduated from the
English course of the Literature College, Waseda University.  He studied versi-
fication under Onoe Shibafune, and later became a prominent poet.  He esta-
blished a poetry magazine, *Sōsaku* or "Original Work", which continues up to
date, having been edited by his widow after his death.  He left "The Voice of
the Sea", "Death or Art?" and several other collections of his own verses; and
wrote many books on poetry.

# 浪 牧 水

朝な朝な　浪の前に來て　こころ踊る
日にけに浪は　新しきかな

## *Nami*

*Asa na asa na　Nami no macni kite　Kokoro odoru
Hini keni nami wa　Atarashiki kana.*

## Waves Bokusui

**Morning after morning
I face the waves of the bay,
And my heart leaps with joy.
So fresh are they every day!**

\*　　\*　　\*　　\*　　\*

"　.　.　.　.　.　.　.　.　.　from a boy,
I wantoned with the breakers—they to me
Were a delight; and if the freshening sea
Made them a terror—'twas a pleasing fear".
From "The Ocean", by George Gordon Byron

# 鴨 牧 水

羽根つらね　浮べる鴨を　うつくしと
静けしと見つつ　こころかなしも

## *Kamo*

*Hane tsurane　Ukaberu kamo wo　Utsukushi to
Shizukeshi to mitsutsu　Kokoro kanashimo.*

### Wild Ducks
Bokusui

**Upon the water, wild ducks float**
**With wings abreast.**
**How beautiful and calm they look!**
**But in my heart wakes sad unrest.**

The beauty and tranquillity of the wild ducks make the poet conscious of his own ugliness and his restless disposition.

わ が 友
牧 水

をち方に　離りゐる友を　おもふとき
かがやく珠を　おもひこそすれ

### *Waga Tomo*

*Ochikata ni　Sakari-iru tomo wo　Omō toki*
*Kagayaku tama wo　Omoi koso sure.*

### My Friends
Bokusui

**Remembering**
**My friends in distant parts,**
**I think at once**
**Of gems with brilliant hearts.**

松 風
牧 水

聞きゐつつ　樂しくもあるか　松風の
いまはゆめとも　うつつとも聞ゆ

## *Matsu-Kaze*

*Kiki-itsutsu   Tanoshiku mo aruka   Matsu-kaze no*
*Ima wa yume tomo   Utsutsu tomo kikoyu.*

### The Wind Rustling through Pines     Bokusui

The wind rustling through the pines,
How pleasant it is to hear!
Dream-like or vision-like,
It comes now to my ear.

## 白　鳥　　　　　牧　水

白鳥は　かなしからすや　空の青
海の青にも　そまず漂ふ

### *Shiratori*

*Shiratori wa   Kanashikarazu ya   Sora no ao*
*Umi no ao ni mo   Somazu tadayō.*

### The White Bird     Bokusui

Is not the white bird sorrowful?
It drifteth free,
Blending with neither the blue of the sky
Nor the blue of the sea.

"The white bird" means "a seagull". A white gull, drifting lonesomely in the blue sea and under the blue sky, symbolizes the poet himself who feels lonely, being companionless in the poets' circles.

眼 の な き 魚　　　　　　　牧 水

海底に　眼のなき魚の　棲むといふ
眼のなき魚の　戀しかりけり

*Me no naki Uo*

*Una-zoko ni　Me no naki uo no　Sumu to yū*
*Me no naki uo no　Koishi kari keri.*

### Eyeless Fish　　　　　　Bokusui

They say at the bottom of the sea
There dwell eyeless fish.
How I feel drawn toward
Those eyeless fish!

The poet is so dazzled by the glare of society that he envies those eyeless
fish which are dull, annoyed with no visual phenomena.

幾 山 河　　　　　　　牧 水

幾山河　越えさりゆかば　寂しさの
はてなむ國ぞ　今日も旅ゆく

*Iku Yamakawa*

*Iku yamakawa　Koe-sari yukaba　Sabishisa no*
*Hatenan kuni zo　Kyō mo tabi-yuku.*

### How Many Mountains and Rivers?  Bokusui

How many mountains, how many rivers
Are still to be crossed before I gain
The land where loneliness comes to an end?
To-day, as ever, I travel on.

This verse is carved on a stone of medium size as a so-called *kahi* (歌碑) or "poem-monument" in the Sembon-Matsubara or One Thousand Pine Grove in the suburbs of Numazu, a sea-coast town in Shizuoka Prefecture.

A poet's masterpiece is often carved as a poem-monument by his pupils and admirers, so that throughout Japan are to be seen numerous monuments of this kind.

### 雲ふたつ  牧 水

雲ふたつ　合はむとしては　また遠く
わかれて消えぬ　春の青空

### Kumo Futatsu

*Kumo futatsu　Awan to shite wa　Mata tōku*
*Wakarete kienu　Haru no aozora.*

### Two Clouds  Bokusui

Two clouds drew close to join one another,
Then drifted apart again, far and high,
And melted to nothingness—what was left?
The blue spring sky.

This verse seems to suggest something in human life.

たんぽぽ　　　　　　牧 水

多摩川の　砂にたんぽぽ　咲くころは
われにもおもふ　ひとのあれかし

### Tampopo

*Tama-gawa no　Suna ni tampopo　Saku koro wa
Ware nimo omō　Hito no arekashi.*

## Dandelions　　　　Bokusui

When dandelions bloom
　　In the Tama's dry river-bed,
Oh, how I wish that I might have
　　A belovèd!

滿　月　　　　　　牧 水

ありがたや　今日盈つる月と　知らざりし
この大き月　海にのぼれり

### Mangetsu

*Arigataya　Kyō mitsuru tsuki to　Shirazarishi
Kono ōki tsuki　Umi ni noboreri.*

## The Full Moon　　　Bokusui

Happy for me that I did not know
　　It would be a full moon to-night,
Until this great orb rose over the sea,
　　Round and bright!

おろかなり　　　　　　　　　牧　水

おろかなり　阿呆鳥の　啼くよりも
わがかなしみを　ひとに語るは

### Oroka Nari

*Oroka nari　Ahō-garasu no　Naku yori mo*
*Waga kanashimi wo　Hito ni kataru wa.*

### How Silly!　　　　　　　　Bokusui

**Ah! it is sillier**
**Than the cawing of a senseless crow,**
**To talk to other men**
**About my sorrow.**

土　岐　善　麿

**Toki Zenmaro** (1885–　　)

Zenmaro is the second son of Toki Zenjō, a scholarly priest of the Shinshū Sect at Asakusa, Tōkyō.  On finishing the English course at Waseda University in 1908, he joined the editorial staff of the *Tōkyō Asahi*, and he is now the chief of the Investigation Section of the paper.  He has published about ten collections of his verses, a collection of his essays and "An Account of Travelling Abroad".  He has been engaged for many years in a movement for the Romanization of the Japanese language.

大　　鐘　　　　　　　　　善　麿

大鐘の　まひるのひびき　松にこもり
櫻にこもり　ひろがりてゆく

### Ōgane

*Ogane no   Mahiru no hibiki   Matsu ni komori*
*Sakura ni komori   Hirogarite yuku.*

#### A Great Temple Bell          Zenmaro

The sound of the great temple bell,
    Booming at midday,
Lodges in cherry-bloom and pine,
    And then spreads far away.

グラフ ツェペリン          善 麿

人類の　ながい間の　夢が今こそ　現實の空を
飛んできた　グラフ ツェペリン

### Graf Zeppelin

*Jinrui no   Nagai aida no   Yume ga ima koso*
*Genjitsu no sora wo   Tonde kita   Graf Zeppelin*

#### Graf Zeppelin          Zenmaro

A long, long dream of humankind
    Is flying now across the welkin
Of actual reality —
    The great Graf Zeppelin.

### 銀 光 の 巨 體          善 麿

あの銀光の　巨體がいつまでも　絶えず
あたまの中の　おほ空を飛んでゐる

### Ginkō no Kyotai

*Ano ginkō no   Kyotai ga itsumademo   Taezu*
*Atama no naka no   Ōzora wo tonde iru.*

## The Mighty Silver Bulk                    Zenmaro

That mighty silver bulk,
In my mind's eye,
Is still sailing ever
Across the sky.

This was composed when Der Graf Zeppelin, the great airship, commanded by Dr. Eckener, visited Japan in August, 1929.

エヂプト ギーゼ の スフインクス        善 麿

動くなと　ここにすゑられて　しまつたままの
恐ろしい　退屈さ

### Ejiputo Giize no Sufinkusu

*Ugokuna to   Koko ni suerarete   Shimatta mama no*
*Osoroshii   Taikutsusa.*

## The Great Sphinx at Gizeh, Egypt     Zenmaro

What terrible ennui
It must have suffered on this spot,
Since here they set and left it fixed,
Saying "Move not!"

"The Great Sphinx at Gizeh, Egypt"—Toki Zenmaro
Handwritten by the poet

四 賀 光 子

**Shiga Mitsu-ko** (1885–    )

A native of the village of Shiga in Shinano Prefecture, Mitsu-ko is the wife of Ōta Mizuho, the poet. She is a graduate of the Tōkyō Women's Higher Normal School, and teaches in a Tōkyō girls' school. Her pen-name, Shiga, was adopted from the name of her native village.

家　畜　　　　　　光 子

喰べ喰べて　外に思ひも　なかるらん

飼はるるものの　幸を思ふ

### Kachiku

*Tabe-tabete　Hoka ni omoi mo　Nakaruran*

*Kawaruru-mono no　Saiwai wo omō.*

### Domestic Animals　　Mitsu-ko

They eat and eat,
And seem to think of nothing else;
I envy these home pets
Their happiness.

故　郷　　　　　　光 子

みづうみも　いでゆもわれに　何ならん

母ありて今日　歸る故郷

### Furusato

*Mizuumi mo　Ideyu mo ware ni　Nani naran*

*Haha arite kyō　Kaeru furusato.*

### My Old Home                                    Mitsu-ko

For lakes and hot springs
What do I care?
I am going home to-day,
And my mother is there.

柳 原 燁 子

**Yanagiwara Aki-ko** (1885–    )

The second daughter of Count Yanagiwara Sakimitsu, Aki-ko studied at the
Peeresses' School, and took lessons in versification from Sasaki Nobutsuna.   At
the age of twenty-seven, she married a millionaire named Itō, but after ten
years' unhappy union she was divorced.   She has published several collections
of her own verses, novels, dramas and essays.

### 神はいづこに                                    燁 子

われはここに　神はいづこに　ましますや
ほしのまたたき　さびしき夜なり

### *Kami wa Izuko ni*

*Ware wa koko ni   Kami wa izuko ni   Mashi-masu ya
Hoshi no matataki   Sabishiki yo nari.*

### Where Are the Gods?                             Aki-ko

" Here am I.   Where are ye,
Merciful Gods? " I cry.
It is a lonely night,
With twinkling stars in the sky.

This verse was written in the greatest crisis of the poetess' life, when everything in the world was for her the cause of sorrow and resentment.  She had no one of whom to ask help; nobody seemed to care for her.  One still night when stars were twinkling, she wept and exclaimed repeatedly, "Oh, merciful gods, where are ye?  Pray help me!"

## 物 思 ふ 頃　　　　　　　　　燁 子

忘れむと　君いひまさば　辛らからむ
わすれじといはば　なほ悲しけむ

### *Mono-omou Koro*

*Wasuren to   Kimi iimasaba   Tsurakaran
Wasureji to iwaba   Nao kanashiken.*

### When I was Lost in Thought　　　　Aki-ko

**If he should say, "I will forget",
How pained my heart would be!
Yet if, "I never will forget",
Then sadder far for me!**

Needless to say, this was composed when the poetess found herself in a love-dilemma.

## 花　　　　　　　　　　　　　燁 子

花さきぬ　ちりぬみのりぬ　こぼれぬと
われしらぬまに　日へぬ月へぬ

### *Hana*

*Hana sakinu   Chirinu minorinu   Koborenu to
Ware shiranu ma ni   Hi henu tsuki henu.*

### Flowers
Aki-ko

The flowers bloomed and dropped;
The fruit grew ripe and fell,
The days and months went slipping by,
Or ever I could tell.

わ が 魂
燁 子

骨肉は　父と母とに　まかせきぬ
わが魂よ　誰にかへさむ

### Waga Tamashii

*Kotsuniku wa　Chichi to haha to ni　Makase kinu
Waga tamashii yo　Tare ni kaesan.*

### My Soul
Aki-ko

Bones and flesh to my parents may
Submitted be;
But oh, my soul, to whom, to whom
Shall I give back thee?

わ が 歌
燁 子

筆をもて　われは歌はじ　わが魂と
命をかけて　歌生まむかも

### Waga Uta

*Fude wo mote　Ware wa utawaji　Waga tama to
Inochi wo kakete　Uta uman kamo.*

## My Verses
Aki-ko

I would not verses write
By means of pens at all;
I would give birth to them
With my life, with my soul.

## 船
樺 子

船ゆけば 一筋しろき 道のあり
われにはつづく 悲しびのあと

### *Fune*

*Fune yukeba   Hitosuji shiroki   Michi no ari
Ware ni wa tsuzuku   Kanashibi no ato.*

## A Ship
Aki-ko

A ship in its course,
A white line leaving—
My course in life,
With its track of grieving!

## 平 野 萬 里
**Hirano Banri** (1885-    )

Born in a village of Saitama Prefecture, Banri graduated from the College of Engineering, Tōkyō Imperial University, in 1908.   Later he visited Europe and America twice.   He is an official of the Commerce and Industry Department. From early days he has been a contributor to the "Morning Star" and the "*Subaru*", poetry magazines.

海                                          萬 里

海ぞ鳴る　アダムの裔の　人間よ

悔い改めよ　大海ぞ鳴る

## Ō-Umi

*Umi zo naru   Adam no sue no   Ningen yo*

*Kui-aratame yo   Ō-umi zo naru.*

## The Ocean                              **Banri**

**The ocean is roaring.**

**Oh, men, the descendants**

**Of Adam, repent!**

**The ocean is roaring.**

The ocean is roaring.  It is a warning voice.  Oh, hear this voice and give up your selfishness, hatred and petty strifes.

武 藏 野 の 風                          萬 里

風吹けば　荻の葉そよぎ　いさぎよし

風もろともに　武藏野を行く

## Musashino no Kaze

*Kaze fukeba   Ogi no ha soyogi   Isagiyoshi*

*Kaze morotomoni   Musashino wo yuku.*

"The Evening Haze"
—Shibafune

In the poet's own handwriting

"The Breeze in Musashi Plain"
—Banri

In the poet's own handwriting

### The Breeze in Musashi Plain          Banri

How fresh and pure all is!
The reed leaves swaying as the wind may please!
I stroll along upon Musashi Plain,
Together with the breeze.

The *ogi* is a kind of reed.

### 赤倉 に て          萬 里

またしても　色の褪せたる　雲の來て

山の中途に　幕を引く秋

### *Akakura Nite*

*Mata shite mo　Iro no asetaru　Kumo no kite*
*Yama no chūto ni　Maku wo hiku aki.*

### At Akakura          Banri

Again a faded cloud has come
And drawn a curtain
Half-way up the mountain.
It is autumn.

### 臼 井 大 翼

**Usui Taiyoku** (1885–    )

Born in a village in Shimōsa Province, Taiyoku graduated from the Law
College, Imperial Tōkyō University. He is a lawyer. He edits the poetry ma-
gazine, *Haōjū* or "The Cactus".

## 元 旦 の 雪　　　　大 翼

降り暮れて　元旦の雪は　もの音の
隣もとほく　積りたるらし

### Gwantan no Yuki

*Furi-kurete　Gwantan no yuki wa　Mono-oto no*
*Tonari mo tōku　Tsumoritaru rashi.*

### The Snow on New Year's Day　　Taiyoku

The falling snow, with which
　　Twilight closed in on New Year's Day,
Seems to have drifted up so deep,
Even the sounds from neighbours' houses
　　Come faint and far away.

## 夏 の 日　　　　大 翼

夏の日の　ひそまり深く　思へれば
たのしきことは　むかしにありき

### Natsu no Hi

*Natsu no hi no　Hisomari fukaku　Omoereba*
*Tanoshiki koto wa　Mukashi ni ariki.*

### A Summer Day　　Taiyoku

Amid the stillness of a summer day,
　　I ponder, deep in reverie,
How all the pleasures of my life belong
　　To long-past days, an ancient history.

## 依 田 秋 圃

### Yoda Shūho (1885–    )

A native of Tōkyō, Shūho graduated from the practical course of forestry in Imperial Tōkyō University, and for several years was a prefectural inspector of forests. He has published two or three collections of his own verses. He is the selector of verses for the magazines, *Akebi* and *Sanrin*.

## 田 園 の 風 景　　　　秋 圃

戸に立ちて　背を呼ぶ妻の　遠聲の
麥の穗風に　乘りて來れり

### *Den-en no Fūkei*

*To ni tachite　Se wo yobu tsuma no　Tōgoe no*
*Mugi no hokaze ni　Norite kitareri.*

### A Rural Scene　　　　Shūho

The distant voice of a wife at her door,
Calling her husband,
Has reached him, wafted by the breeze
Which lightly brushes the ears of barley.

## 富　　士　　　　秋 圃

知らぬ間に　雨は晴れ居り　菜の花の
夕照る上に　富士の嶺を見る

### *Fuji*

*Shiranu mani　Ame wa hare-ori　Na no hana no*
*Yū teru ue ni　Fuji no ne wo miru.*

## Mount Fuji   Shūho

**All unawares, the rain has cleared,**
**And over the golden rape flowers,**
**Bathed in the setting sun,**
**Mount Fuji towers.**

A fascinating scene, a suitable subject for a water-colour painter.

## 石 川 啄 木
### Ishikawa Takuboku (1886–1914)

Takuboku was the son of the chief priest of a Buddhist village temple in Iwate Prefecture.  He entered the Morioka Middle School, but owing to his father's narrow circumstances, left it two or three years later.  While attending school, he devoured novels and poems.

In his twenty-first year he became a school teacher in Morioka; but soon resigned and crossed over to Hokkaidō, where he lived a journalist's life for some two years.  When twenty-three years old, Takuboku went up to Tōkyō, where, struggling against poverty, he wrote several novels but could find no publisher.  Later he became a proof-reader of the *Tōkyō Asahi*.  The appearance, in 1911, of a collection of his verses, "A Handful of Sand", brought him sudden fame as a poet.  Then his pen became busy with writing poems, novels and essays; but he died of some illness before he had enjoyed his reputation three years.

## 打 ち あ け て   啄 木

打ちあけて　語りて何か　損をせし
ごとく思ひて　友と別れぬ

### *Uchi-akete*

*Uchiakete  Katarite nanika  Son wo seshi*
*Gotoku omoite  Tomo to wakarenu.*

## Unbosoming Myself    Takuboku

Freely to a friend of mine
    I opened all my heart,
And felt as if some loss I had suffered,
    When we did part.

*Nani-ka son wo seshi* or "suffered some loss" means "lost some money".
Needless to say, the poet regrets having unbosomed himself.

## 砂    啄 木

いのちなき　砂のかなしさよ　さらさらと
握れば指の　あひだより落つ

### Suna

*Inochi naki　Suna no kanashisa yo　Sara-sara to*
*Nigireba yubi no　Aida yori otsu.*

### Sand    Takuboku

How pitiful
    The lifeless sand!
When grasped, it rustles down
    Between the fingers of my hand.

## 花    啄 木

友がみな　われよりえらく　見ゆる日よ
花を買ひ來て　妻としたしむ

### *Hana*

*Tomo ga mina   Ware yori eraku   Miyuru hi yo*
*Hana wo kai-kite   Tsuma to shitashimu.*

### Flowers                    Takuboku

To-day it seems to me that all my friends
    Have won distinction more than I in life;
However, I have flowers bought
    And love my wife.

### 生　命　　　　　　啄　木

そんならば　生命か欲しく　ないのかと
醫者に言はれて　だまりし心

### *Inochi*

*Sonnaraba   Inochi ga hoshiku   Nai no ka to*
*Isha ni iwarete   Damarishi kokoro.*

### Life                    Takuboku

Asked by my physician
    "Then, to live long
You have no wish?"
    My heart was silent.

### 兵　士　　　　　　啄　木

一隊の　兵を見送りて　かなしかり
何ぞ彼等の　うれひ無げなる

### Heishi

*Ittai no   Hei wo mi-okurite   Kanashi kari*
*Nanzo karera no   Urei nage naru.*

### Soldiers                     Takuboku

As I watched
A squad of soldiers marching by,
Sadness came o'er me suddenly—
So care-free seemed that company!

Evidently, the poet envies the cheerful-looking soldiers, and surely there is a deeper meaning—the thought of the possible sufferings of those light-hearted boys.

### 百　　姓　　　　　　啄　木

百姓の　多くは酒を　やめしといふ
もつと困らば　何をやめるらむ

### Hyakushō

*Hyakushō no   Ōku wa saké wo   Yameshi to yū*
*Motto komaraba   Nani wo yameruran.*

### Farmers                     Takuboku

It is said that most of the farmers
Have given up drinking;
If they should have a harder time,
What would they then give up, I'm thinking!

空　　　　　　　　　　　　　　啄 木

この四五年　空を仰ぐと　いふことが

一度もなかりき　かうもなるものか

## Sora

*Kono shigonen　Sora wo aogu to　Yū koto ga*

*Ichido mo nakariki　Kō mo naru mono ka.*

## The Sky　　　　Takuboku

**For these few years,**

　　**Not even once have I**

　　　**Looked upward to the sky.**

**Oh! have I come to this?**

Overwhelmed by stress of work and financial difficulties, the poet had forgotten the blue sky. Then by some chance, he looked upward and broke into the above pathetic verse.

母　　　　　　　　　　　　　　啄 木

たはむれに　母を脊負ひて　そのあまり

軽きに泣きて　三歩あゆます

## Haha

*Tawamureni　Haha wo seoite　Sono amari*

*Karuki ni nakite　Sampo ayumazu.*

### My Mother
**Takuboku**

Just for fun I carried
My mother on my back,
But could not even walk three steps
For weeping that she proved so light.

### こころよき仕事
啄木

こころよく　我にはたらく　仕事あれ
それを仕遂げて　死なんと思ふ

#### Kokoroyoki Shigoto

*Kokoroyoku　Ware ni hataraku　Shigoto are
Sore wo shitogete　Shinan to omō.*

### A Congenial Task
**Takuboku**

I wish to find a task
At which I can work happily.
I would accomplish it
And then would die.

### はたらく
啄木

はたらけど　はたらけど猶　わが生活
樂にならざり　ぢっと手を見る

#### Hataraku

*Hatarakedo　Hatarakedo nao　Waga kurashi
Raku ni narazari　Jitto te wo miru.*

### I Work                    Takuboku

I work and work, but still,
No better fare.
Bewildered, on my hands,
I can but stare.

In ancient times we said, "No Poverty can overtake Industry"; but nowa-
days, too often a man cannot make his circumstances easier, however hard he
works.

### クリスト                    啄木

クリストを　人なりといへば　妹の
眼がかなしくも　われをあはれむ

### Kurisuto

*Kurisuto wo　Hito nari to ieba　Imōto no
Me ga kanashiku mo　Ware wo awaremu.*

### Christ                    Takuboku

I said unto my sister,
"Christ was but a man".
Her eyes looked on me sadly
Pitying me.

### 熱烈な戀                    啄木

柔かに　積れる雪に　熱てる頬
埋むるごとき　戀して見たし

### Netsuretsu na Koi

*Yawaraka ni   Tsumoreru yuki ni   Hoteru hō*
*Uzumuru gotoki   Koi shite mitashi.*

## Passionate Love                    **Takuboku**

I wish to feel a love
Which might be likened to
Burying a hot cheek
In a soft drift of snow.

### 故 郷 の 訛                    啄 木

故郷の　訛なつかし　停車場の
人ごみの中に　そを聽きに行く

### Kokyō no Namari

*Furusato no   Namari natsukashi   Teishajō no*
*Hito-gomi no naka ni   So wo kiki ni yuku.*

## The Accent of My Old Home           **Takuboku**

For the accent of my home,
   Oh, how I long!
I go to the station
   To hear it in the throng.

### 北 原 白 秋
#### Kitahara Hakushū (1886-    )

A native of Yanagawa, Kyūshū, Hakushū attended the English course,
Waseda University.  He is one of the most celebrated contemporary poets.  He
has written eighty volumes, consisting of poems, folk-songs, essays and novels.

## 天 の 河 白 秋

天の河　棕梠と棕梠との　間より
幽かに白し　闌けにけらしも

### Ama-no-Gawa

*Ama-no-gawa　Shuro to shuro to no　Aida yori*
*Kasukani shiroshi　Fuke ni kera shimo.*

### The River of Heaven (The Milky Way)　Hakushū

The River of Heaven
Gleams dimly white
Between two hemp-palms.
Late grows the night.

## 土 の 鳩 白 秋

過ぎし日の　幼な遊びの　土の鳩
吹きてならさな　月のあかりに

### Tsuchi no Hato

*Sugishi hi no　Osana-asobi no　Tsuchi no hato*
*Fukite narasana　Tsuki no akari ni.*

### A Clay Dove　Hakushū

Oh, by the light of the moon,
　Again I would blow a clay dove,
Which, in my childhood's days,
　I used to blow and love.

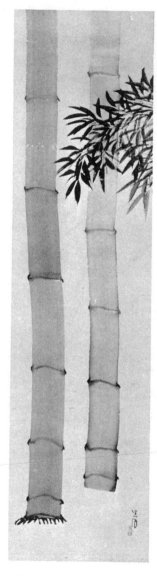

**Bamboos**

By Gengetsu (矢澤弦月),
a contemporary painter

The glorious moon has turned the world into a beautiful dreamland. Entranced by the sight, the poet becomes a child, so to speak, and is almost inclined to blow an earthen toy flute in the shape of a dove, which he used to blow when a little boy.

夏　來　る　　　　　　　白　秋

山羊の乳と　山椒のしめり　まじりたる
そよ風吹いて　夏は來りぬ

### Natsu Kitaru

*Yagi no chichi to Sanshō no shimeri   Majiritaru*
*Soyokaze fuite   Natsu wa kitarinu.*

### Summer Has Come　　　　Hakushū

**Summer has come to us, borne on
Breezes gentle and vagrant,
Which with the odour of moist Japanese
Pepper and goat's milk are fragrant.**

A refreshing breeze of early summer is blowing and seems to smell of goat's milk and moist Japanese pepper. This is evidently due to the poet's fancy. Be that as it may, delightful summer has come wafted by the breeze.

螢　　　　　　　　白　秋

晝なが'ら　幽かに光る　螢ひとつ
孟宗の藪を　出でて消えたり

### Hotaru

*Hiru nagara   Kasukani hikaru   Hotaru hitotsu*
*Mōsō no yabu wo   Idete kietari.*

### A Firefly

Hakushū

A firefly faintly glowing,
Though it was day,
Emerged from a grove of bamboo trees
And vanished away.

Mōsō (孟宗) is an abbreviation for *mōsō-chiku* (孟宗竹). The *mōsō-chiku* is
the largest, most beautiful and most valuable of bamboos. Its stems are used
for making a variety of utensils and its young shoots are eatable.

### パンと薔薇

白 秋

麭麴を買ひ　紅薔薇の花　もらひたり
爽かなるかも　両手に持てば

### Pan to Bara

*Pan wo kai　Beni-bara no　Hana moraitari
Sawayaka naru kamo　Ryōte ni moteba.*

### Bread and Roses

Hakushū

I have bought bread;
I have received red roses.
How happy do I feel, all these
In my two hands holding!

### 春 の 鳥

白 秋

春の鳥　な啼きそ啼きそ　あかあかと
外面の草に　日の入る夕

**"A Clay Dove"—Hakushū**

In the poet's own handwriting

**"A Firefly"—Hakushū**

In the poet's own handwriting

Erratum    Page 741    Line 11
For 赤き日さして    Read 赤き日のさし

### Haru no Tori

*Haru no tori   Na naki-so naki-so   Aka-aka to*
*Tono-mo no kusa ni   Hi no iru yūbe.*

## Spring Birds                                       Hakushū

Sing no more, spring birds,
　　Oh, birds, stop crying;
The grasses on the open field
　　The scarlet evening sun is dyeing.

## 水　　車                                             白　秋

ゆく水に　赤き日さして　水ぐるま
春の川瀬に　やまずめぐるも

### Mizuguruma

*Yuku-mizu ni   Akaki hi sashite   Mizuguruma*
*Haru no kawase ni   Yamazu meguru mo.*

## A Waterwheel                                        Hakushū

Upon the running water
　　The bright red sun is burning;
And ceaselessly, in springtime spate,
　　The waterwheel keeps turning.

## 吉　井　勇

**Yoshii Isamu (1886-　　)**

A native of Tōkyō, Isamu studied some years in the Literature College, Waseda University.  He began to write poems in his Middle School days.  He has published a few collections of poems, some dramas and novels.  He edits a magazine devoted to poetry

### 翡　翠　　　　　勇

止め給へ　君が締めたる　帶止の
翡翠の色は　悲しみの色

### Hisui

*Yame tamae   Kimi ga shime taru   Obidome no*
*Hisui no iro wa   Kanashimi no iro.*

### A Chrysoprase　　　　Isamu

O lady, lay it by—
　　That girdle-clasp's fair stone—
The colour of the chrysoprase
　　Is sorrow's own.

### 悲　　　　勇

悲しみに　心は舵を　失ひぬ
南を北と　して辿り行く

### Kanashimi

*Kanashimi ni   Kokoro wa kaji wo   Ushinainu*
*Minami wo kita to   Shite tadori-yuku.*

### Grief　　　　　　　　　　　　Isamu

Grief doth overwhelm!
My mind hath lost its helm;
It drifteth forth,
Mistaking south for north!

### 戀 の 足 あ と　　　　　　　　　勇

砂やまの　麓にのこる　足のあと
戀の足あと　なほ消えずあり

### *Koi no Ashi-ato*

*Suna-yama no　Fumoto ni nokoru　Ashi no ato
Koi no ashi-ato　Nao kiezu ari.*

### The Footprints of Love　　　　　Isamu

The footprints yet remain
At the base of the sandy hill;
The footprints of Love
May be seen here still.

The poet is surprised and pleased to find his own footprints and those of his sweetheart at the foot of a sandhill, where they had taken a stroll together the previous day.

### 大　海　　　　　　　　　　　　勇

若やかに　ひねもす歌ふ　大海の
こえを聞かんと　山の傾く

## Ō-umi

*Waka-yakani Hinemosu utō   O-umi no*
*Koe wo kikanto   Yama no katamuku.*

### The Great Sea                    Isamu

The mountain is leaning down
To hear the song—
The voice of the great sea,
Singing youthfully all day long.

### 橋 田 東 聲
### Hashida Tōsei (1886–1930)

A native of a village in Kōchi Prefecture, Tōsei graduated from the Law College, Imperial Tōkyō University, and was an official of the Education Department. He wrote several books on Japanese poetry.

### 春                    東 聲

木に花さき　陽はうらうら照る　眼をあげよ
この天地に　かなしみはあらず

## Haru

*Ki ni hana saki   Hi wa uraura teru   Me wo ageyo*
*Kono ametsuchi ni   Kanashimi wa arazu.*

### Spring                    Tōsei

The trees are all in bloom;
The sun shines sheen.
Lift up your eyes!  In heaven and earth
No shadow of sorrow is seen.

## 木 下 利 玄

**Kinoshita Toshiharu** (1886–1925)

Toshiharu graduated from the Literature College, Imperial Tōkyō University. In his youth he became a pupil of Sasaki Nobutsuna and later came to be known as a poet. He left several collections of his verses.

### 秋 う ご く 利 玄

遠方に　鍛冶屋かねうつ　音すみて
秋ややうごく　八月のすゑ

### *Aki Ugoku*

*Empō ni　Kajiya kane utsu　Oto sumite*
*Aki yaya ugoku　Hachigatsu no sue.*

### Autumn Stirs Toshiharu

The hammers of a smithy far away
A clear sound hither send;
Mark! autumn has begun to stir
Already now at August's end.

### 燒 場 利 玄

吾子一人　燒場に殘して　夜と云ふに
われ等大人は　かへらんとする

### *Yakiba*

*Ako hitori　Yakiba ni nokoshite　Yo to yūni*
*Warera otona wa　Kaeran to suru.*

### The Crematory — Toshiharu

We older people are now to go back,
    In the crematory
Leaving my child—though dark is the night—
    Solitary.

### 古 泉 千 樫
#### Koizumi Chikashi (1886–1927)

Born the son of a farmer in a village of Chiba Prefecture, Chikashi began to write verse in his early youth, and afterwards became a pupil of Itō Sachi-o, the poet. For some years he was a clerk in the Imperial Life-Saving Association. On the establishment of the poetry magazine, *Araragi* or "The Yew", he became a contributor to it. Later he started a poetry society, *Aogaki-Kwai*, over which he presided until his death. He published many books, including a few collections of his verses and essays.

### 靜 か な 雨 — 千 樫

ふる里の　雨しづかなり　母も吾も
悲しきことは　今日はかたらず

### Shizuka na Ame

*Furusato no　Ame shizuka nari　Haha mo ware mo*
*Kanashiki koto wa　Kyō wa katara zu.*

### Quiet Rain — Chikashi

Quietly falls the rain
    At my old home.　To-day
Not a single word about sad things
    My mother and I will say.

**White Herons**

By Bunchō (谷文晁 1764–1841)

*Ame* or "the rain" means "the spring rain", which is generally mild and is considered one of the joys of the season.

鷺 の 群 　　　　　　千 樫

鷺の群　かすかぎりなき　鷺のむれ
騒然として　寂しきものを

### Sagi no Mure

*Sagi no mure   Kazu-kagiri naki   Sagi no mure*
*Sōzen to shite   Sabishiki mono wo.*

## A Flock of Herons                    Chikashi

Behold! the flock of herons—
The flock of numberless herons—
Clamorous truly they are,
And yet how lonely!

山 田 葩 夕
**Yamada Haseki** (1886–　　)

A native of Mino Province, Haseki is a schoolmaster.  He is a pupil of Kaneko Kun-en and edits "The Green Zone", a poetry magazine.

雲 雀 　　　　　　葩 夕

遙々と　國を思へば　わがまうへ
雲雀長閑に　舞ひのぼるかな

## *Hibari*

*Harubaruto   Kuni wo omoeba   Waga ma-ue*
*Hibari nodokani   Mai-noboru kana.*

## A Lark

**Haseki**

As I was thinking of my native place
    So far, far distant, very longingly,
Behold!—right over me a singing lark
    Soared circling high, in quiet ecstasy.

### 渡 邊 湖 畔
**Watanabe Kohan** (1886–    )

A native of Sado Island, Kohan is the president of the Sado Electric Light Company.  His real name is Kinzaemon, Kohan being his *nom de plume.*

### 旅

湖 畔

一人の　吾を知るなく　はた吾を
裏切るも無し　旅は安かり

## *Tabi*

*Ichinin no   Ware wo shiru naku   Hata ware wo*
*Uragiru mo nashi   Tabi wa yasukari.*

### Travelling

**Kohan**

While travelling
    I am all free from care.
No man knows me;
    No man betrays me there.

萬 造 寺 齊

**Manzōji Hitoshi** (1886-　　)

A graduate of the English Course, Tōkyō Imperial University, Hitoshi is a
professor at the Ōtani University, Kyōto.

牡　　丹　　　　　　　齊

「改まれ、我心よ」と　祈るかな

牡丹さく日は　春きたる日は

### Botan

*Aratamare　Waga kokoro yo to　Inoru kana*

*Botan saku hi wa　Haru kitaru hi wa.*

### Peonies　　　Hitoshi

**When peonies bloom,**

**At the coming of spring,**

**How fervently I pray, "Oh heart,**

**A new life bring"!**

さ す ら ひ　　　　　齊

さすらひの　願ひはあれど　子等と別れ

ひとりとなれば　何ぞ寂しき

### Sasurai

*Sasurai no　Negai wa aredo　Ko-ra to wakare*

*Hitori to nareba　Nanzo sabishiki.*

### Wandering

Hitoshi

I love a roaming life,
But when I find myself alone,
From all my children separate,
Oh, how I am forlorn!

## 九 條 武 子

### Kujō Take-ko (1887-1928)

The second daughter of Abbot Myō-nyo (明如) of the Hongwanji Temple of the Western Branch, Take-ko married Baron Yoshimasa Kujō at the age of twenty-two. The following year, accompanying her husband, she sailed to Europe, where she stayed for a year and a half. Then returning home to Japan alone, she lived a solitary life for ten long years until Yoshimasa came back. During those years, she consoled herself by literary pursuits, taking lessons in poetry from Sasaki Nobutsuna. Among his numerous pupils she shone brilliantly, and soon became widely known as both a poet and a beauty. As President of the Buddhist Women's Society of the Western Hongwanji, President of the Tōkyō Shinshū Sect Women's Society and President of the Rokkwa-en Reformatory, she exerted her influence in social and charitable works. She left the *Kin-Rei* or "Gold Bells" and two other collections of her verses, and a collection of her essays, all of which have won great popularity. The following verse refers to her coming home alone from Europe.

## 別 れ

武 子

かりそめの　別れとききて　おとなしう
うなづきし子は　若かりしかな

### *Wakare*

*Karisome no　Wakare to kikite　Otonashū
Unazukishi ko wa　Wakakarishi kana.*

### Parting
Take-ko

Hearing the parting was to be
For but a little while,
I gave a gentle nod; ah me,
How young and innocent I was!

### 來　客
武　子

わびてくらす　この夕暮を　人は來ぬ
砂の中より　玉得たる如し

### *Raikyaku*

*Wabite kurasu　Kono yūgure wo　Hito wa kinu
Suna no naka yori　Tama etaru gotoshi.*

### A Visitor
Take-ko

This lonely evening,
　Time hanging heavy on my hands,
Comes a visitor, like a jewel
　Out of the sands.

### わ　が　心
武　子

わが心　しる人なしと　寂しらに
いへどわれだに　えしらじよくは

### *Waga Kokoro*

*Waga kokoro　Shiru hito nashi to　Wabishira ni
Iedo ware dani　E-shiraji yokuwa.*

### My Mind
Take-ko

I say dejectedly,
　"Alas! none knows my mind!"
But even I myself
　Don't know it well, I find.

### 天　　地
武 子

數に足らぬ　われとしおもへど　をりふしは
　この天地を　狹しとも見る

### Ame-Tsuchi

*Kazu ni taranu　Ware toshi omoedo　Orifushi wa*
*Kono ame-tsuchi wo　Semashi tomo miru.*

### Heaven and Earth
Take-ko

I do not consider myself
　Worth counting at all;
But sometimes, even for me,
　Heaven and Earth seem too small.

### わ が 足 あ と
武 子

大きなる　ものの力に　引かれゆく
　わが足あとの　覺束なしや

### Waga Ashi-ato

*Ōki naru　Mono no chikara ni　Hikareyuku*
*Waga ashi-ato no　Obotsuka nashi ya.*

### My Footsteps      Take-ko

Guided though they be
By the power of the Great One,
Oh, how uncertain are my footsteps!

*Ōki naru mono* or, literally, "the Great One" means "Buddha".

### 大正十二年の大震火災      武 子

母のごと　頼む大地の　叛逆に
なすすべもなし　人の子あはれ

### *Taishō Jūni-Nen no Dai Shin Kwa Sai*

*Haha no goto　Tanomu daiji no　Hangyaku ni
Nasu sube mo nashi　Hito no ko aware.*

### The Great Earthquake and Fire of 1923      Take-ko

Betrayed by the great Earth,
Which like their mother, thro' and thro'
They had relied upon—alas, alas,
For sons of men, all at a loss, who know not what to do!

### 春 歸 る      武 子

みわたせば　西も東も　霞むなり
君はかへらす　また春や來し

### *Haru Kaeru*

*Mi-wataseba　Nishi mo higashi mo　Kasumu nari
Kimi wa kaerazu　Mata haru ya koshi.*

### Spring Has Come Again          Take-ko

Mists fill all the air,
    East and west, where'er we see—
Spring has, indeed, come back again,
    But he does not return to me.


### ざ れ 言          武 子

十年を　侘びて人待つ　ひとりゐに
ざれ言いはん　すべも忘れし


### *Zaregoto*

*Jūnen wo   Wabite hito matsu   Hitori-i ni
Zaregoto iwan   Sube mo wasureshi.*


### Joking          Take-ko

Ten long years lonely have I lived,
    My love awaiting wearily;
Until I have forgot the way
    Of joking merrily.


### 若 山 喜 志 子
#### Wakayama Kishi-ko (1888–    )

Kishi-ko is the widow of Wakayama Bokusui, the poet. Since the death of her husband, she has been editor of the *Sōsaku* or "Original Work", a poetry magazine established by him.

## 雜 木 林　　　喜 志 子

故郷の　雜木林　葉の散る
ころの戀しさよ　心鳥となりつつ

### *Zōki-Bayashi*

*Furusato no　Zōki-bayashi　Ha no chiru*
*Koro no koishisa yo　Kokoro tori to nari-tsutsu.*

### The Copse　　　Kishi-ko

How I long for the copse at my old home!—
　My heart becoming a bird, as it were,—
When tinted leaves are fluttering
　Down off the trees over there.

## コ ス モ ス　　　喜 志 子

コスモスの　一重の花の　つつましき
姿をぞ願ふ　われの起居に

### *Kosumosu*

*Kosumosu no　Hitoe no hana no　Tsutsumashiki*
*Sugata wo zo negō　Ware no tachi-i ni.*

### The Cosmos Flower　　　Kishi-ko

Oh, that I,
　In my demeanour,
Might be like the modest single-petalled
　Cosmos flower!

## 桶　屋　　　　　　喜志子

櫻紅葉　ひらりひらりと　散るなかに
桶屋唄ひて　桶たたきをり

### *Okeya*

*Sakura-momiji　Hirari-hirari to　Chiru nakani*
*Okeya utaite　Oke tataki ori.*

### A Cooper　　　　　Kishi-ko

**Tinted cherry leaves**
**Drop fluttering, fluttering;**
**Amid them sings a cooper,**
**At the tub he is hammering.**

A cooper, carrying split bamboos, intended for binding the staves of tubs, often walks in the street, looking for jobs, such as mending tubs or casks.

Such a cooper, singing a popular song, is mending a tub in the yard of a house, where the leaves of a cherry-tree, tinted by frost, are fluttering down on the ground.

*Sakura momiji* do not mean "cherry flowers and maple leaves", but "cherry leaves tinted scarlet, like frost-bitten maple leaves".

## 大 き 月　　　　　喜志子

をさな子の　吾子の驚き　指す方に
見るもおどろく　大き月の出

### *Ōki Tsuki*

*Osanago no　Ako no odoroki　Sasu kata ni*
*Mirumo odoroku　Ōki tsuki no de.*

### A Great Moon
Kishi-ko

Where my little child,
In wondering surprise,
Pointed—see a marvellously
Great moon rise!

### 銀やんま
喜 志 子

銀やんま　つと室内に　通りぬけ
ゆくへは知らす　初秋の空

### Gin-Yamma

*Gin-yamma　Tsuto shitsunai ni　Tōri-nuke*
*Yukue wa shirazu　Hatsu-aki no sora.*

### A Silver Dragonfly
Kishi-ko

A silver dragonfly sped through the room
And took its flight
Into the early autumn sky,
Whither I know not — out of sight.

### 痩　烏
喜 志 子

かしましく　唏くよと見れば　やせ鴉
トマト一つを　啄ばみ合へり

### Yase-Garasu

*Kashimashiku　Naku yo to mireba　Yase-garasu*
*Tomato hitotsu wo　Tsuibami aeri.*

### Lean Crows Kishi-ko

What shrill loud cries!
See, some lean crows
Are pecking at
One tomato.

### 尾 山 篤 二 郎
**Oyama Tokujirō (1888–    )**

A native of Kanazawa, Tokujirō studied English at a private school in his city. From his youth he began to write verse, and has published several collections of his own. He edits a poetry magazine, "Nature".

### 荒 れ た 庭 篤 二 郎

柚子一つ　赤く殘りて　庭荒れぬ
見る影もなき　ものの親しさ

### Areta Niwa

*Yuzu hitotsu    Akaku nokorite    Niwa arenu*
*Miru kage mo naki    Mono no shitashisa.*

### A Wild Garden Tokujirō

My garden, with but one red *yuzu* left,
Is in sore neglected plight,
Yet there is something dear to me
In this lorn sight.

The *yuzu* is a kind of citron.

見知らぬ人の聲　　　　　篤二郎

打ち語る　人の聲音を　緣無くきけば
人よりも蟲の　聲まさりたり

### Mishiranu-Hito no Koe

*Uchikataru   Hito no kowane wo   En-naku kikeba*
*Hito yori mo mushi no   Koe masaritari.*

## The Voices of Strangers　　　Tokujirō

The voices of strangers
Talking together,
To my uninterested ear,
Less charming sound than insect notes.

香　川　不　抱
### Kagawa Fuhō (1888–1920?)

Born in a village of Kagawa Prefecture, Fuhō studied at the Marugame Middle School.  During his school days he joined the *Shinshi-Sha* or the New Poetry Society and began to contribute his verses to the *Myōjō* and the *Subaru,* poetry magazines.

硝　子　戸　　　　　不　抱

我が行けば　必す我を　映しけり
かの硝子戸ぞ　君にまされる

### Garasu-do

*Waga yukeba   Kanarazu ware wo   Utsushi-keri*
*Kano garasu-do zo   Kimi ni masareru.*

### The Door of Glass
**Fuhō**

That door of glass, whene'er I pass,
Reflects me faithfully.
Oh, kinder far than e'er you are—
That door of glass!

### 原 阿 佐 緒
**Hara Asao (1888–    )**

Born in a village in Miyagi Prefecture, Asao studied versification under Yosano Hiroshi and his wife and Saitō Mokichi and has published several collections of her verses.

### わ が 怨 言
**阿 佐 緒**

言おほく　わが恨むをば　鳥の啼く
ほどにも君は　思はざるらむ

### *Waga Uramigoto*

*Koto ōku   Waga uramu woba   Tori no naku
Hodo nimo kimi wa   Omowazaruran.*

### My Complaint
**Asao**

Not even so much thought
As he gives to a bird's song,
Will he grant to the many words
Of my complainings long.

睡れる子　　　　　阿佐緒

春の夜の　花の息とも　やわらかに
身をそそるかな　子の寝たるいき

## Nemureru-Ko

*Haru no yo no   Hana no iki tomo   Yawarakani*
*Mi wo sosoru kana   Ko no netaru iki.*

## My Child in Sleep　　　**Asao**

**The sweet breath of my child in sleep**
**Thrills me with soft delight,**
**Like to the balmy breath of flowers**
**On a spring night.**

長島豐太郎
**Nagashima Toyotarō** (1888–　　)

Toyotarō was first a pawnbroker; now a publisher.

獅子つかひ　　　　　豐太郎

獅子つかふ　若き女は　その夫子と
獅子住む檻の　傍らに寝る

## Shishi-Tsukai

*Shishi tsukō   Wakaki onna wa   Sono seko to*
*Shishi sumu ori no   Katawara ni neru.*

## A Lion Performer

Toyotarō

The young woman,
A lion-performer,
Sleeps by the cage
With her husband.

This verse seems to suggest the conquest of danger and the victory of love.

中 村 憲 吉

**Nakamura Kenkichi** (1889–1934)

A native of a village in Hiroshima Prefecture, he graduated from the Law College, Tōkyō Imperial University; was on the editorial staff of the *Ōsaka Mainichi* for five years; later was engaged in the industry of *saké* distilling, his father's business; and published three collections of his verses.

比叡山にて

憲 吉

しののめに　山ふかき鳥を　聞くものか
比叡寺にゐるを　寝て忘れたる

### Hi-ei-Zan Nite

*Shinonome ni　Yama-fukaki tori wo　Kiku-mono ka
Hi-e-dera ni iru wo　Nete wasuretaru.*

## On Mount Hi-ei

Kenkichi

What is this I hear at dawn?
　The birds of mountain depths that sing their lay?
I had forgotten while I slept
　That I was in a temple on Hi-ei.

松 村 英 一

**Matsumura Ei-ichi** (1889-    )

Ei-ichi is a native of Tōkyō and took lessons in versification from Kubota Utsubo.  He edits a poetry magazine and has published several literary books, including two collections of his own verses.

鷺　　　　　　　英 一

四五十羽　群れたる鷺は　白し白し
木の上にくだり　しづまりにけり

### Sagi

*Shigojippa   Muretaru sagi wa   Shiroshi-shiroshi*
*Ki no e ni kudari   Shizumari ni keri.*

### Herons                    Ei-ichi

**A flock of herons, forty or fifty—**
**White, white, how white!—**
**They flew down on the trees**
**And suddenly grew quiet quite.**

蟲　聲　　　　　　英 一

蟲聲の　庭に絶えしは　いつよりぞ
人のねむれる　夜半におもほゆ

### Mushi no Koe

*Mushi-goe no   Niwa ni taeshi wa   Itsu yori zo*
*Hito no nemureru   Yowa ni omohoyu.*

### Insects' Voices
Ei-ichi

Ah! when had the insects' songs
Ceased to be heard in the garden?
I wondered so,
At midnight, when men were sleeping.

### 玩　具
英　一

わが部屋を　とりかたづくと　見出しし
亡き子が玩具　棄てもかねつる

### Omocha

*Waga heya wo　Tori-katazuku to　Mi-idashishi*
*Naki ko ga omocha　Sute mo kanetsuru.*

### A Toy
Ei-ichi

When I tidied my room,
I found a toy of my lost child;
Ah, I cannot bring myself
To throw it aside.

### 矢　代　東　村
#### Yashiro Tōson (1889–　　)

Born in a village in Chiba Prefecture, Tōson studied in the Japan University,
and is a lawyer. He is a regular contributor to the magazine, "Poetry". Tōson
does not observe the traditional regulation of five lines and thirty-one syllables,
and often writes in colloquial Japanese. He is a proletarian poet.

暑　さ　　　　　　東　村

今日も　朝からこの暑さだ　けれども
暑さのことなんか　いつて居られようか　仕事は待つ

## Atsusa

*Kyō mo Asa kara kono atsusa-da　Keredomo*
*Atsusa no koto nanka　Itte orareyō ka　Shigoto wa matsu.*

## The Heat　　　　　　Tōson

To-day again it is intensely hot
Since early morn!
But can we talk of heat?
No, no, our work awaits us!

扇　子　　　　　　東　村

おれたちより　もつと暑い　仕事場にある
人達を考へて見ろ　扇子はへんだ

## Sensu

*Oretachi yori　Motto atsui　Shigoto-ba ni aru*
*Hitotachi wo kangaete miro　Sensu wa hen da.*

## Fans　　　　　　Tōson

Think of the people
Toiling in workshops
Much hotter than ours.
How ridiculous are our fans!

## 菊 池 知 勇

### Kikuchi Chiyū (1889-    )

Kikuchi Chiyū was born in a village of Iwate Prefecture. After graduating at a Normal School, he joined the *Sōsaku-sha*, the "Society for Writing Novels", and later started a poetry magazine called *Nuhari*. He has published two collections of his own verses and written several books, including "*Manyō Shū* for Children", and some school text books.

## 魚 一 つ                         知 勇

藻の上に　浮びうごかぬ　魚一つ
かすかなれども　鰭ふれり見ゆ

### Uo Hitotsu

*Mo no ue ni    Ukabi ugokanu    Uo hitotsu
Kasuka nare domo    Hire fureri miyu.*

### A Fish                         Chiyū

Lo! motionless on the water-weed
A fish is floating!
No, although very slightly,
Its fins are moving.

## 錦 織 く ら 子

### Nishigori Kura-ko (1889-    )

The wife of Nishigori Sadao, Chief of the Educational Section of the Congregational Church, Kura-ko was a primary school teacher in her younger days and later studied at the Kyōritsu Women's Divinity School at Yokohama. She has published a collection of her verses, "The Whispers of My Soul".

聲 な き 聲　　　　　　　　く ら 子

森に來て　星を仰きつ　祈るとき
聲なき聲を　たましひにきく

## Koe Naki Koe

*Mori ni kite   Hoshi wo aogitsu   Inoru toki*
*Koe naki koe wo   Tamashii ni kiku.*

## Voiceless Voices　　　　　**Kura-ko**

When to the woods I come
And pray with eyes uplifted to the stars,
Within my deepest soul
I hear a voice which voiceless is.

生 命 の 扉　　　　　　　く ら 子

春の呼吸　いとやはらかに　かゝる時
生命の扉　おのづから開く

## Inochi no Tobira

*Haru no iki   Ito yawarakani   Kakaru toki*
*Inochi no tobira   Onozukara aku.*

## The Doors of Life　　　　　**Kura-ko**

Comes, with most tender touch, to me
　　The breath of Spring—
Then, of themselves, the doors of Life
　　Wide open swing.

今 井 邦 子

### Imai Kuni-ko (1890–    )

Born in Tokushima, Awa Province, Kuni-ko began to evince poetic talent at seventeen. She studied versification under Ōta Mizuho, Maeda Yūgure and Shimaki Akahiko and now she is known as a prominent poetess of the *Araragi* School. For a time she was on the editorial staff of the *Chū-ō*, a Tōkyō newspaper. She is the wife of Imai Takehiko, an M.P. She has published a few collections of her own verses.

観 音 の 像                           邦 子

立ちならぶ　み佛の像　いま見れば
みな苦しみに　耐へしみすがた

### *Kwannon no Zō*

*Tachi-narabu    Mi-Hotoke no zō    Ima mireba*
*Mina kurushimi ni    Taeshi misugata.*

### Images of Kwannon                 Kuni-ko

Images of the Goddess, ranged in line—
When now I look at them, their holy faces
Seem all of suffering, meekly borne,
To show the traces.

These lines were composed when the poetess visited *Sanjū-San-gen-dō*, the Buddhist Temple of the 33,333 images of Kwannon, the Goddess of Mercy, in the southeastern suburbs of Kyōto. It is so called because of the 33 (*Sanjū-san*) spaces between the pillars of the temple. The original temple, erected in 1132 by order of the Ex-Emperor Toba, was destroyed by fire in 1249, but was rebuilt in 1251 by order of the Emperor Go-Fukakusa.

The verse means: When I now calmly and reverentially look up at the numerous images of the Goddess of Mercy, standing side by side, I—who have resigned myself to my destiny after long sufferings and have attained a mental attitude of serene happiness—I see in their beautiful faces of serene calmness and great benevolence the traces of the patient endurance of sufferings, which she suffered voluntarily for the sake of all mankind.

"Their faces" means the Goddess of Mercy's countenance of perfect beauty, of forbearance, great benevolence and profound tranquillity, which was by no means her natural countenance but was attained after long endurance of suffering. It is the poetess' deep insight which has enabled her to perceive the innermost depths underlying the Goddess' expression.

睡れる子等　　　　邦　子

吾子ふたり　ならばせて寝て　蚊帳ぬちに
見れどもあかぬ　その寝顔あはれ

### Nemureru Kora

*Ako futari　Narabasete nete　Kaya-nuchi ni
Miredomo akanu　Sono negao aware.*

## My Children in Sleep　　Kuni-ko

Beneath the mosquito-net, side by side,
I have laid my two children to sleep,
Nor ever can weary of looking upon
Their dear faces in slumber deep.

水　鳥　　　　邦　子

つくづくと　心親む　水鳥の
つがひ相寄る　枯葦のかげに

## *Mizutori*

*Tsukuzuku to   Kokoro shitashimu   Mizutori no*
*Tsugai ai-yoru   Kare-ashi no kage ni.*

### Waterbirds                                    Kuni-ko

Upon a pair of waterbirds, my eyes
　　Attentively, with friendly glances, rest,
As in the shade of withered reeds they sit,
　　So lovingly, abreast.

A pair of waterfowl sitting lovingly abreast in the shade of withered reeds
in the winter sun—what a peaceful sight!  The poetess breathes sighs of quiet
bliss.  This verse suggests to the translator an old couple lovingly gazing at
pot flowers and sipping tea, in the verandah of their quiet retreat.

## 妹 の 墓                                        邦 子

水そそげば　おのづからにし　涙ながる
　　この墓まこと　久惠の墓か

### *Imōto no Haka*

*Mizu sosogeba   Onozukara nishi   Namida nagaru*
*Kono haka makoto   Hisae no haka ka.*

### My Younger Sister's Tomb            Kuni-ko

My tears rolled fast, of themselves,
　　When water I poured on the ground.
Can this be really Hisae's grave—
　　This grave-mound?

*Mizu* or "water" means *aka no mizu* or lustral-water.

When the poetess returned to her native town and visited the grave of her younger sister, who had recently died while the poetess was in Tōkyō, and poured lustral water on it, the pent-up tears suddenly rolled down her cheeks. At that moment the grief-stricken poetess, in a dreamy mood, wondered if it was really Hisae's grave. It might be a mistake! And yet the grave-post with her name upon it was standing before her eyes.

楠　田　敏　郎

**Kusuda Toshirō** (1890-　　)

Born in Miyazu, Kyōto Prefecture, Toshirō studied versification from his early days, and at twenty became a pupil of Maeda Yūgure, the poet. For some years he was a newspaper man. He edits a poetry magazine.

労　働　者　　　　　　　敏　郎

唄はせて　置くと知らぬ間に　仕事の

はかどるのを　誰が考へついた

*Rōdōsha*

*Utawasete　Oku to　Shiranu ma ni　Shigoto no*

*Hakadoru no wo　Tare ga kangae-tsuita.*

### Labourers　　　　　　Toshirō

I wonder who first hit on the idea
That labourers accomplish much unwittingly,
If they are set to singing songs,
At work.

きほふ心　　　　　　　　敏郎

きほふ心も　いまはむなしく　なりけらし
時をぬすみて　ねぶるたのしさ

## Kiō Kokoro

*Kiō kokoro mo   Ima wa munashiku   Nari kerashi
Toki wo nusumite   Neburu tanoshisa.*

### The Spirit of Rivalry　　　Toshirō

**To rival other men no longer
Seems to be my chief employ—
Only to snatch time to sleep
Is my great joy.**

茅　野　雅　子

**Chino Masa-ko (1890–　　)**

Born in Ōsaka, Masa-ko graduated from the Japan Women's University.
Later she married Chino Shōshō, a German scholar and a poet. She visited
Europe. She now teaches at her Alma Mater. She has published two collections
of her verses. She has also written some short stories and juvenile songs.

春　の　月　　　　　　　　雅子

春の夜の　月のなかにも　かくれまし
おもふと君に　つげえたるのち

## Haru no Tsuki

*Haru no yo no   Tsuki no naka nimo   Kakiremashi
Omō to kimi ni   Tsuge etaru nochi.*

### The Spring Moon                Masa-ko

Oh, I shall long to hide myself
Within the moon of the spring night,
After I dare to own
My love to you.

### こころよし                雅 子

こころよし　城の如くに　仰ぎたる
男の子も我に　涙すと聞く

### *Kokoroyoshi*

*Kokoroyoshi　Shiro no gotoku ni　Aogi-taru*
*Onoko mo ware ni　Namida-su to kiku.*

### I Feel Joyful                Masa-ko

With joy I hear that he
To whom as to a castle high
I reverently raised my eye,—
Has wept for me.

### 丹羽安喜子
#### Niwa Aki-ko (1890-      )

The wife of Niwa Toshihiko, a managing director of the Kwansai Trust Company; a pupil of Yosano Aki-ko; a regular contributor to the *Tōhaku* or "Camellia", the famous poetry magaine edited by Yosano Aki-ko.

四 十 雀　　　　安喜子

四十雀　山の木の間に　よき音して
歌へど彼も　子をば護れり

## Shijūgara

Shijūgara　Yama no ko no ma ni　Yoki ne shite
Utaedo kare mo　Ko wo ba mamoreri.

## The Great-Tit　　Aki-ko

Among the trees upon the hill
The great-tit sweetly sings, and yet
Her little ones to watch and guard
Does not forget.

Evidently the tit symbolizes the poetess herself, who constantly writes verses and who is at the same time a model of maternal affection.

十 月 の 海　　　　安喜子

津浪して　我の流しし　翠翡ゆゑ
斯くも青きか　十月の海

## Jūgatsu no Umi

Tsunami shite　Ware no nagashishi　Hisui yue
Kaku mo aoki ka　Jūgatsu no umi.

### The October Sea                    Aki-ko

**Ah, how green is the sea**
**Of this October day!**
**Is it due to my chrysoprase**
**Which the tidal wave washed away?**

On September 7, 1934, Ashiya in Settsu Province, where the poetess lives, was visited by a tidal wave, which seriously damaged her house, carrying away many valuables. She has written some two hundred touching verses on the disaster and this is one of them.

### 植 松 壽 樹

**Uematsu Hisaki (1890–    )**

A native of Tōkyō and a graduate of the Economics College, Keiō University, Hisaki is a teacher of Japanese at a Middle School.

### 挽　歌                    壽 樹

なきがらの　實の顔の　安けさに
笑はむとして　われ泣きにけり

### *Banka*

*Nakigara no　Minoru no kao no　Yasukesa ni*
*Warawan to shite　Ware naki ni keri.*

### A Dirge                    Hisaki

**Looking on the peaceful face**
**Of Minoru, who was dead,**
**I tried to smile,**
**But wept instead.**

This is a dirge on Suda Minoru, a classmate of the poet.

## 營所の喇叭　　　　　壽 樹

寝よと吹く　營所の喇叭　かなしくも

奈良の月夜を　鳴りわたりつつ

### *Eisho no Rappa*

*Neyo to fuku　Eisho no rappa　Kanashikumo*

*Nara no tsukiyo wo　Nari-watari-tsutsu.*

### The Bugles of Barracks　　　**Hisaki**

**The bugles of the barracks,**

**Sounding the call to sleep,**

**Reverberate mournfully**

**In Nara's moonlit night.**

The following *haiku* (a seventeen syllable verse) by Iwaya Sazanami is on the same theme.

名月や　あたら寝よとの　喇叭吹く

*Meigetsu ya　Atara neyo to no　Rappa fuku.*

**The harvest moon is shining, but alas !**
**The bugle blows the call to sleep.**

## 蝶　　　　　壽 樹

夏の日の　光の中に　飛びてゐし

蝶ふと見えす　柳の青さ

## Chō

*Natsu no hi no   Hikari no naka ni   Tobite ishi*
*Chō futo miezu   Yanagi no aosa.*

### A Butterfly    Hisaki

A butterfly a-dancing in
        The light of summer sun, oh,
Suddenly has disappeared—
        Green, green is the willow!

## まっしろの蝶    壽 樹

眞夏空　ひかり溢れて　みちの上に
蝶一つ飛ぶ　まっしろの蝶

### Masshiro no Chō

*Ma-natsu-zora   Hikari afurete   Michi no ue ni*
*Chō hitotsu tobu   Masshiro no chō.*

### A Snow-White Butterfly    Hisaki

The sunlight overflowed
        Through the midsummer sky,
And overhead above the road—
        A single snow-white butterfly.

杉 浦 翠 子

**Sugiura Midori-ko** (1891–　)

The wife of Sugi-ura Hisui, a famous painter, Midori-ko studied versification under Saitō Mokichi for some years, and has published a few collections of her own verses. She is a regular contributor to a poetry magazine, *Kōran* or "The Fragrant Orchid".

## 車 前 草　　　　翠 子

信濃路や　君に愛せられつつ　ゆく道は
車前草さへも　踏まじとぞする

### Ōbako

*Shinano-ji ya　Kimi ni aiserare tsutsu　Yuku-michi wa
Ōbako sae mo　Fumaji tozo suru.*

## Plantains　　　　Midori-ko

**I would not even tread
Upon the plantains,
As, in your love enfolded, I walk over
Shinano's mountains.**

Evidently this verse is addressed to her husband.

## 我 が 魂　　　　翠 子

我が魂　ここに來りて　泣けばとて
野山は寂しく　山は答へす

## Waga Tamashii

*Waga tamashii   Kokoni kitarite   Nakeba tote*
*Noyama wa sabishiku   Yama wa kotaezu.*

### My Soul                                          Midori-ko

**Though here my soul has come**
**Making a bitter cry,**
**The fields and mountains lonely are,**
**And the mountains do not reply.**

This seems to be pure imagination, for the poetess in reality enjoys her
husband's affection and domestic happiness.

田 波 御 白

**Tanami Mishiro** (died 1915)

A native of Tochiki Prefecture, Mishiro studied for some time at the Lit-
erature College, Tōkyō Imperial University.   He was a pupil of Kaneko Kun-en.

辭　世　　　　　御 白

わが知れる　限りの人に　愛せられ
死にゆくことの　何ぞうれしき

### Jisei

*Waga shireru   Kagiri no hito ni   Aiserare*
*Shini-yuku koto no   Nanzo ureshiki.*

### The Death-Verse          Mishiro

Ah! how joyful,
> To death to go,
Loved by everyone
> Whom I know!

土 屋 文 明

**Tsuchiya Bunmei** (1891–     )

Born in a village of Gumma Prefecture, Bunmei graduated from the Literature College, Imperial Tōkyō University; and he is now a teacher of Japanese literature. He took lessons in versification from Itō Sachio, and he edits *Araragi* or "The Yew", a poetry magazine.

嫌 は し 人          文 明

曉の　月の光に　思ひいづる

厭はし人も　死にて戀しき

### *Itowashi Hito*

*Akatsuki no　Tsuki no hikari ni　Omoi-izuru*
*Itowashi hito mo　Shinite koishiki.*

### A Disagreeable Man          Bunmei

I thought about a man I had disliked,
> As at the break of day pale moonlight shone;
And strangely did my heart long after him,
> Now he was dead and gone.

初　　彈　　　　　　　　文　明

初彈命中に　國の存亡はかかるといふ　その時の
砲術長を思ひ　涙ながるる

### Shodan

*Shodan meichū ni　Kuni no sonbō wa kakaru to yū*
*Sono toki no　Hōjutsuchō wo omoi　Namida nagaruru.*

### The First Shell　　　　　　Bunmei

**Upon the first shell fired depends**
**The nation's destiny, 'tis said; and so**
**When on the master-gunner of that time I think,**
**My tears o'erflow.**

This verse refers to the Battle of the Japan Sea fought between Japan and Russia on May 27, 1905.

水　町　京　子
**Mizumachi Kyō-ko** (1891–　　)

A native of the city of Takamatsu, Kyō-ko studied at the Tōkyō Women's Higher Normal School and took lessons in versification from Onoe Shibafune. She has published a collection of her verses.

### 光 の 中 の 鳥　　　　　　京　子

雨霽れて　俄かにあかるむ　光の中
峽こえて飛ぶ　鳥のはろけさ

### Hikari no Naka no Tori

*Ame harete   Niwakani akarumu   Hikari no naka*
*Kai koete tobu   Tori no harokesa.*

### A Bird in the Sun's Ray          Kyō-ko

On the clearing up of the rain,
    The mountain glowed in the sun's clear ray;
Then over the vale through the sea of gold
    A bird soared, oh, how far away!

### 岡 本 か の 子

#### Okamoto Kano-ko (1893-    )

A native of Tōkyō, Kano-ko studied at the Sakurai English School.  After graduation she wedded Okamoto Ippei, a famous caricaturist.  She has published several collections of her own verses, and some novels and dramas.

### 浪 の 音          か の 子

浪の音よ　かなしくな鳴りそ　百千年
ひとおもひつつ　われは生くべし

### Nami no Oto

*Nami no oto yo   Kanashiku na nariso   Momochitose*
*Hito omoi tsutsu   Ware wa iku-beshi.*

### The Sound of Waves          Kano-ko

O, sound of waves, let not your voice
    Come mournfully to my ears!
I will live on, remembering him,
    A hundred, nay, a thousand years.

富士の麓にて　　　　　　か の 子

富士が嶺は　今日は見えねど　麓野に
宿るこころは　おほらかにして

## Fuji no Fumoto nite

*Fuji ga ne wa　Kyō wa miene do　Fumoto-no ni*
*Yadoru kokoro wa　Ōraka ni shite.*

## At the Foot of Mount Fuji　　　Kono-ko

**The peak of Mount Fuji**
**Cannot to-day be seen;**
**Yet at an inn on the field at its foot**
**I am happy and serene.**

The peak of Fuji, no doubt wrapt in clouds, cannot be seen; yet the poetess is not disappointed, probably because of the sense that she is in the bosom of the peerless mountain.

黄 金 の 蜂　　　　　　か の 子

日もすがら　牡丹にこもり　去りやらぬ
黄金の蜂の　腹のふくらみ

## Kogane no Hachi

*Himosugara　Botan ni komori　Sari-yaranu*
*Kogane no hachi no　Hara no fukurami.*

### The Golden Bee
Kano-ko

How swollen its abdomen is!
   The golden bee which, all through the hours
Of daylight, has buried itself
   In peony flowers.

### 上 田 英 夫
**Ueda Hideo** (1894–    )

Hideo is a native of a village in Hyōgo Prefecture, and a graduate of the Literature College, Imperial Tōkyō University. He is a professor of Japanese literature at the Kumamoto High School.

### 秋　晴
英 夫

秋晴と　今日もなるらし　あかときの
宿近く來て　鳥さはに啼く

### *Akibare*

*Akibare to　Kyō mo narurashi　Akatoki no*
*Yado chikaku kite　Tori sawani naku.*

---

### Fine Autumn Weather
Hideo

To-day, too, promises
   Fine autumn weather;
At daybreak many birds have flocked
   Near to my inn, chirping together.

## 村 野 次 郎

**Murano Jirō** (1894–    )

A graduate of the Commerce College, Waseda University, he is engaged in export and import trade; and edits the *Kōran* or "Fragrant Orchid", a poetry magazine.

## 春　雨 次　郎

風に消えて　降るとも見えぬ　春雨の
また光りをり　庭にふりつつ

### Harusame

*Kaze ni kiete　Furu tomo mienu　Harusame no*
*Mata hikari-ori　Niwa ni furitsutsu.*

### The Spring Rain Jirō

The breezes seemed to have carried away
　The soft spring rain,
But now in the garden falling,
　It sparkles again.

## 靄のちまた 次　郎

うろくづの　なまめけるがに　灯に映えて
人流れゆく　靄のちまたを

### Moya no Chimata

*Urokuzu no　Namamekeru gani　Hi ni haete*
*Hito nagare-yuku　Moya no chimata wo.*

### Misty Streets
Jirō

The people stream through misty streets at night,
    Among gay lights aglow;
Like passing shoals of beautiful fish they seem,
    That through sea-water swimming go.

### 土 田 耕 平
#### Tsuchida Kōhei (1895–    )

A native of the town of Kami-Suwa in Nagano Prefecture, Kōhei finished
the Middle School course in Tōkyō and was a primary school teacher for some
years.  He studied versification under Shimaki Akahiko and is now well known
as a poet.  He has published two collections of his verses.

### 菫
耕 平

春さらば　菫を摘みて　おくらむと
思ひしものを　人はむなしき

### Sumire

*Haru saraba　Sumire wo tsumite　Okuran to*
*Omoishi mono wo　Hito wa munashiki.*

### Violets
Kōhei

I meant to gather violets
    And send them to her when the spring came round;
But ah! on earth
    She is no longer found.

月 　　　　　　耕 平

寢ねぎはに　ふたたび見むと　おもひたる
み空の月は　雲がくれにし

## *Tsuki*

*Ine-giwa ni   Futatabi min to   Omoitaru
Misora no tsuki wa   Kumo-gakure nishi.*

## The Moon 　　　　Kōhei

**I meant to see it again**
**Just before falling asleep,**
**But the moon in the solemn sky**
**'Mong clouds has hidden deep.**

米 田 雄 郎

**Yoneda Yūrō (1895–　　)**

Yūrō studied in the Literature College, Waseda University; a pupil of Maeda Yūgure, the poet; the chief priest of the Gokurakuji Temple in Ōmi Province.

眞　實 　　　　　雄 郎

行くところ　眞實ならば　綠なす
山あり川あり　なつかしきかも

## *Shinjitsu*

*Yuku-tokoro   Shinjitsu naraba   Midori nasu
Yama ari kawa ari   Natsukashiki kamo.*

### Truthfulness
Yūrō

If thou art truthful to the core,
Wherever in the world thou art,
Green hills there are, and crystal streams;
All things bring joy unto thy heart.

### をさなご
雄 郎

をさなごは　床にめざめて　うぐひすの
朝の音色を　まねてゐるかも

### Osanago

*Osanago wa　Toko ni mezamete　Uguisu no*
*Asa no ne-iro wo　Manete iru kamo.*

### The Little Child
Yūrō

Listen, the little one waking in bed,
With childish voice—
"Hō-hō-kekyo!"—is imitating
The morning song tones of an *uguisu*.

### 鈴 木 康 文
**Suzuki Yasubumi** (1896–　　)

Yasubumi is a farmer in Sakaemura, Sōsa County, Chiba Prefecture. He is a regular contributor to *Kanran* or "The Olive", a poetry magazine edited by Yoshi-ue Shōryō, whose pupil he is.

**A Cowboy**

By the late Hyakusui（故平福百穗）
From an art print by Mr. Ōtsuka Minoru
（大塚稔氏巧藝版）

## 田 作 り　　　　康 文

みたりの子　並べて聞けど　田作りの
わが業つぐと　いふ子のなしも

### *Ta-Tsukuri*

*Mitari no ko　Narabete kike do　Ta-tsukuri no*
*Waga waza tsugu to　Yū ko no nashi mo.*

### Farming　　　Yasubumi

I asked my three sons, sitting side by side,
　If they were willing to succeed
To rice-field farming; but alas, not one
　Answered, consenting my old life to lead.

## 牛 の 背　　　　康 文

野歸りは　牛の背に乗り　うらたぬし
今日なりし歌を　口ずさみつつ

### *Ushi no Se*

*No-gaeri wa　Ushi no se ni nori　Uratanushi*
*Kyō narishi uta wo　Kuchizusami tsutsu.*

### On a Bull's Back　　　Yasubumi

Returning homeward from the field,
　My bull I mounted joyfully,
Reciting in an undertone
　Lines which to-day had come to me.

## 西 村 陽 吉

**Nishimura Yōkichi (1892–    )**

A native of Tōkyō, Nishimura Yōkichi had no school course other than elementary education. He is the managing director of the Tō-undō, a publishing company. He has published four collections of his own verses, and edits a poetry magazine, *Geijutsu to Jiyū* or "Art and Liberty".

## 俺 の 住 居                      陽 吉

空が晴れて　今夜の月が　まるく出た
涼しい風だ　俺の住居だ

### Ore no Sumai

*Sora ga harete   Konya no tsuki ga   Maruku deta*
*Suzushii kaze da   Ore no sumai da.*

### My Dwelling-Place                      Yōkichi

**The sky has cleared;**
**This evening's moon has risen, a perfect round.**
**The wind is cool.**
**This is my dwelling-place!**

This verse consists entirely of colloquial and rather common language. For instance, *ore* (俺) or "I" is vulgar. Of course there is no English equivalent for *ore*.

## 篠 懸                      陽 吉

篠懸の　大きな葉っぱが　落ちてゆく
人夫の鋏が　夏を刈りこむ

### *Suzukake*

*Suzukake no   Okina happa ga   Ochite yuku*
*Nimbu no hasami ga   Natsu wo kari-komu.*

### Plane-Trees                    Yōkichi

The large leaves of the plane-trees
Come falling down.
The labourers' great shears
Are clipping summer short.

Most of the recent short verses of this poet do not observe the traditional
regulation of five phrases and thirty-one syllables, and are in colloquial Japanese.
They may well be called free verses.

### 駄　馬                    陽　吉

むしやむしやと　草を喰べてる　駄馬の顔
近よつてみて　笑ひも浮ばぬ

### *Daba*

*Musha-musha to   Kusa wo tabe-teru   Daba no kao*
*Chikayotte mite   Warai mo ukabanu.*

### A Pack-Horse                    Yōkichi

An old pack-horse
Was munching grass!
I nearer drew, and saw his face,
But no smile came to me.

The moment the poet saw this pitiful old pack-horse, he thought of hungry, worn-out old workmen.

日　曜　　　　　　　　　陽　吉

日曜は　土窖にあく　窓のやうに
私の生活に　蒼空をくれる

### Nichiyō

*Nichiyō wa　Anagura ni aku　Mado no yōni
Watashi no kurashi ni　Aozora wo kureru.*

### Sunday　　　　　　　Yōkichi

**Sunday, like a window
Opening out of a cellar,
Gives a blue sky
To my daily life.**

大 悟 法 利 雄

**Daigobō Toshi-o (1898–　　)**

A native of a village in Ōita Prefecture, Toshi-o studied versification under Wakayama Bokusui; and since the poet's death, he has been on the staff of the poetry magazine *Sōsaku* or "Original Work", as assistant of Mrs. Wakayama, its editor.

ほ ほ 笑 み　　　　　利　雄

ほほ笑みて　話しかけむと　する顔に
われも明るく　笑みかへしたり

## *Hoho-Emi*

*Hoho-emite   Hanashi-kaken to   Suru kao ni*
*Ware mo akaruku   Emi-kaeshi tari.*

### A Bright Smile                     Toshi-o

To a face which was about
    To address me
    With a smile,
I gave a bright smile instantly.

## 少 女 子                          利 雄

少女子は　美しきぞよき　しからぬは
　咲くべき草に　花咲かぬ如

### *Otomego*

*Otomego wa   Utsukushiki zo yoki   Shikaranu wa*
*Sakubeki kusa ni   Hana sakanu goto.*

### A Young Girl                      Toshi-o

A beautiful girl is all right ;
    But a girl without beauty's dower
Is like to a plant which ought to bloom,
    Yet has no flower.

## 光                               利 雄

とこしへに　われの心の　光なれ
　この一年を　しかありしごと

## *Hikari*

*Tokoshieni   Ware no kokoro no   Hikari nare*
*Kono hito-tose wo   Shika arishi goto.*

### The Light                                    Toshi-o

Be the light of my heart,
For ever, my dear,
As you have been
For this one year.

## 面　影                                    利　雄

面影は　目交に珠と　見ゆれども
珠にあらねば　手にもとられず

## *Omokage*

*Omokage wa   Manakai ni tama to   Miyure domo*
*Tama ni araneba   Te ni mo torarezu.*

### Her Image                                    Toshi-o

In image like a shining gem
My eyes behold her,
But since no gem she is, alas!
My hand cannot enfold her.

## そ　よ　風                                    利　雄

電燈を　消せば月夜の　庭の木に
吹くとしもなき　そよ風の見ゆ

### Soyokaze

*Dentō wo   Keseba tsukiyo no   Niwa no ki ni*
*Fukuto shimo naki   Soyokaze no miyu.*

## A Light Breeze                    Toshi-o

Putting out the electric light,
    Among the garden trees,
Bathed in the brilliant moon,
    I saw the lightest breath of breeze.

### 秋　動　く                    利　雄

雲に水に　秋動くとふ　野尻湖の
寫眞したしき　今朝の新聞

### Aki Ugoku

*Kumo ni mizu ni   Aki ugoku tou   Nojiri-ko no*
*Shashin shitashiki   Kesa no shimbun.*

## Autumn Stirs                    Toshi-o

"In clouds and water Autumn stirs!"—
    Dear memories awake,
Seeing this heading in the morning paper,
    Over a photo of Nojiri Lake.

In town the heat of midsummer is still intense. To the poet's delight, in one of the morning newspapers a photograph of Lake Nojiri, in the northern mountainous province of Shinano, appears, accompanied by the heading "Autumn stirs in clouds and in water".

中　學　生　　　　　　　　　　利　雄

就職や　失業にまだ　遠ければ
中學生は　いとも朗らか

## Chūgakusei

*Shūshoku ya　Shitsugyō ni mada　Tōkereba*
*Chūgakusei wa　Itomo hogaraka.*

### Middle School Boys　　　Toshi-o

Looking for employment
　　And loss of jobs still far away,
The boys of Middle Schools
　　Are very bright and gay.

中　原　綾　子
**Nakahara Aya-ko (1898–　　)**

A native of the city of Nagasaki, Aya-ko studied versification under Yosano
Aki-ko, and has published two or three collections of her own verses. She
edits a poetry magazine.

我　が　心　　　　　　　　綾　子

わが心　少さき鳥屋に　入れられた
舞はぬ孔雀の　あはれさに似る

## Waga Kokoro

*Waga kokoro　Chiisaki toya ni　Irerareta*
*Mawanu kujaku no　Awaresa ni niru.*

### My Heart          Aya-ko

Alas! my heart is like
    A peacock in a narrow cage,
Which cannot spread its feathers out
    To fullest advantage.

This verse states the sorrow of a woman whose circumstances do not allow her to display her personal and spiritual beauty to full advantage.

### 手 弱 女          綾 子

願はくば　王も額づく　美女となれ
　鬼もしたがふ　手弱女となれ

### *Taoyame*

*Negawakuba　Ō mo nukazuku　Bijo to nare*
　*Oni mo shitagō　Taoyame to nare.*

### Gentle Women          Aya-ko

May you become beautiful women
    Before whom even kings may bow—
Such gentle women as might make
    Ogres, even, submission vow.

It is idle for women to endeavour to compete with men in the same fields. They should conquer men with their beauty or gentleness as women.

劔　　　　　　　　　綾子

あなかしこ　劔は疾くも　錆びよかし
人間の世の　榮光のため

## Tsurugi

*Anakashiko　Tsurugi wa toku-mo　Sabi yo kashi*
*Ningen no yo no　Eikō no tame.*

## Swords　　　　　　Aya-ko

**May swords become quickly**
**Rusted completely,**
**For the honour and glory**
**Of the world of mankind!**

薔　薇　　　　　　　綾子

媚びながら　あなどることを　許さじと
思へる薔薇の　美しき刺

## Bara

*Kobi-nagara　Anadoru koto wo　Yurusaji to*
*Omoeru bara no　Utsukushiki toge.*

## The Rose　　　　　Aya-ko

**Even though coquettishly**
**It may pose,**
**It will not brook a slighting touch—**
**The lovely thorny rose!**

中 村 孝 助

**Nakamura Kōsuke** (1901–      )

Kōsuke is engaged in farming at his own village in Chiba County, Chiba Prefecture. He contributes to "Art and Liberty", a poetry magazine.

繭                                       孝 助

おちおちと　夜も眠らす　繭とれど
絹の着物も　持てぬ妹

## Mayu

*Ochi-ochi to    Yoru mo nemurazu    Mayu tore do*
*Kinu no kimono mo    Motenu imōto.*

### Cocoons                    Kōsuke

My sister reels the silk cocoons;
　　No quiet sleep at night has she;
But ah, she cannot even have
　　One silken dress, her own to be!

# SUPPLEMENT

---

### 今 中 楓 溪

**Imanaka Fūkei** (1883–    )

A native of a village in Ōsaka Prefecture, Fūkei graduated from the Hiro-
shima Higher Normal School.  He is head instructor at a girls' school in his
prefecture.  He has published three collections of his own verses and edits a
poetry magazine entitled *Wakana* or "Young Herbs".

皇儲殿下の御降誕          楓 溪

ひたまちし　皇子は大皇子　天つ日と

曉かけて　み光させり

### *Kōcho Denka no Gokōtan*

*Hitamachishi    Miko wa Ōmiko    Amatsu-hi to*
*Akatsuki kakete    Mi-hikari saseri.*

### On the Birth of the Crown Prince          Fūkei

The hallowed Baby for whose blissful birth
We waited with expectancy—
A Crown Prince proved to be, who did appear
At break of day with the sun's brilliancy.

The Emperor is sometimes called *Amatsuhi-tsugi* or "The Sun-Goddess'
Successor"; hence the phrase " with the sun's brilliancy ".

東郷元帥をいたみまつりて　　　　楓　溪

現身の　元帥はあはれ　逝きませど

永久に生きます　われらの國に

### Tōgō Gensui wo Itami-matsurite

*Utsusomi no　Gensui wa aware　Yukimasedo*

*Towani ikimasu　Warera no kuni ni.*

### An Elegy on Admiral Tōgō　　　Fūkei

**Alas! in mortal form**

**The Admiral has passed away,**

**But in our land**

**For ever will he living stay.**

Admiral Tōgō (1847–1934) was the Nelson of Japan, who destroyed the
Russian fleet commanded by Rozhdestvensky on May 27, 1905.

### 萩　の　花　　　　楓　溪

庭隈に　眞萩のさけば　扉によりて

嫁ぎし吾子の　一人をおもふ

### Hagi no Hana

*Niwa-kuma ni　Ma-hagi no sakeba　To ni yorite*

*Totsugishi ako no　Hitori wo omō.*

### Lespedeza Flowers　　　Fūkei

The lespedezas have bloomed fair
　　Down in my garden's corners;
Gazing at them I muse upon
　　One of my married daughters.

The sight of the graceful lespedeza flowers, one of the "Seven Autumn Herbs", brings to the poet the lonesome atmosphere of autumn, whereupon he longs for his lovely daughter who is away in married life.

### 長男五逸に　　　楓溪

節儉に　常はあるべし　いやしくも
書買ふ錢は　惜しむべからず

### Chōnan Goitsu ni

*Tsuzumayakani　Tsune wa arubeshi　Iyashikumo*
*Fumi kō zeni wa　Oshimu bekarazu.*

### Lines Sent to my Eldest Son Goitsu　　　Fūkei

Ever in common ways
　　Practise economy;
But when you purchase books, in any case,
　　Use not your money sparingly.

# INDEX OF POETS

(Vol. I includes pages 1–448 ; Vol. II pages 449–799)

# ERRATA （正 誤）

| | | Errors | Corrected |
|---|---|---|---|
| Page 11 | Line 24 | Go-Mizuno-o | Go-Mino-o |
| P. 50 | L. 14 | 飢ゑたる | 飢ゑたる |
| ,, | L. 18 | Tabi-bito | Tabito |
| ,, | L. 19 | tabi-bito | tabito |
| P. 59 | bottom | whom | who |
| P. 61 | L. 16 | さやけども | さやけども |
| P. 62 | L. 4 | 秋山の | 秋山に |
| P. 75 | L. 10 | 栗田 | 栗田 |
| P. 78 | L. 8 | 飢え | 飢ゑ |
| P. 101 | L. 16 | まかみたけびて | きかみたけびて |
| P. 114 | L. 7 | いた㕝らに吹く | いたづらに吹く |
| P. 130 | L. 5 | をの妻 | おの妻 |
| P. 141 | L. 20 | 時はあれども | 時はあれど |
| P. 148 | L. 8 | Iratsume | Otome |
| P. 160 | L. 13 | Atarashiki | Aratashiki |
| P. 168 | L. 13 | spirng | spring |
| P. 169 | bottom | Yasuyoshi | Michiyasu |
| P. 261 | L. 8 | though | through |
| P. 322 | L. 12 | 山ざぐら | 山ざくら |
| P. 334 | L. 20 | Ogi | Ōgi |
| P. 354 | L. 10 | o | to |
| P. 379 | L. 14 | 西行法師 | 平兼盛 |
| ,, | L. 15 | をくれねは | おくれねば |
| ,, | L. 20 | Priest Saigyō | Taira no Kanemori |

The verse "The Autumn Moon" on Page 379 ought to have been printed on Page 279.

| | | | |
|---|---|---|---|
| P. 414 | L. 11 | uchi | naka |
| P. 450 | L. 3 | うぐひすのなく | うぐひすなくも |
| P. 508 | bottom | How pitiful! | All praise to them! |
| P. 522 | L. 10 | 尼望東 | 望東尼 |
| P. 547 | L. 2 | こゑのみ | こゑのみ |
| ,, | L. 13 | きづなきは | きずなきは |
| P. 560 | L. 9 | Akatsuki | Akebono |
| ,, | L. 10 | ,, | ,, |
| P. 588 | L. 21 | 松のこえ | 松のこゑ |
| P. 596 | L. 5 | kuchibashi | hashi |
| P. 626 | L. 7 | おち方に | をちかたに |
| P. 663 | L. 10 | 雉子のこえ | 雉子のこゑ |
| P. 665 | bottom | 盆唄のこえ | 盆唄のこゑ |
| P. 677 | L. 17 | Nanto | Nanito |
| ,, | L. 20 | know not | I know not |
| P. 679 | L. 16 | Akatsuki | Akebono |
| P. 692 | L. 6 | 草かけらふは | 草かけろふは |
| P. 710 | L. 5 | Ōki na abu | Ōki abu |
| P. 718 | bottom | ひろがりてゆく | ひろがりゆく (six syllables) |
| P. 732 | L. 10 | 生命か | 生命が |
| P. 736 | L. 2 from bottom | 熱てる頬 | 熱てる頬を |
| P. 737 | L. 2 | Hoteru hō | Hoteru ho wo |
| P. 741 | L. 10 | 赤き日さして | 赤き日のさし |
| ,, | L. 13 | Akaki hi sashite | Akaki hi no sashi |
| P. 743 | bottom | こえ | こゑ |
| P. 745 | L. 8 | 八月のすえ | 八月のすゑ |
| P. 761 | L. 2 | やわらかに | やはらかに |
| P. 796 | L. 18 | 少さき | 小さき |
| ,, | ,, | 入れられた | 入れられて |

昭和十一年六月五日印刷
昭和十一年六月十日發行

著作者兼發行者　　宮　森　麻　太　郎

發　賣　所　　九　善　株　式　會　社
東　京　市　日　本　橋　區　通　二　丁　目

印　刷　者　　古　橋　照　太　郎

印　刷　所　　株式會社　東　京　築　地　活　版　製　造　所
東　京　市　京　橋　區　築　地　三　丁　目　十　番　地

——(定　價　金　拾　圓)——